"Kimball suffers from more strange diseases than any three people you know...
Somebody is going to have to answer for this book. If I were you, I'd get the hell out of town."
Hunter S. Thompson on George Kimball's first adventure in the book trade — Only Skin Deep.

GW00976301

GEORGE KIMBALL
AMERICAN AT LARGE

WITH AN INTRODUCTION BY TWO-TIME WORLD HEAVYWEIGHT BOXING CHAMPION
GEORGE FOREMAN

ALL ROYALTIES FROM THE SALE OF THIS BOOK WILL GO DIRECTLY TO THE CHILDREN'S
MEDICAL & RESEARCH FOUNDATION, **OUR LADY'S CHILDREN'S HOSPITAL, CRUMLIN**

RED ROCK PRESS

First published 2008
Red Rock Press
Glengyle
Claremont Road
Howth
Dublin 13
Ireland
redrockpress@eircom.net www.redrockpress.ie

|ACKNOWLEDGEMENTS|

This publication of this book is as a direct result of the generous support of The Irish Times, its sports editor Malachy Logan, and David Doran, chief executive of the Children's Medical & Research Foundation, Our Lady's Children's Hospital, Crumlin. The publisher and author would like to thank George Foreman, retired former world heavyweight boxing champion; Keith Duggan, Irish Times journalist and author; Marek Wystepek of Getty Images and Simon McCormick, farmer, for their generous and valuable contributions.

This edition published 2008 © George Kimball
The moral right of the author has been asserted.
A catalogue record for this book is available from the British Library.
ISBN 978-0-9548653-6-8
Photographs: All photographs from Getty Images/Getty Images Collections, with the exception of the following. Author portrait, cover and page 10: Laura Vaccaro Seeger. Muhammad Ali, page 12: author's personal collection. Marge Marash, page 13: Laura Vaccaro Seeger. Marvin Hagler, Mike Tyson, George Kimball, page 13: Angelo Carlino. Malachy Logan, page 15: The Irish Times.
Cover photograph Ross Kinnaird, Getty Images. The Stars and Stripes fly at half-mast in honour of the late Byron Nelson during the second round of the WGC American Express Championship in 2006.
Printing J.H.Haynes, Sparkford, Somerset.
Printing liaison Hugh Stancliffe.

THIS BOOK IS FOR MY FOURSOME FROM HELL: FINBAR FUREY, KEVIN HAUGH, PAT RUDDY, AND NIALL TOIBIN. MAY THEY CONTINUE TO LEAD ME ASTRAY...

Also by George Kimball

Only Skin Deep
1968

Sunday's Fools
Tromped, Stomped, Kicked and
Chewed in the NFL
(with Tom Beer)
1974

Eamonn Coghlan
Chairman of the Boards
2008

Four Kings
Leonard, Hagler, Hearns, Duran
and the Last Great Era of Boxing
2008

All of the material in this collection
originally appeared in pages of
The Irish Times since the column's
inception in 1997.

F or thirty-five years, including a quarter-century spent as a columnist for the *Boston Herald*, George Kimball fulfilled a boyhood ambition by earning his living at an occupation that did not involve manual labour. Criss-crossing the globe to enjoy sporting events while spending other people's money, he covered Super Bowls, World Series, and NBA Finals, Olympic Games, racing classics, and NCAA Final Fours, as well as thousands upon thousands of boxing matches, some 380 of which were for world titles.

Along the way he received numerous awards, including 'Best Column' designations from United Press International, the Golf Writers Association of America, the Boxing Writers Association of America, and *Boston Magazine*, as well as the Nat Fleischer Award for Excellence in Boxing Journalism. He retired from the newspaper dodge in 2005, but has continued to write his popular 'America at Large' column for *The Irish Times*. He has two children, Darcy and Teddy Kimball, stepsons Kim, Chris, and Jeremy Seeger, and four grandchildren. A member of the European Club at Brittas Bay and the St. Andrews Golf Club in Scotland, he lives in New York with his wife, Marge Marash, M.D.

American at Large is the first published collection of George Kimball's work since his first published newspaper story appeared — in the *Murray (Kentucky) Democrat* — more than half a century ago

INSIDE

Woods

Bonds

4

Foreword

Former world heavyweight boxing champion, George Foreman, on his long friendship with Kimball. **6**

Introduction

Irish Times sports journalist, Keith Duggan, profiles the author and talks to him in his Manhattan home. **10**

Acknowledgement

David Doran of the Children's Medical & Research Foundation on their work at Our Lady's Hospital. **22**

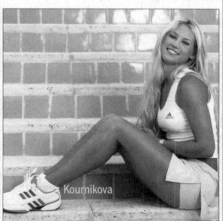

Kournikova

FOREWORD BY GEORGE FOREMAN

TWO-TIME WORLD HEAVYWEIGHT CHAMPION OF THE WORLD

Ireland is a country that has a special place in my heart, and if it weren't for George Kimball I wouldn't have got there. When I was about to fight Gerry Cooney in 1990, George introduced me to an Irish priest named Father Joe Young. A few  years before that, Kimball had taken Cooney to Ireland, where he'd met Father Joe, and when he came out of retirement to fight me, Gerry had invited Father Joe to come to Atlantic City to watch it. When we met then, I promised Father Joe then that some day I would come to Limerick.

A few years later George came down to Texas to visit me at my ranch outside Marshall, where I was training for another fight. One day we were sitting out on the porch, chewing the fat when the subject of Ireland came up again, and I told him "We've put this off long enough. Why don't you just make the arrangements and we'll go together?"

Continued on next page

Main photograph: George Foreman in 2008. Inset: George Foreman entering the ring for his bout with Evander Holyfield in 1991.

Continued from previous page: So in the spring of 1999 I visited Ireland for the first time. On one of our first nights there, JP McManus hosted a big dinner for us in Adare. I own some horses myself, so we went down to Tipperary and toured one of the magnificent stud farms there, and on the way George and Eamonn Coghlan took me to see the Rock of Cashel and told me all about the legends of St. Patrick and the King of Munster. I even got to stay in a magnificent old castle on that trip.

George Foreman hits Michael Moorer with a right during their world title fight in 1994. Foreman knocked out Moorer in the 10th round to become the oldest ever heavyweight champion of the world, aged 45.

But in between, George and Eamonn made sure I learned there was another Ireland you wouldn't find on any tourist maps. Before I left on the trip I'd read Frank McCourt's *Angela's Ashes*, and when I asked George "Limerick isn't like that anymore, is it?" he told me that there were places it was even worse, and that I should try to imagine one of our desperate inner-city American ghettos. The only difference, he said, was that in Southill, the kids would have blue eyes.

When I spent a couple of days in Father Joe's impoverished parish in Southill, I saw what he meant. It was an eye-opening experience for me, one I'll never forget, and one of the high points of that trip came when Father Joe invited me to share the pulpit at his church and I was able to preach to the children of Southill.

And later on, when we got to Dublin, I also got to visit Our Lady's Hospital for Sick Children in Crumlin. I knew about that place in advance, because just a year earlier I'd flown up to Boston to help Kimball by appearing at a golf tournament he was running to raise funds for the kids there.

I'd known George Kimball since 1971, well before I won the heavyweight championship for the first time, but it wasn't until I made my comeback years later that we became friends. I don't know whether he was picking with his head or with his heart, but I do know that back in 1994 he was just about the only boxing writer in the world to predict that I was going to beat Michael Moorer when I surprised the world by becoming the oldest heavyweight champion in history, and when he and his wonderful bride Marge got married, he invited me to come to New York and officiate at the ceremony.

For many years I'd known George as one of the more accomplished sportswriters

in America, but until we went there together I hadn't realised that, thanks to his weekly "America At Large" column in *The Irish Times*, he held a similar position of respect among his readers in Ireland.

Each of these columns was written for a daily newspaper, usually in response to specific events, but when you read them as a body of work you can't help but notice recurrent themes that I think reveal as much about George Kimball as his commentary does to illuminate the landscape of sports.

He has an amused tolerance, for instance, for the renegades who cut corners playing fast in loose with the rules in certain games, but he seems to believe that a special place in Hell is reserved for a man (or a woman) who would cheat at golf.

He has deep-seated appreciation when it comes to history, tradition and sportsmanship, a fondness for good books and bad movies, for fast women and slow horses, but he doesn't try very hard at all to conceal his contempt for (in no particular order) self-promoters, pompous officials, hypocrites, show-offs and braggarts, for George W. Bush, the War in Iraq, racial injustice, drug cheats in general, and for Barry Bonds in particular.

I'd always hoped that some day those columns might be collected in a book, and now that it's finally going to happen, I can't tell you how pleased I am.

George Foreman.
Houston, Texas.
2008.

George Kimball on the streets of New York: he writes every morning and roams Manhattan with Marge (his wife) when there is music or a play worth seeing — although he leaves the vampire hours to the younger generation.

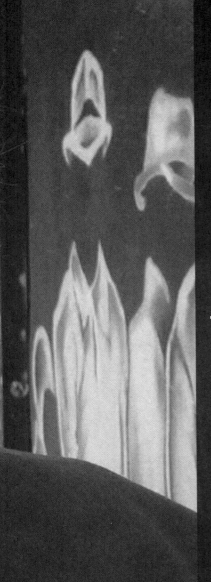

GEORGE KIMBALL

RIGHT TIME
RIGHT PLACE
RIGHT MAN

INTRODUCTION BY KEITH DUGGAN

When George Kimball was young, his post was sent to The Lion's Head on Sheridan Square in Manhattan's Greenwich Village, and for years the now-vanished drinking house provided the address on his passport. Persuading Kimball, who has lived in a bewildering variety of international and American locations, to pinpoint precisely where "home" means to him is no easy task.

But when he talks about the rambunctious days when the 1960s were flipping toward the bloody, restless 1970s and The Lion's Head was a bohemian hang-out of newspaper people, musicians, novelists, waiter/writers, waiter/actors and plain old eccentrics, it sounds as if that pub — and those years of agitation and possibility — gave him as great a sense of belonging as any of his more conventional addresses.

Continued on next page

Continued from previous page: "It had this very evocative feel, you know, walls covered in dust jackets of books by many writers who drank in there and just a great gang of people," he remembers.

We met in the apartment he shares with his wife, Marge, in an impressive turn-of-the-(20th)-century Manhattan brownstone, with a dauntingly narrow staircase opening into an airy, two-storey apart-ment, the white walls decorated in memo-rabilia, all alcoves and unexpected turns and brightness, even on a charcoal and moody autumn noontime.

"It was an eatery and there were periods when the food was quite good and others when it was f****** inedible. Once the dinner crowd was gone, musicians would come in and sit around the dining tables and these sing-songs would go on all night, but apart from that, it was just a great place to drink and talk. But it was not at all pretentious. That was the appeal."

Having retired last year from the *Boston Herald* after 25 years writing a nationally acclaimed column and having been then diagnosed with oesphageal cancer, Kimball continues to live *carpe diem*, speaking of his illness with disarming ease and resolute calm while talking animatedly of his plans for whatever months and years are ahead.

When he was diagnosed with cancer, the most immediate casualty might have been the beloved Lucky Strike cigarettes that have journeyed with Kimball through decades of cutting-edge sports writing. But after he quizzed his consultant, Kimball discovered persisting with the habit — though deeply unfashionable and perhaps even perverse — would negligibly decrease his chances of recovery. So having agreed to sit down for a pow-wow about his working life, he smoked with impunity at a breakfast table laid out with fresh coffee, muffins and apple turnovers.

And like many committed smokers, Kimball has a wonderfully mellow voice that would make you want to listen even if he hadn't lived the kind of life that makes most of us wonder if we are living at all. The reason those roaring nights at The Lion's Head came so readily to him was that just a week earlier he and Marge had attended what was a reunion of that place and period in what is now The Kettle of Fish. And although Jessica Lange did not show up to relive her days as a cocktail waitress and Lion's Head cognoscenti Malachy McCourt and Pete Hamill were, as New Yorkers put it, "out of town," the return of so many of the patrons of the early 1970s produced, to Kimball's surprise, an automatic sense that the old fizz of ideas and fun was still there.

"Yeah, I mean, it was like a typical night at The Lion's Head. Even the no-smoking shit did not bother you because you would go out on the pavement and the conversation might be even better. And Marge and I wondered how the place ever closed if it did so well. Mismanagement, I guess, is the answer. And we wondered why can't we do this every night.

"But, of course, the thing was scheduled to begin at eight. And it didn't kick off until 10. And I kept saying, 'Hey, don't they realise we are all *old*? Don't they know this is our *bedtime*?'"

And through plumes of smoke and rain bucketing down on to the roof decking behind him, Kimball laughs at time's joke. His, the classic baby-boomer generation and self-appointed guardians of America's future, were supposed to be the gang that did not get old, and as he talks about a quarter-century covering world title fights and Boston's Red Sox, Bruins and Celtics, it seems like a good bet that Kimball never hit the hay before 2.00am throughout the 1980s — if he managed to catch any sleep at all.

Born in 1943 in California, he attributes the wanderlust of his adult years to a childhood that was both strict and privileged as the family followed George E. Kimball the Second, a colonel in the US Army, on postings in Europe, the South China Seas and throughout the US.

Kimball was not overtly rebellious, but the discipline and order inculcated by his father led to a yearning for some kind of lifestyle that would facilitate the very opposite of that rigid structure.

Far page: former world heavyweight champion of the world, Muhammad Ali, spars with Teddy Kimball (above) 1994, and cuddles Darcy Kimball (below) poolside at Caesars Palace, 1986. This page: Marge Marash, George's wife (top).
Spring 1986: reigning world middleweight champion of the world, Marvin Hagler, with soon to be world heavyweight champion of the world, Mike Tyson and George Kimball, at an awards ceremony during which Kimball received the Nat Fleischer award for Excellence in Boxing Journalism.

By the time he arrived at the University of Kansas with no clear calling in life, the nascent Vietnam War draft riots consumed his energies and ideas and he spent most of the mid-1960s participating in and helping organise rallies and protests.

The first of several career arrests occurred in Lawrence, Kansas. The arresting officer was a one-man institution named Rex Johnson, an old-fashioned law-enforcer with a withered arm and a low tolerance for beatnik students. In 1970, a few years after his maiden arrest, Kimball got his name on the ballot paper as the Democratic nominee and ran against Johnson using the slogan, "Douglas County Needs a Two-Fisted Sheriff."

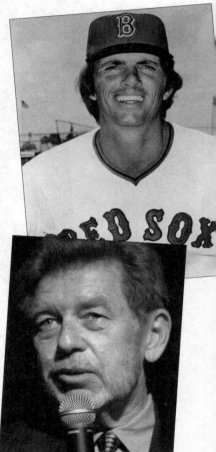

"I got about 2,000 votes of about 16,000 cast. Though if everyone who has claimed in the last 35 years to have voted for me actually did, I would have won. But Rex Johnson is still alive and I gather he has mellowed out a lot. Someone did a story revisiting that time not so long ago and when they asked Johnson about that election, he said, 'Well, he's not the worst sonofabitch that ever ran against me.'"

That stunt was partly for theatre, but the passionate anti-war stance and the constant instinct to agitate against right-wing policy, against authority, was genuine. It was also embarrassing for Kimball's father, a significant player in the US Army.

"He was pretty displeased about it," the son admits now. "But a couple of things helped calm that down. One is that my younger brother Tim had actually gone to Vietnam and came back nearly as committed against the war as I was. And my father never talked much about this, but he ended up doing a second tour as the military attaché to the American embassy in Laos, basically a spy. And I don't know what he got involved in, but there were goings-on that he did not like. And he lost all his enthusiasm for the war. He became very disenchanted.

"In later years, we would play golf and talk baseball, but never talked about it. I guess he would have preferred I had not been arrested and compiled a huge FBI file and it probably had an effect on his career. He hoped to wind up a general and that didn't happen. If he blamed us for that, he never said so."

When not involved in the sway and heat of the counter-cultural movement, Kimball was compelled by the vague knowledge that he "was always going to write something and not work the nine-to-five beat."

At college, the eminent poet Edward Dorn took an interest in his ability, and though Kimball has always loved the form, he stopped because he realised he "was merely writing very good Ed Dorn poems." He even penned an erotic novel for commercial benefit, gleefully producing a bound hardback cover of *Only Skin Deep* from a stacked library with the triumphant introduction: "And this is the dirty one."

And — probably because he took on all-comers as he found them — his entrance into the world of American journalism seems to have been precipitated by an extraordinarily influential group of people. In the early 1970s Hunter S Thompson wrote him a letter (which is included in Thompson's *Fear and Loathing in America*) explaining he was urging Jann Wenner of *Rolling Stone* to solicit longer pieces from Kimball, mainly out of belief in Kimball's talent, but also so he could prove to the magazine editor there was another somebody out there "as demonstrably f*****-up as I am."

Regular *Rolling Stone* pieces followed and an acquaintance with John Landau (later to become Bruce Springsteen's producer) led to features on literature, music and sport for the *Boston Phoenix* and a Pulitzer nomination in 1973.

He was 36 years old by the time the *Boston Herald* swooped and made him a columnist, boxing to become his speciality. It was — and remains — almost unheard of for a US newspaper to bring in a columnist "cold" — and it was not a universally popular decision in the sports department.

"Guys were very resentful at first. Understandably. Tim Horgan, the senior columnist I displaced, and I eventually became friends, but it took time. I mean, there were guys who spent a whole career there who felt they had paid their dues."

Far page: Bill Lee, Red Sox pitcher and countercultural icon. Journalist, author and friend Pete Hamill (bottom). This page: author, friend and raconteur Malachy McCourt (top). Irish Times sports editor and friend Malachy Logan (bottom).

By 1986, Kimball had won the Nat Fleischer award, the highest accolade for boxing writing. He was a seasoned survivor in the nocturnal, trans-American nomadic lifestyle that consumes US sportswriters, chasing the Red Sox and the Celtics and Patriots on night flights across the Great Plains and regularly checking in to the megawatt neon of Vegas for a heavyweight fight during that late, magical period before boxing cannoned towards oblivion.

He was in Candlestick Park for the 1989 earthquake in San Francisco. He was ringside in London for the Alan Minter-Marvin Hagler fight that precipitated a riot and in Madison Square Garden the night the Riddick Bowe-Andrew Golota bout kicked off another melee. He watched the late decline of Ali, wincing as Ken Norton took him apart in New York, and recalls "sitting beside Red Smith at the old Boston Garden to watch Ali-Holmes on closed-circuit television."

In Atlantic City in 1980, he was having a drink with the boxing writer Mike Katz in a wintry establishment when the proprietor informed them a special guest would like to meet them. Upstairs, sitting around a plain table drinking tea and amaretto was a boxing man of their acquaintance and the great Joe DiMaggio. The baseball legend quizzed the boxing experts earnestly about their predictions. Asked if the encounter intimidated him, Kimball shrugs, "Well, not really, because I had been sitting with Joe DiMaggio butt naked in a sauna a few years before that."

His career — and a personality that has never been overly impressed by celebrity — took him to genuinely friendly terms with Ali. Among the mementos in his apartment are two wonderful photographs taken in the early 1980s, when Ali still shone with the last vestiges of his startling freshness and beauty, his great arms cuddling Kimball's two children, Teddy and Darcy.

His years in Boston brought him into contact with both ends of the Irish-American spectrum, from the notorious, grizzly hoodlum Whitey Bulger to the Kennedy dynasty. Throughout the 1980s, he lived at 122 Bowdoin Street on Beacon Hill — the address on JFK's licence when he was assassinated. The Kennedys had kept an apartment there since the 1940s and Kimball became friendly with Joe Kennedy jnr.

We speak of Teddy Kennedy's doomed bid for the Democratic nomination in 1980 and his unforgettable concession speech that included the *"And may it be said of us, both in dark passages and in bright days"* valedictory and is maturing into one of the great American political oratories. You enquire if Kennedy wrote the address himself and whether Kimball had any involvement in its drafting.

"No, no, I wish I could claim that I had," he says. "Thing was, right after that broadcast, a friend called me up shouting 'I could tell you wrote that f***** thing,' though I didn't. I did work with his campaign team for a couple of months and I was there when that speech was drafted and I knew what would be in it."

He has played golf with Michael Jordan. He remains friends with Sugar Ray Leonard and when he and Marge married a few years back, George Foreman

The legedary baseball player, Joe DiMaggio, with whom Kimball spent some time in a state of undress.

performed the ceremony.

Like Zelig, Kimball is the guy in the background of every historic photograph. Although you are pretty certain he didn't feature on the cover of *Sergeant Pepper's Lonely Heart Club*, after a few hours of sitting with him, you find yourself wanting to check just to make sure. He tailed the rise of Larry Bird's charismatic, blue-collar Celtics basketball team and watched the Red Sox blow the 1986 World Series when a ball a child would have caught somehow jinked through the legs of poor Bill Buckner.

And through all that, he was fortunate enough to have become a sportswriter of influence in the waning days when American sports reportage was the dominant voice of the medium, when there was still some semblance of respect between the athletes and those who wrote about them and before 1,000 camera angles dissected every play until all mystery had ceased.

"It will never happen again," he says of the fraternity that existed between the stars and those who, as Jimmy Cannon put it, "godded 'em up" through newspaper ink. "We have become some kind of pond scum to 'em now. It was partly the money. When I started covering baseball games, I wasn't making a lot of money. But neither were the players. So you end up in a strange city and you go buy one another beers.

"Probably the closest friendship I had was with Bill Lee. He was a left-handed pitcher for the Sox known as 'The Spaceman'. He was light years ahead of his time, a counter-cultural icon before people knew what that was. For instance, during the bussing issue in Boston, when the schools were desegregated, Bill just spoke off the cuff about it, saying that Judge Garrity, who had ordered the desegregation, was the only one who could stand up with any guts. Bill had a lifestyle.

"And a lot of players in the league liked to smoke weed then but the Sox had this whole coterie — The Buffalo Head Gang, they called it. And we all hung out and I guess there were a lot of illegal substances taken in those days and every town had a jazz place or two you could go to and unwind. And then the coverage of sports just exploded and a lot of stuff became fair game. The whole performance-enhancing drugs issue meant that athletes got cautious and mistrustful. And I guess a new generation of journalists arrived who weren't guys who would go smoke a joint with a player but would rather turn him in if they got the chance."

Boozing went with the territory and allowances were made for that culture that would seem absurd today. There was a famous story of a Boston writer who ended up in Las Vegas and "got so f***** up that he filed a report on an ice hockey game that he wasn't even at. And he wasn't fired," marvels Kimball.

Another episode involved a sportswriter named Jack Welch, who at a fight in Vegas passed out at ringside before the fighting began. The veteran was blissfully comatose throughout the event and, in the confusion, colleagues filed three separate

The King of Gonzo, Hunter S. Thompson who urged *Rolling Stone* publisher, Jan Wenner, to commission material from Kimball.

stories to his bemused sports desk.

Kimball admits he drank hard and the culture probably contributed to at least some of the incidents that led to overnight jailhouse sojourns, but he was always controlled enough to wait until after the sport was over. Others had no such discipline, the most celebrated freefall into a fugue state being executed by Hunter S. Thompson.

In his *America at Large* column in *The Irish Times,* which began life at the behest of sports editor Malachy Logan in 1997, Kimball has written with acerbic humour and elegiac hindsight about the histrionic and heedless behaviour of the cult hero. (No passage hints at the anarchic behaviour of the day as slyly as one random night at Superbowl VIII, when Thompson began cutting up a sheet of paper with a Swiss army knife and then, as Kimball writes, carefully "depositing the resultant bits of confetti into his drink. When Leigh Montville, then of the *Boston Globe* asked what he was doing, I replied, correctly, 'blotter acid'. Montville groaned. Hunter was supposed to be our designated driver that night.")

Thompson's death, through a self-inflicted gunshot wound last year, was popularly portrayed as the true-to-self conclusion of a remorselessly dangerous and uncompromisingly nuts existence. But Kimball sighs as he thumbs through a hardback collection of Thompson's when asked if he was surprised by the suicide of the guy who was always up for the party.

"I was. I was. The thing with Hunter was not that he did extraordinary amounts of drugs, but that he did them all the time. Like, at a Superbowl press conference he would be tripping. And he didn't go around boasting about it, but people could tell. I think he created this monster he felt obliged to live up to. And he always got into trouble. People did beat the shit out of him quite regularly.

"I hadn't seen him for quite a few months, but I was surprised. And they had this private gathering at the Hotel Jerome and then the big event where they shot him out of the rocket and Johnny Depp paid for the whole thing. And I had no desire to be part of that. It was a big circus. I think the fact that his writing was deteriorating was part of the reason and he was in a lot of physical pain too, which a lot of people did not know about."

Out of the blue, in 1991, Kimball stopped drinking, leaving a restaurant in Denver and deciding that was that. "Didn't even know it was my last beer. And I had drunk my share of whiskey too. It was time. As Malachy McCourt says when someone offers him a drink, 'No thank you, I've had enough.'"

The 1990s raced on; the glittering sports events got even brighter. They knocked the ramshackle Boston Garden, which remains Kimball's favourite venue. "Just wonderful. That smell of old beer and 30-year-old cigars and elephant shit. You could walk in there blindfold and know where you are. Mind you, Fenway Park has the same distinctive smell."

He watched Ali become older and develop the giveaway shakes and other luminaries fade. He kept hammering out those elegant, formal columns, kept smoking and noticed his younger colleagues stayed out late less and less.

And on it raced until retirement and illness, those twin rogues, tapped him on the shoulder last year. The day arrived when his picture was no longer in the *Boston Herald*.

"I had been worried that because the whole game and the public image that goes with this, sort of defined who I was, it would be hard to overcome," he concedes. "You know, it was strange suddenly not being in the daily paper and not out hobnobbing with these guys. And it was a pleasant surprise to discover I felt great about that."

The early-morning work habits persist — including his weekly column for *The Irish Times* newspaper, which as recently as August included arguably the perfect newspaper column, sports or otherwise, headed *The True Tale of the Original Contender*.

He writes every morning and roams Manhattan with Marge when there is music or a play worth seeing — although he leaves the vampire hours to the younger generation. If he has a worry, it is about his children and the country they are about to inherit, which seems much more troubled and grave and dour than the America of his youth.

"It was a much better time to be young then," he says, wistful for the only time. "Oh God, I have no doubt. I sit around and watch my kids and in a lot of ways, they wish they had been around then, in the 1960s. Because however much we were lashing out then, there was always this confidence and belief that we were on the right track. People felt we were just troublemakers and agitators, but subsequent events proved us right.

"And I remember saying even back then, I spent three years in Germany as a teenager and never met anyone who had been a Nazi. And I said then that 20 years from now, you are not going to find anyone who will say they supported this war. And apologists for Vietnam are few and far between."

His dear wish, beyond writing projects yet to be realised, is that he gets to see his kids a little further set on the road to life. They are both young adults now and George talks of them with pride, not least of the volunteer work they have undertaken with relief agencies, which suggests they have at least inherited some of the altruistic ideals he has carried from that fading period of peace and love.

"Guess so," he breathes. "Mind you, Teddy is just back from volunteer work in New Delhi, where they had to send him home because they found some pot in his room. So I guess that is not all he inherited."

George Kimball laughs happily about this as sheets of rain pour steadily across New York.

And then he lights up.

This article first appeared in The Irish Times.

ACKNOWLEDGEMENT
BY DAVID DORAN

It is helpful to paraphrase that other great American columnist, Art Buchwald, to gain an understanding of why sport has such a hold on all of us: "Americans are a broadminded people. They'll accept the fact that a person can be an alcoholic, a dope fiend, a wife beater, and even a newspaperman; but if a man isn't into sport there's something wrong with him."

Another newspaper peer of George Kimball's, the famous Pulitzer Prize winning journalist, Russell Baker said "In America, it is sport that is the opiate of the masses."

However, those of us who have feasted weekly on George's column for the past  decade understand that while sport certainly raises something primeval in man, it is the ability to capture the sporting moment and set the scene, as George has done in this marvellous book that sets sports journalism apart as a special skill.

This compendium of articles puts George Kimball at the apogee of his profession and, by following his take on a particular event, championship or joust, we can learn to see sporting heroes in a new light and truly understand the significance of their achievements.

Who was it that said "nothing increases your golf score like witnesses?" What we do know from this anthology is that George Kimball was there. He was that witness. But, we do not get just the straightforward narrative of the event; we see it through the prism of George's eyes and his evocative words.

I was fortunate to be given the opportunity to meet some of the subjects of George Kimball's column. For a decade George organised a celebrity golf classic in his own township of Hingham, Massachusetts for the benefit of The Children's Medical & Research Foundation.

There is a rationale for supporting research into serious childhood illness and disease because research, wherever it is carried out, benefits sick children and their families, no matter where on this planet they are situated. But, only George could bring such a raft of personalities to inaccessible Hingham, for what is a somewhat inaccessible charity as far as most sports personalities are concerned.

The explanation as far as I can see lies in the fact that the book has been mis-titled: *George Kimball American at Large* does convey a certain flavour of the contents of the book and indeed the man; but the spirit of the author, his approach to life and his physique might have been more accurately captured if it read *Larger Than Life Sized American.*

I remember sitting beside George Foreman at dinner after a snow bedevilled golf classic one April at the South Shore Country Club in Hingham (the annual classic there was timed to coincide with the weekend of the Boston Marathon) trying to recall the most notable bouts of that famous slugger's career so as to make polite conversation.

I was mystified when the conversation seemed to focus on the merits and features of some grill with which George Foreman seemed to be identified and about which I knew nothing.

That was a side of George Kimball that few saw. The willingness to throw himself into organising a fundraiser by calling on the many friendships he had built over the years. George Foreman, an early subject but lately a TV personality and promoter of a specialised grill selling millions of units, had become a lifelong friend.

This book is another such example – the proceeds once again dedicated to paediatric research at our Children's Research Centre in Dublin.

Thank you George!

David Doran.

Chief Executive Officer, Children's Medical & Research Foundation,

Our Lady's Children's Hospital, Crumlin.

PART I

DOPERS, DOPES, AND OTHER MISCREANTS

Barry Bonds of the San Francisco Giants warms up in the on-deck circle prior to batting against the Washington Nationals in 2007. Bonds was indicted on four counts of perjury and one count of obstruction of justice for lying about steroid use in front of a Federal Grand Jury. Bonds' case is expected to go to trial in 2009.

Robinson — going down in history

At approximately nine o'clock last Saturday night, Eugene Robinson pulled his rented Ford Taurus over to the curb on Biscayne Boulevard and invited a fetching young lady to climb into the front seat beside him. During the process of the negotiation which shortly ensued, Robinson offered the lady in question $40 to perform on him an act one Monica Lewinsky is said to have performed, free of charge, on the President of the United States.

Seconds later, Eugene Robinson was wearing handcuffs. The lady, it seems, was no lady at all, but an undercover policewoman working the street as a vice squad decoy.

Twenty-five other men were apprehended that night in Miami for approximately the same offence, including one who was wanted for three murders in Pennsylvania, but not all of them put together created the furor Robinson's arrest did.

For one thing, Eugene Robinson is the acknowledged leader of the Atlanta Falcons' defence, and was scheduled to start at strong safety against the Denver Broncos in Super Bowl XXXIII less than 24 hours later.

On the very morning of his arrest, Robinson had attended a "Prayer Breakfast" where he had received the Bart Starr Award for "high moral character" from Athletes in Action, an organisation of prominent Christian sporting figures.

And, almost predictably, Robinson ensured that his place in Super Bowl history would remain forever secure the following evening when he became the unchallenged goat of the game.

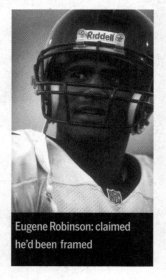

Eugene Robinson: claimed he'd been framed

Just after Atlanta's usually-reliable Danish place-kicker Morten Andersen had missed a field goal that would have made the score 10-6, Robinson bungled his coverage of Denver wide receiver Rod Smith. When John Elway found Smith with a pass, the play turned into an 80-yard foot-race between the two men, which Robinson lost. The touchdown made it 17-3 and the Broncos never looked back.

Now, not only was Robinson guilty of creating what every big-game coach tries to avoid — the dreaded Super Bowl Distraction — but also of inflating the market on Biscayne Boulevard, where his offer served to jack up the price of the act in question by a good $15 for the rest of the weekend.

If nothing else, Robinson supplied fodder for America's late-night talk-show hosts. Three days later the monologues of Jay Leno and David Letterman were still dominated by Eugene jokes.

Atlanta coach Dan Reeves, himself a born-again Christian, announced that he "loved Eugene unconditionally" and forgave him his transgression. The forgiveness of his team-mates may be longer in coming. Although he apologised to the Falcons players before and after the game, Robinson also admitted that he had not slept a wink the night before the game, a circumstance which may have contributed to his confusion on the pivotal touchdown play.

Moreover, younger Atlanta players who had looked to Robinson for leadership could not help but feel a certain resentment. It had taken the Atlanta team 32 years just to reach the Super Bowl. Robinson had played in the last two with the Green Bay Packers. A team-mate who allowed himself to think "he's already got his ring, and he just cost me my chance to get mine" may not have been far wrong.

Robinson's transgression was complicated by the fact that he was accompanied in Miami by his wife and two young children. Predictably, he claimed that he had been framed.

"I will be found innocent, but not righteous, in this deal," he said after the game. "But what I want to do now is apologise to my Lord Jesus Christ, secondly to my wife and kids, and thirdly to my team-mates and the entire Atlanta Falcons organisation."

At the same time, Robinson claimed the episode had not affected his performance in the Super Bowl.

"I was extremely focused on the game," he insisted. "It didn't affect my play because it was pretty much therapeutic."

This, of course, is pure balderdash. Robinson said later that a friend had reminded him that "confession is good for the soul, but bad for the reputation".

"Reputation, I can deal with that," he vowed.

Perhaps, perhaps not. A Miami police spokesman said this week that Robinson, whose previous record is spotless, may escape charges by entering a diversion programme for first offenders, but if he genuinely believes that all of this will go away the instant the arrest is expunged from the record, he's nuts.

Robinson has ensured that if Super Bowls are played 100 years from now his name will still come up in conversation. With one thoughtless act he has joined the pantheon of heroes, villains, and distraction-creators whose names arise every year when the NFL winnows the field down to its final two teams:

Max McGee, the fun-loving Green Bay back-up receiver who became the unlikely hero of Super Bowl I when he was unexpectedly pressed into service after spending the night carousing in the company of a young lady. (McGee, fortunately, was a bachelor; Robinson could be one again soon enough.)

Joe Namath, the New York Jets quarterback who brashly "guaranteed" victory for his 17-point underdog team in Super Bowl III — and then delivered.

Thomas (Hollywood) Henderson, the fun-loving Dallas linebacker who said of Pittsburgh quarterback Terry Bradshaw: "Bradshaw is so dumb he couldn't spell 'cat' if you spotted him the 'c' and the 't'. (Bradshaw proved to be so dumb that he won four Super Bowls, including both meetings with Hollywood's Cowboys.)

Stanley Wilson, the Cincinnati fullback and reformed drug addict who relapsed on the eve of Super Bowl XXIII and didn't turn up again until two days after the game — in a crack-induced stupor. Wilson, ironically enough, slipped off the wagon on Biscayne Boulevard in Miami. He bought the pipe-load of crack that started his downfall 10 years ago not two blocks from where Robinson stopped his car last Saturday night.

If Robinson prays long and hard enough, the Lord may, as he so earnestly believes, forgive him. His wife and children might eventually forgive him, too. Even the law may eventually let him off the hook. But if he thinks his name isn't going to come up every January as long as Super Bowls are played, he is plainly deluding himself.

February 04, 1999

Red mist from a yellow flag

No matter how many American football games you've watched, the question has probably never occurred to you before: Those brightly-coloured yellow handkerchiefs the officials toss around to signal penalties? What prevents them from, you know, being picked up by a gust of wind and blowing clear across the stadium and into, say, Lake Erie?

Until last Sunday afternoon Orlando Brown probably hadn't given much thought to this imponderable aerodynamic riddle, either. Brown, a 6 ft 7 in, 350lb offensive tackle for the Cleveland Browns, learned the hard way that the zebras' penalty flags fly as far as they do because they are weighted with buckshot.

Early in the second period of Cleveland's 24-14 loss to Jacksonville on Sunday afternoon, match referee Jerry Triplette spotted a false start on the Cleveland line and fired his weighted handkerchief in Brown's direction. His aim was true.

Struck in the right eye by the penalty flag, Brown staggered off the field in obvious pain. The eye swelled shut almost immediately, but as he returned to take his place in the huddle, the player's vision was not so impaired that he did not spot Triplette taking a few hesitant steps in his direction.

At that point the enraged Brown, who for reasons entirely devoid of irony answers to the nickname "Zeus," flung the referee to the ground, and might have done even graver damage had he not been restrained by team-mates.

Immediately ejected from the contest, Brown was taken to The Cleveland Clinic, where he remains hospitalised. Fears that he may lose his eyesight have been exacerbated by the disclosure that his father, Claude Brown, went blind from glaucoma in 1993, and that the condition is hereditary.

None of which should excuse his attack on the referee. In his day job, Triplette is employed as a treasurer for an energy corporation. He had immediately apologised to Brown after the incident. No one has claimed that he intentionally threw his flag at the player, but the fact remains that some football officials seem to regard the handkerchief toss as some class of Olympic field event in which they might be judged both on distance and style points.

Moreover, it might be noted that between knee pads, thigh pads, rib pads, shoulder pads, helmet, and face mask, a player's eyes are just about the only part of his body that is not protected from flying objects.

Some NFL players do wear optional plexiglass visors attached to their helmets. Granted, those who wear these shields generally do so to discourage opponents

Orlando Brown reacts after getting hit by the penalty flag.

from gouging them in the eye during pile-ups and not as protection from scatter-armed officials. One is still forced to wonder why Orlando Brown, given a family history that made him more vulnerable than most to eye injury, did not.

The episode now seems to have taken on a life of its own. On one hand, the hardliners are demanding that the NFL send a message by suspending Zeus for the entire 2000 season. (That Brown will miss Sunday's season finale against the Colts appears a foregone conclusion).

Others, particularly Brown's team-mates, suggest that the entire incident was provoked by a trigger-happy official and that the potential loss of an eye ought to be punishment enough.

The debate seems to have blurred all perspective, even to the point that the NFL head office, normally decisive in matters of this sort, has been eerily silent. The minimum punishment for physical contact with an official is supposed to be a $10,000 fine — loose change to a player like Brown, whose contract calls for him to be paid $27 million over six years.

Four times in the past, players have been suspended for one game for zebra abuse. Three seasons ago, Raiders' guard Steve Wisniewski was also fined $20,000 for the same infraction — the most severe punishment meted out to date.

Listen to Cleveland fans and players and you'd find yourself believing that the NFL employs a pack of vigilantes in striped shirts who amuse themselves by taking target practice on Browns players.

Listen to the law and order faction and you'd think Orlando Brown was the next logical step in a league in which the Carolina Panthers did not officially waive Rae

Carruth until he was officially charged with first-degree murder last week — fully six weeks after he was implicated in the drive-by shooting of the mother of his unborn child.

Nor should Brown's family ophthalmological history be a mitigating factor in whatever decision commissioner Paul Tagliabue ultimately hands down — if and when he makes a decision at all.

At the same time, is it outrageous to suggest that the league adopt a policy ordering their officials to direct penalty flags away from miscreants, rather than toward them? Or that, perhaps, the first order of business going into the next millennium might be to use something less dangerous and outmoded to weight down the zebras' handkerchiefs?

I mean, nobody has even remotely suggested that the referee intentionally threw the flag at Brown. But after watching the episode on videotape it is apparent that neither did he try very hard *not* to hit him.

A statement released from the hospital on Tuesday sounded suspiciously more like the work of Brown's PR department than Zeus himself:

"My actions were based upon an incredible amount of pain which affected my judgement," it read in part. "This situation was very scary due to my father's blindness and having to deal with that for many years.

"My injury and those facts still do not justify pushing an official. I regret what has happened a great deal. Nothing like this will ever happen again."

Brown, of course, should be punished. He has already been fined $5,000 once this season, for jumping on a Saints' player and punching him in the back on the final play of an October 31st Cleveland win.

But when it was suggested that Zeus might benefit from anger counselling, team-mate Derrick Alexander pointed out, "if that is the case, then all of us need help, because on Sundays we're all out there trying to kill each other."
December 23, 1999

Truth is swept aside by Hurricane

Just when you think you've heard the last of Rubin Carter, he goes out and reinvents himself again. This time around the ex-pug known as "The Hurricane" is apparently trying to cast himself as the black Forrest Gump.

In his latest version of his life story, Carter helped shape history as he crossed paths with virtually every important historical figure of the early 1960s: Martin Luther King. Malcolm X. Steve Biko.

Hounded at every turn by FBI director J Edgar Hoover himself, who "targeted (Carter) for destruction just like the Kennedys, Malcolm X, Martin Luther King Jr and

Jeff Panigia protests against the Academy Award nomination for the movie "The Hurricane" in March, 2000. Panigia is the grandson of the girlfriend of one of the people allegedly murdered by boxer Rubin Hurricane Carter.

HURRICANE MURDERS THE TRUTH!

PLEASE!

NO Oscar
to a film
that trashes
good people

www.graphicwitness.com/carter

countless other political activists," Carter nonetheless managed a second career on the side, that of smuggling guns to Nelson Mandela and the African National Congress.

As preposterous as these claims might be, all of them appeared, unchallenged, in print this week following a public appearance by Carter in Kansas City. After a lecture-*cum*-book-signing for the most recent version of his "autobiography," Carter invited *Kansas City Star* columnist Jayson Whitlock up to his hotel suite, where he spun this revision of history. And here's the worst part of it all: Whitlock fell for it — hook, line and sinker.

In the six weeks since the Academy Awards, everyone from actor Denzel Washington to producer Norman Jewison to Carter himself has blamed, with some justification, the media backlash against the half-truths and fabrications implicit in the cinematic version of *The Hurricane* for the film's (and Washington's) failure to garner an Oscar. Many academy members apparently felt that a vote for the movie, or for Washington's portrayal, would represent an endorsement of its flawed historical perspective.

In any case, Carter has apparently reassessed his position and hit the road with his latest version of his life story.

When one reads a newspaper account of Carter which includes the phrase "wrongfully accused and convicted twice for murders he did not commit," alarm bells ought to go off right away. Rubin Carter might claim he did not kill three people in a Paterson, New Jersey, saloon back in 1965, but people familiar with the particulars of the case believe he did — and that includes the descendants of the victims.

Moreover, Whitlock was toying with the sensibilities of his readers when he wrote that "Carter spent two decades in New Jersey state penitentiaries before his convictions were overturned and he was released in 1985".

It goes beyond mere semantic quibbling to point out that Carter's conviction was never "overturned," but, rather, set aside. There's a big difference. As we have previously taken pains to point out, the prosecution indisputably cut some corners in their efforts to convict him, resulting in a trial that by no standard could have been labeled fair, but not even the federal judge who ordered Carter's release claimed he wasn't guilty of the 1965 crime.

Conveniently overlooked is the fact that Carter would never have been tried a second time had he not rejected a prosecution deal following his first release. After Bob Dylan, *et al*, managed to secure his release in 1976, New Jersey prosecutors offered to drop the charges if Carter took and passed a lie detector test. He refused. Significantly, Al Bello, the eyewitness who placed Carter at the scene of the murders, *did* pass a polygraph test.

In real life, Rubin Carter was a middling middleweight (he won just seven of his last 15 fights), a small-time street criminal and stick-up artist who eventually graduated to multiple homicide, yet Whitlock proclaims his "remarkable journey from exalted boxer to convicted triple murderer to global freedom fighter" without evincing so much as a trace of embarrassment.

"His class and graciousness amazed me," gushed the newsman.

Carter managed to persuade Whitlock that "the US government" engaged in a systematic persecution that resulted in his eventual imprisonment.

"The FBI followed me everywhere I went," claimed Carter.

Strange, isn't it, that his lengthy rap sheet contains not a single federal arrest or conviction. His last transgression preceding the murders was for a street mugging.

Although Carter did have one fight in Transvaal, in 1965, there is no evidence that he ever met Biko, who would have been 18 years old at the time — and don't you suppose that if he had, that little historical titbit would have wound up in the film version of The Hurricane?

Equally ludicrous is Carter's claim that he was actively engaged in smuggling guns to the ANC, although perhaps that would explain the live .32 calibre bullet and shotgun shells — both precisely matching the weapons used in the Paterson killings — found in Carter's car literally minutes after the murders. Presumably the ammunition rolling around under the seat that night was on its way to Nelson Mandela.

Like the Kennedys and J Edgar Hoover, Biko, Malcolm, and Martin Luther King are all conveniently dead and in no better position to dispute Carter's claims than are the decedents in the Lafayette Grille on the night in question.

It strains all credulity that Carter would be making these claims now, and even more outrageous that Jayson Whitlock would so naively represent them as factual, but the real culprit, it seems to us, is the Kansas City Star, the newspaper which willingly printed this fanciful claptrap. Isn't there an ombudsman in the house?

May 11, 2000

It's all in the brawl game

When it comes to sporting violence, we Americans tend to be a fairly blase lot. The very notion that a soccer game could inspire tribal warfare in the stands is regarded with mild amusement and whenever a Third World soccer war spills over to result in tens or even hundreds of deaths, the carnage is treated as a curiosity of the order of an earthquake in Turkey or a train wreck in India. We don't understand hooligans, we like to think we don't have hooligans, and it doesn't affect us. Ergo, it might as well never have happened.

Even the obligatory bench-clearing brawl at our baseball games is an almost ritualistic form of combat, waged within the bounds of clearly understood rules. When a player on one team takes exception to something a fellow on the other team has done (usually this would involve a batter deciding a pitcher has deliberately tried to hit him), the principals are required to go at it in *mano-a-mano* combat (i.e., no bats), while the other members of the two sides pair off and grapple with one another in sort of a dignified scrum around home plate.

These rules of combat can occasionally result in an amusing spectacle. At New York's Yankee Stadium, for instance, both the home team and visiting bullpens are located beyond the fence in left-centre field and the occupants of the two warm-up areas must enter and leave through a common gate.

When a fight breaks out in the infield, decorum requires the combatants on both sides first race over a hundred yards to the scene of the pig-pile, and square off only then. One such Donnybrook broke out between the Yankees and the Red Sox 25 years ago, and when Boston relief pitcher Tom House raced to the entranceway, it was to discover the late James Augustus (Catfish) Hunter politely holding the gate open for him.

"See ya in there, kid," said the Yankee pitcher.

That long-ago brawl is memorable for two other reasons. One was it was one of the few baseball fights in my experience to have resulted in a serious injury: While the melee was in progress, Yankee third baseman Graig Nettles body-slammed Bill Lee, dislocating the Boston pitcher's business shoulder. ("He was never the same pitcher again," opined one of Lee's former managers in a recent autobiography.)

The other was the New York fans demonstrated their allegiance by offering token participation. Once the most serious miscreants had been ejected and the game recommenced, a Boston outfielder came perilously close to being wounded by a hypodermic needle heaved onto the field by a dope-addled New York partisan from the left-field upper deck.

Although New York fans are by reputation among the nation's most passionate, it would be a stretch to call Yankee Stadium a dangerous place. (Although Frank Cashen, then the general manager of cross-town rivals Mets, once did just that. After he referred to Yankee Stadium as "Fort Apache," Yanks owner George Steinbrenner retaliated by calling Cashen "a puffy-faced little man.")

Indeed, the most frightening night I ever experienced in The House That Ruth Built wasn't at a baseball game at all, but at a prize fight. The third encounter between Muhammad Ali and Ken Norton at Yankee Stadium unfortunately coincided with a New York Police strike and the only evidence of the constabulary that night was on the picket lines outside.

Gangs of freely-roaming toughs took this as a licence to circulate through the crowd robbing patrons. Red Smith, the late dean of American sportswriters, was relieved of his wallet that night and I had to personally intercede with the stadium security personnel to help Harold Lederman, one of the ringside judges, escape through the visiting-team dugout after the fight lest he be lynched by angry Norton partisans.

Be that as it may, an awkward incident at Yankee Stadium last weekend ought to have shaken our smug sensibilities, but instead it appears to have been viewed only with a disturbingly tolerant amusement.

In the fourth inning of Sunday's game against the Cleveland Indians, New York's Derek Jeter smashed a home run into the right-field stands. The ball bounced into a runway, setting in motion a foot-race between several fans in pursuit of the souvenir.

The winner of this little dash turned out to be a stockily-built adult wearing a blue Yankees T-shirt. The television camera zoomed in as he picked up the baseball and held it aloft over his head. As he raised his arms in celebration, his shirt rose to reveal a holstered handgun strapped to the side of his trousers.

The MSG network even showed a replay of the home run, finishing up by circling the weapon on a telestrator.

"What's up with that,?" wondered broadcaster Al Trautwig. "I have a feeling that's making the highlights tonight."

It did indeed. Two New York TV stations, as well as ESPN's SportsCenter showed the footage on that evening's newscast. The fact television had picked up the pistol, of course, also alerted the constabulary working the stadium detail that afternoon. Before the game was over the man had been visited by both NYPD officials and Yankee security personnel, who ran a check on him.

It was determined he was an off-duty corrections official (i.e., a prison guard) and that he was licensed to carry the gun.

So they let him keep it.

Now, why anyone would feel the need to bring a deadly weapon to a baseball game attended by over 47,000 alcohol-fuelled fans ought to be baffling enough, but why the security people wouldn't make him check it at the door once they knew he was packing is utterly mind-boggling.

And we think sports fans in the *rest* of the world are nuts?

June 07, 2001

Hunting Dolphins with heavy artillery

It was 10 years ago this month that Irving Fryar and Hart Lee Dykes, both of whom had been first-round draft choices of the New England Patriots, made a late-night visit to the Club Shalimar, a now defunct Rhode Island nightclub with a deservedly unsavoury reputation.

Whether the football players came looking for trouble or, as they themselves would later claim, were met with unprovoked hostility, remains unlearned a decade later. What we do know is that shortly after their arrival they had been asked to leave. Although the bouncer on duty was larger than either of the wide receivers, he was somewhat hampered by a broken leg, and had his right leg encased in a plaster cast.

Determined not to let his affliction be a handicap, the bouncer gave Dykes a clout with his crutch and knocked him stone cold on the bar's front step. Fryar thereupon raced to his car and retrieved an unlicensed .38-calibre pistol from his glove compartment. While he did not fire it, he was taking aim as he crouched behind the vehicle when the constabulary arrived and arrested him.

Fryar was hauled away to the sneezer and Dykes to the hospital. The latter, in fact, sustained injuries sufficiently serious that the episode effectively ended his NFL career. Fryar went on to find religion and became an ordained minister, but it didn't help him much that night. I recall writing at the time that only a pair of Patriots players could bring a gun to a crutch fight and still lose.

Just as it remains one of life's unsolved mysteries that boxers should require bodyguards, the fascination with firearms harboured by NFL players appears to know no bounds. Although they are bigger and stronger than their counterparts in almost any team sport around the world, football players as a group spend more time trafficking with arms dealers than do the armies of some nations.

As the season approaches each autumn, the public relations officers of the 31 NFL teams routinely ask their players to submit to a questionnaire, listing their hobbies and off-field interests, presumably in order to humanise them in the media guide for the upcoming season.

A surprising number list "hunting" among their favourite pursuits, although from my limited knowledge of their arsenals, many of the players in question appear to believe that bear, elk, and mountain lions must travel in armoured personnel carriers. I mean, what can you actually hunt with a bazooka?

All of which brings us to this week's subject, the unfortunate saga of Damien Robinson.

Robinson is a 27-year-old safety for the New York Jets, having spent his first half dozen NFL seasons with the Tampa Bay Buccaneers. When Herman Edwards, the Bucs' longtime secondary coach, became the head coach of the Jets this year, he made it one of his first orders of business to sign Robinson as a free agent.

As most of the world knows by now, the events of September 11th have led to enhanced, and sometimes draconian, security measures across the US. Patrons entering a stadium for a Sunday afternoon football match have been advised to arrive two hours before kick-off to allow searches of their vehicles entering the car-park and their person as they pass through the stadium gates. These precautions are in effect throughout America, but particularly so at sporting events in the New York area.

Why Robinson might have supposed that a player would be exempt from the same scrutiny is somewhat baffling, but when he arrived at the Giants Stadium players' parking lot for last Sunday's game against the Miami Dolphins, he was in the process of exchanging pleasantries with the gendarmes when the bomb-sniffing dog that one of the guards had on a leash began to bark excitedly, displaying significant interest in the contents of Robinson's sport utility vehicle.

The guards asked the player to pull over so they might inspect his truck. When they did, the search discovered that Robinson had in the boot a Bushmaster .223 assault rifle, three high-capacity 30-round magazines, and two boxes of ammunition containing another 200 rounds.

While the cops were trying to figure out whether Robinson planned to use his machinegun against the Dolphins or was merely preparing himself in case the Taliban showed up at halftime, they reminded him that possession of both the assault rifle and the ammunition were illegal under New Jersey law.

Damien Robinson: running foul of New Jersey laws.

Robinson was booked on the spot (the authorities maintain a temporary jail-*cum*-courtroom at the stadium on game days) but released on $7,500 bail and allowed to play the game, in which he recorded six tackles and deflected a Miami pass in the Jets' win. He was then arraigned Sunday night and freed on his own recognisance, but potentially faces five years in prison if the Passaic County prosecutor elects to pursue the case and he is convicted.

In addition to running afoul of New Jersey's laws, Robinson also apparently violated NFL directives by attempting to smuggle his arsenal into the stadium parking lot.

"We have a policy on guns and weapons that says you must not possess guns or any other kind of weapons while travelling on league-related business or on the premises of a stadium or a club facility," said an NFL spokesman. "Violation of the policy is grounds for punishment, including suspension."

The Jets themselves appear to have headed off discipline by the league. On Tuesday they announced they had fined Robinson a week's pay, which under the terms of his $10 million, five-year contract, comes out to roughly $30,000.

Robinson's explanation was that he'd gone to the shooting range and forgot he

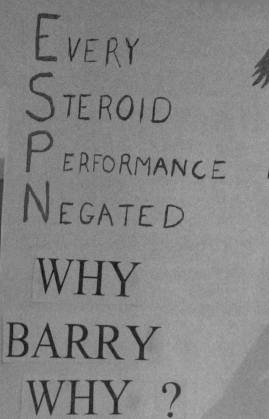

EVERY

STEROID

PERFORMANCE IS

NEGATED

WHY

BARRY

WHY ?

A young fan leaves little to the imagination.

had the weapon in his truck.

"It was very innocent in that respect — he genuinely forgot he'd left it there," said Robinson's agent Jimmy Gould. "It's an innocent mistake."

In case you were wondering whether the ongoing proceedings might affect Robinson's availability for Sunday's game against the unbeaten Rams, rest easy. You can bet your booty he's going to play.

"It's a mistake he made and obviously he will pay the price for it," said Edwards, the Jets' coach. "Knowing Damien — I have been around him for some time — this is really uncharacteristic of him. I know what kind of person he is, a good man, I don't think he had any intent about this. He forgot."
October 18, 2001

Bush now setting his sights on Bonds

Whether he was trying to divert attention from his misguided adventures in Iraq or attempting to create a new election issue, the former president of the Texas Rangers startled a joint session of Congress and a nationwide television audience last month when, in the midst of his annual State of the Union address, he made an abrupt left (or was it right?) turn and sailed into what sounded like a direct attack on Barry Bonds.

"To help children make right choices, they need good examples," said George W Bush. "Athletics play such an important role in our society, but, unfortunately, some in professional sports are not setting much of an example.

"The use of performance-enhancing drugs like steroids in baseball, football, and other sports is dangerous, and it sends the wrong message — that there are short-cuts to accomplishment, and that performance is more important than character. So tonight I call on team owners, union representatives, coaches, and players to take the lead, to send the right signal, to get tough, and to get rid of steroids now."

If he hoped to win votes by claiming the moral high ground on the issue he could have saved his breath. A recent poll commissioned by USA Today asked baseball fans whether their interest would be diminished were Major League stars identified as confirmed steroid users. Nearly half of the electorate responded that it would make no difference at all.

Two weeks ago US Attorney General John Ashcroft personally appeared at a grandiose announcement that the Justice Department had obtained a 42-count indictment against BALCO, the California drug lab which ranks as the world's foremost distributor of tetrahydrogestrinone (TGH), the designer steroid which this week proved the undoing of British sprinter Dwain Chambers, and which imperils the participation at least half a dozen of America's Athens Olympic hopefuls.

Four individuals were also indicted in the federal probe, including BALCO founder, CEO, and Bonds nutritionist Victor Conte and Greg Anderson, the San Francisco slugger's "personal trainer" who has for several seasons enjoyed a free run of the Giants' clubhouse as the most prominent member of Bonds's travelling posse.

The names of Bonds, the Yankees' Jason Giambi, and newly-acquired New York outfielder Gary Sheffield all appeared on BALCO's client list obtained when the feds raided the lab, and all three were subpoenaed to testify before the Grand Jury which produced the Conte and Anderson indictments.

Under a newly-adopted scheme in which baseball was supposed to clean up its own mess, all major leaguers were tested for steroids last season. The arrangement was supposed to be that it would be a one-shot deal if fewer than five per cent tested positive.

Neither TGH nor its ancient cousin andro were among the substances tested for, but seven per cent of the players failed the test anyway. In keeping with its agreement with the Players Association, the names of those stupid enough to be caught despite advance warning have been withheld by Major League Baseball.

Significantly, in the first season following mandatory testing, not a single major league player hit as many as 50 home runs last summer, the first time that has happened since 1993. (In a mini-press conference in the Giants' dugout when he reported to spring training in Arizona last week, Bonds, who shattered baseball's single-season record when he hit 73 homers in 2001, offered an explanation which was, to say the least, original: Bonds, who hit 45 last year, claimed the baseballs used in 2003 were for some reason "softer" than in preceding seasons.

When Giambi showed up at the Yankees' complex in Tampa his appearance, if not his chemical composition, had been so visibly altered over the off-season that all three New York tabloids felt obliged to run headlines over pictures of his new body. "Here's the Skinny," trumpeted the *Post*. The *Daily News* described the transformation as "Slim Fast," while *Newsday* described the first baseman as "The Thin Man".

Giambi claimed he had lost approximately 15 lbs from last year's playing weight by "cutting out fast food," thereby shifting the focus from BALCO to McDonald's.

Sheffield, also in a denial mode, offered to urinate on the spot, while Bonds said: "They can test me every day if they choose to," a grandstand claim if ever there was one, since, (a) the Players Association wouldn't allow it, and, (b) said testing wouldn't include Andro, THG, or whatever "nutritional supplement" BALCO might have cooked up over the winter in its ever-vigilant attempt to stay one step ahead of the law.

Suffice it to say the questions being asked at major league camps right now will continue to be asked all season, particularly should Bonds, deprived of his nutritionist, and Giambi, deprived of his Big Macs, experience significant statistical free-falls. In Mesa, Arizona, Chicago Cubs manager Dusty Baker compared the current inquisition to "McCarthyism".

Baker was for 10 seasons Bonds's manager in San Francisco, and now manages Sammy Sosa, who, while not connected to the BALCO probe, continues to be regarded with suspicion. (Sosa, who was caught red-handed using a doctored bat last summer, is at the very least a confirmed cheat.)

At his initial meeting with the press a few days ago, Baker pleaded ignorance. Straining credulity, he said he'd never seen evidence of steroid use among any of his players and that, moreover, "I wouldn't know what somebody using steroids even looks like."
February 26, 2004

Testifying to being caught in the middle

Whew!

This past Monday morning in Las Vegas, a federal jury returned guilty verdicts against South Carolina boxing promoter Bobby Mitchell and journeyman heavyweight Thomas "Top Dawg" Williams. The pair was convicted on one count each of conspiracy to commit sports bribery, sports bribery, and attempted sports bribery. Each faces a five-year prison term and could be fined as much as $250,000.

To my immense relief, the jurors managed to reach this conclusion without any help from me.

The last thing any newspaperman wants is to *become* the story, which is why it was so unsettling to receive a phone call last month from Kevin Tate, the Federal Deputy Public Defender who was Williams' court-appointed defence attorney on the case.

The government's star witness was Robert (The Middleman) Mittelman, a boxing bottom-feeder who had helped engineer the outcomes of several fights and then, in the face of overwhelming evidence, flipped and ratted out his co-conspirators. Mittelman pleaded guilty to similar charges last spring, but his sentencing has been deferred several times, presumably pending the extent of his cooperation with the prosecution of Mitchell and Williams.

I had had a long conversation with Mittelman in Athens during last summer's Olympics, in the course of which he had made several statements Tate thought might be useful to his client, to wit: when I had asked the convicted fight-fixer how he'd managed to retain his passport, he had replied, "Let's just say I'm on very friendly terms with the federal government right now."

Mittelman had also speculated, somewhat cheerfully, on the sentence he might receive: "Right now I'm supposed to be sentenced in October. I may not do any time at all, and at worst I'm probably looking at a year."

Since Mittelman's first-hand testimony figured to be the most damning evidence against Williams, Tate hoped to discredit the fixer's credibility by demonstrating that the government might have influenced his account by promising him leniency. And, presumably, he hoped I might aid him in that demonstration.

Over the course of several days in August, accounts of my encounter with Mittelman had appeared in dispatches I filed from Athens for the *Boston Herald,* for *The Irish Times,* and for the website *TheSweetScience.com.* Tate began by asking whether the quotes attributed to Mittelman were accurate (they were), and then asked whether I would be willing to attest to their veracity on the witness stand. The government, he explained, would fly me to Las Vegas and see to my accommodation.

In other words, the United States Department of Justice, having already spent tens of thousands of dollars prosecuting the case, now wanted to spend (at least) another thousand attempting to discredit it by bankrolling my testimony to assist the indigent Williams' court-appointed attorney's defence strategy.

I've never been particularly comfortable with the notion of journalists being compelled to testify under subpoena, but in this instance there did not appear to be any compelling First Amendment issue. I wasn't being asked to give up a source, but merely to confirm that what I had written was accurate. After consulting with my legal adviser, I agreed I would appear provided my testimony would be limited solely to confirming the veracity of what I had written.

Although Mittelman, at the trial, admitted to having arranged 11 fixed fights with the defendants, including Williams' March 2000 loss to Brian Nielsen in Denmark, the fight at the heart of the prosecution's case was Williams' knockout loss to Richie "The Bull" Melito at the Paris Las Vegas on the undercard of the Evander Holyfield-John Ruiz WBA heavyweight title fight on August 12th, 2000.

I'd covered the card at the Paris Las Vegas that night, but would have made a damned unreliable witness when it came to Melito v Williams. I didn't see it, and practically nobody else did, either. Originally scheduled for five o'clock in the afternoon, it was mysteriously moved up an hour amid whispers that something odoriferous was afoot. Melito's first-round knockout of Williams took place at 4.0 that afternoon, an hour before the doors were opened to the public.

Kevin Tate apparently thought better of compelling my testimony, and while the trial proceeded without me, my stories did come up in his cross-examination of Mittelman. To his credit, the fight-fixer did not attempt to deny anything he'd said to me in Greece.

Mittelman conceded, as he had admitted in last summer's guilty plea, that he had been paid $1,000 to arrange the loss, and that Williams had received $10,000 for agreeing to lie down for Melito.

If Tate had hoped to discredit Mittelman's testimony, he apparently failed. Mitchell and Top Dawg were convicted. Seven other boxers were paraded through the courtroom, and each admitted to having thrown fights against Melito in exchange for financial consideration.

"By returning guilty verdicts against both men, the jurors in Las Vegas have spoken that criminal conduct of this kind violates an important public trust in the integrity of sports," said prosecutor Daniel G Bogden after the trial.

Mitchell and Williams have been released on bail pending their sentencing next February. Mittelman also remains on the street. His latest sentencing date is December 6th. It will be instructive to see how much time the respective parties receive for essentially the same offence.

In the meantime, I keep thinking about one other thing Robert Mittelman said to me that night in Athens.

"Look, I made a mistake," he said. *"But I'm not a career criminal."*
November 11, 2004

Baseball drug testing hooks a big fish at last

Outside the boundaries of Suffolk County, Massachusetts, St Patrick's Day is not a legal holiday in the United States, so on March 17th, while festivities were under way in Boston and New York, a parade of another sort was taking place in Washington, DC, and at the conclusion of the proceedings, Rafael Palmeiro might have been elected its Grand Marshal.

A congressional sub-committee investigating the preponderance of steroids in professional sport summoned a bevy of baseball stars past and present. Mark McGwire might have been stupid enough to leave a vial of androstenedione on show in his locker, but he wasn't so dumb he didn't realise the implications of committing perjury under oath.

While he didn't exactly confess, Big Mac stammered, wriggled, sweated and dodged direct questions that by day's end he stood convicted in the court of public opinion. The widespread conclusion was McGwire had effectively labelled himself a drug cheat.

Palmeiro's presence on the stand stood in contrast to McGwire's. No sooner had the Baltimore Orioles' first baseman been sworn in than he confronted his interlocutor, Rep Tom Davis, pointing at the committee chairman as he declared: "Let me start by telling you this: I have never used steroids. Period. I don't know how to say it more clearly than that. Never."

On Monday, after the news broke Palmeiro had tested positive for stanozolol, ESPN played that clip over and over, interspersed with cuts to another famous finger-wagging denial — that of former President Bill Clinton averring "I did not have sexual relations with that woman."

Caught red-handed this week, Palmeiro sought refuge in the usual dodge: yes, he had tested positive, but no, he had never "knowingly" ingested performance-enhancing drugs. It must have been something in one of his "nutritional supplements." Laughable as his denial might have been, he found an ally in Washington.

That same day the former president of the Texas Rangers was holding forth in an informal gathering of Texas newsmen. Palmeiro had played for the Rangers when George W Bush owned the team, and the president backed his former employee.

Describing Palmeiro as "a friend," Bush declared: "He's testified in public, and I believe him."

It might be noted here the resurgence of interest in the subject had been sparked in a large measure by Bush's digression to the subject of the steroid epidemic in his State of the Union Address. Buttressed by the show of support from the White House, Palmeiro agreed to participate in a tele-conference call with sportswriters later in the day.

"When I testified in front of Congress, I know that I was testifying under oath and I told the truth," he insisted. "Today I am telling the truth again that I did not do this intentionally or knowingly."

Claiming he had no idea how the stanzozolol had got into his body, Palmeiro described the test result as an "embarrassing" situation.

"Why would I do this in a year when I went in front of Congress and I testified and I told the truth?" he pleaded. "Why would I do this during a season where I was going to get to 3,000 hits? I'm not a crazy person."

No, but maybe he thinks the rest of us are.

Another participant in the St Patrick's Day parade on Capitol Hill last spring had been Jose Canseco. Having just published a book entitled *Juiced*, in which he described steroid-sharing sessions with both McGwire and Palmeiro, Canseco was a virtual pariah, but this week's developments shed a new light on his credibility.

Consider, for instance, the fact that in Palmeiro's first four full seasons with the Rangers he hit a grand total of 70 home runs. In 1993, the year Canseco joined Bush's team, his single-season total ballooned to 37, and, following the strike-interrupted 1994 season, he put together consecutive seasons of 39, 39, 38, 43, 47, 39, 47, 43, and 38 home runs.

As he approaches the 10-day suspension resulting from this week's positive finding, Palmeiro has 569 career homers, more than all but eight men who ever played the game, and is one of just four players in history to have accumulated 500 home runs and 3,000 hits.

These benchmark figures, coupled with his strong anti-drug stance, had led to the assumption he was a cinch to be elected to the Hall of Fame when his playing days ended, but that eventuality has been cast into considerable doubt. Two years ago I announced I would refuse to vote for any of the steroid-enhanced candidates when they were presented for election, and many of my colleagues on the panel are now echoing the same sentiment. It sounds as if we will have some allies in Washington.

Rep Christopher Shays, a Bush Republican from Connecticut, was sitting on the panel when Palmeiro testified last March 17th. Shays doesn't have a Hall of Fame vote, but he offered up his personal reaction.

"He ended up being the most outspoken against steroid use and even this guy is in a situation where he's been suspended," marvelled Shays. ". . . Obviously, it calls into question every accomplishment he's had."

The suspension will cost Palmeiro about $164,000 in salary, but the damage to his reputation and legacy will be more devastating.

Palmeiro's apprehension has been labelled "a black eye for the sport," but Major League Baseball has done its best to put a positive spin on the revelation. Even the players' association appeared to be jumping on the bandwagon, as union chief Donald Fehr proclaimed Palmeiro's impending suspension "should serve to dispel doubts about our determination to rid baseball of illegal steroids, or the strength or effectiveness of our testing programme."

Until Palmeiro joined the line-up, the steroid-testing policy initiated this year had yielded minnows like Alex Sanchez and Juan Rincon. Now a big fish has turned up in the net.

August 04, 2005

To pee or not to pee

Some guys just like to be close to the action. You find yourself in conversation with a conservatively-dressed man at a Super Bowl cocktail party and notice the tell-tale bulge beneath his jacket.

"Secret Service?" you guess.

"No," he replies. "I collect piss for the NFL."

Those of us who still harbour old-fashioned notions regarding the purity of sport react with a certain degree of *Schadenfreude* when a drug cheat is brought down. Whether it's Floyd Landis or Justin Gatlin or an obscure Bulgarian shot-putter, the notion that there's one fellow fewer perpetrating fraud on the rest of us is somehow comforting.

What we don't often contemplate, mostly because we choose not to, is the unpleasant process itself. For every culprit nailed by the drug police, hundreds more have been tested, and for all the techniques science has developed to stay abreast of pharmacological developments, the means of collecting specimens remains largely unchanged.

You think it's easy to produce A and B samples on command in the presence of a stranger? Try it sometime.

At the 1993 Millrose Games in New York, Eamonn Coghlan and Marcus O'Sullivan were selected for random testing. Coghlan had just won the Masters Mile, and O'Sullivan had finished second to Noureddine Morceli in the Wanamaker Mile. The pair were corralled by the drug police, herded into a "medical room," and instructed to make water.

When Coghlan reached to take a drink of water out of his bag, he was told he wasn't allowed to drink it.

"Fair enough," he said. "If you won't let me drink my water, bring me some of yours." But when it came time to perform he wasn't able to produce.

"Marcus," he whispered to his countryman, "I can't pee."

"I can't either," confessed O'Sullivan.

The anti-doping official remained in the room with them. O'Sullivan suggested that maybe if they were allowed to take a shower the change in body temperature might expedite the process.

Eamonn Coghlan: no message in a bottle.

"Nope," the drug cop said, "no shower until I collect the specimen."

After another 20 minutes O'Sullivan proposed a compromise.

"How about we go into the shower and run some water on our legs?" he suggested. "You can come with us and watch."

The agent reluctantly agreed, and in the end collected his samples. Both runners tested negatively for performance-enhancing drugs.

The process can even take its toll on those of us from the Fourth Estate. I was in Las Vegas in May of 1995 when Dana Rosenblatt fought Chad Parker in a battle of unbeaten middleweights on the Oscar De La Hoya-Rafael Ruelas card.

Rosenblatt knocked out Parker in the first round. Since the winner was a Massachusetts fighter and I was covering the event for a Boston newspaper, this loomed as the biggest undercard story of the evening from my perspective. I raced to his dressing-room, where I was told the boxer could only be interviewed after he produced his specimen for the anti-doping test.

Rosenblatt had required less than two minutes to dispose of Parker. I couldn't tell you exactly how long it took him to furnish his specimen, but it was at least 45 minutes, because by the time I emerged from the dressing-room and got back to the arena, Jimmy Garcia was being wheeled out on a gurney.

Garcia had been battered into a coma by Ruelas's brother Gabe in the 11th round. He never regained consciousness and died two weeks later. It was the biggest boxing story of the year, and I'd missed all of it because I was waiting for Dana Rosenblatt to pee.

But if the means of collecting drug-test samples is dehumanising for the athlete, consider, for a moment, the plight of the poor fellow who actually has to handle the specimen.

Sure, he gets free tickets to the biggest sporting events in the world, but at the end of the day his experience consists of walking away clutching a couple of lukewarm vials in his hands.

For 15 years this is what Tom Taylor did for a living. A retired federal drug agent, he secured employment with the National Football League with direct oversight of its substance-abuse programme.

His official title, as was those of several other gun-toting ex-feds hired by the NFL, was "drug programme administrator" (DPA). The league office paid him $50 an hour to periodically collect samples from members of the New York Giants.

Now retired, the 77-year-old Taylor is suing the NFL on the grounds that the league failed to make good on benefits which would normally accrue to a long-time employee.

The NFL maintains the DPAs were independent contractors, not *bona fide* employees, and that it should not be held responsible for medical benefits and Social Security contributions.

The Revenue boys have ruled in favour of the urine-collectors; the next step will likely be the courts.

"The doctors and others in the management council were constantly pushing that theme that we were (independent contractors), but of course we were aware we were being micromanaged, and no independent contractors would put up with that kind of nonsense," Taylor told the New York *Daily News* this week. "Inquiry and investigation led us to believe that we were employees and we were not being treated properly."

While the issue remains the object of looming litigation, the NFL is already looking to cover its backside in future disputes. Beginning next month, it will replace the 80 DPAs on its payroll, outsourcing the oversight of its substance-abuse programme to a California drug-testing firm.

Taylor and his cohorts maintain that no "independent" contractor would have been forced to put up with the nit-picking oversight the NFL exercised over the course of his employment.

The league's posture, on the other hand, appears to be that a man performing the duties of a toilet attendant should have expected to be paid like a toilet attendant.

It will be interesting to see how the courts feel.
November 02, 2006

Time to take Big Mac off the Hall of Fame menu

For the past few days I've been eagerly awaiting the arrival of the postman. The ballots for the Baseball Hall of Fame went out on Monday. The day after I get mine it's going straight back, and Mark McGwire's name won't be checked.

When I retired from the daily newspaper dodge a year and a half ago, ensuring that I would continue as a Hall of Fame elector was a priority. I'd done the maths and realised while I might not be around to reject the candidacy of Barry Bonds (at least five years hence), I would probably be afforded the opportunity to give McGwire the thumbs-down for Cooperstown.

And judging from what I've been reading in newspapers this week I'm not alone. The hope is that barring the door to Big Mac will not only send a message but set a precedent, and that each time one of these steroid-addled former players comes up for election he can expect a similar response.

No game on earth relies more on statistical data than baseball, and on numbers alone McGwire's election would be a slam-dunk: no player with more than 534 career home runs has failed to gain induction on the first ballot. McGwire hit 583 of them. He was the first man to hit 70 home runs in a season, a record since surpassed by Bonds, and his average of one homer per 10.61 at-bats ranks him the most efficient in baseball history.

What these statistics might look like in the absence of performance-enhancing substances remains unlearned — and, indeed, McGwire, like Bonds and many other drug cheats, was never caught red-handed. But in the midst of his 1998 assault on the home run record, Associated Press scribe Steve Wilstein reported McGwire kept a vial of androstenedione in his locker.

Andro isn't technically a steroid: it only helps the body *create* steroids. And, McGwire pointed out, it was not at the time included on the list of substances banned by Major League Baseball. (It would, on the other hand, have gotten him tossed out of the Olympics faster than you can say Ben Johnson.)

The curious response to this episode was that many of McGwire's fellow players, and not a few of Wilstein's colleagues, vilified the reporter for having invaded the sanctity of Big Mac's locker — even though the andro had been sitting out in plain sight.

In March of 2005, as it became apparent drug use among Major League players

Baseball giant Mark McGwire in action for the St. Louis Cardinals during the 2000 season. "My lawyers have advised me that I cannot answer these questions without jeopardising my friends, my family, and myself," he said during a Congressional committee investigation into widespread drug abuse.

had reached epidemic proportions, a Congressional committee subpoenaed half a dozen Major League players — including McGwire, but not Bonds. McGwire's tearful testimony that day was at best evasive, and certainly cowardly. After a hand-wringing speech about the importance of setting an example for the nation's youth, he was asked point-blank about his own reliance on performance-enhancing substances.

"My lawyers have advised me that I cannot answer these questions without jeopardising my friends, my family, and myself," he stammered.

Pressed on the issue, McGwire responded: "I'm not here to talk about the past."

I've known Mark McGwire since 1984, when as a rosy-cheeked lad just out of college he visited Boston as a member of the US Olympic team that would win the gold medal in Los Angeles. In an exhibition game at Fenway Park that summer, McGwire hit two home runs. (Another future major leaguer, Will Clark, hit three, but for both players the performance-enhancing instrument involved was an aluminium bat.)

I covered him for much of his big league career, from the time he broke in as a rookie with the Oakland A's through his subsequent heroics with the St Louis Cardinals.

Beginning in 1992, hampered by injuries, his numbers began to tail off, but in a partial season (1995) he abruptly rebounded to hit a remarkable 39 homers in 31 at-bats.

The next season, at the age of 30, a man who had never before hit 50 or more home runs in a single year rattled off preternatural season totals of 53, 58, 58, 70, and 65, before his body began to break down, a disintegration so abrupt it is nearly as damning as the other evidence.

Two years after he hit 135 home runs in two seasons, McGwire was out of baseball.

I'm all for fair play, due process, and the constitutional right against self-incrimination, but in my view McGwire's deeds are incriminating enough to demand approbation. And the Hall of Fame vote is the only weapon at my disposal.

The McGwire apologists point out he was never found to be in violation of any Major League rule or policy and his accomplishments should hence be accepted at face value.

"I'm voting for him because baseball has not declared him ineligible," Tom Powers of the St Paul Pioneer Press wrote yesterday. "I am not a detective, a doctor or a priest. Based on the numbers, he gets my vote. He has 583 career home runs."

Five hundred homers has historically been the benchmark. Fifteen eligible players previously reached that total, and all of them were granted a place of immortality in the Hall. Eleven of those went in on the first ballot.

The electorate consists of 575 present and former members of the Baseball

Writers Association of America, and since a player must be named on 75 per cent of the ballots for induction, McGwire would need 432 votes. A few days ago the Associated Press conducted a straw poll, and learned of 125 prospective voters, 74 concur with our position and will not vote for McGwire, as opposed to 23 who said they will. (Of the remainder, 16 were undecided, five refused to reveal their positions, five were prevented by their employers from voting, and two said they plan to abstain.)

If that form holds, the message should go out loud and clear. The only better result one could hope for is a long shot: if McGwire somehow gets less than five per cent (29 or fewer votes), his name would disappear from the ballot forever.
November 30, 2006

Warblings about Byrd are badly timed

The unmasking of Cleveland pitcher Paul Byrd as a drug cheat would appear to be another feel-good story gone bad, but its timing could have been better — for Byrd, for the Indians, for Major League Baseball, and for George Mitchell.

Byrd is a Bible-quoting journeyman who battled his way back through at least two career-threatening arm surgeries to win, at the age of 36 and with his sixth major league team, 15 games this past season.

That earned him a spot as the fourth starter in both rounds of the Indians' play-off series.

On October 8th, Byrd beat the Yankees 6-4 to clinch a spot in the Championship Series against the Red Sox, and on the night of October 16th, he defeated Boston 7-3 to give the Indians a commanding, 3-1 lead in the best-of-seven series for the American League pennant.

Byrd did not pitch again, nor did the Indians win another game, but last Saturday the news broke that between 2002 and 2005 the pitcher had purchased nearly $25,000 worth of human growth hormone (HGH) via the internet from a Florida "anti-aging clinic" implicated in supplying drugs to numerous athletes.

Records indicated that during the period in question Byrd had taken delivery of 13 separate shipments of HGH, along with hundreds of syringes. The drugs had been "authorised" with a prescription written by a Florida dentist whose licence was suspended (for "fraud and incompetence") in 2003, and were shipped to the pitcher's Georgia home, to his former team's spring training headquarters in Florida and to a team hotel in New York. Apparently Byrd even brazenly stored some of the contraband drugs in a refrigerator in the team clubhouse.

Although Byrd was not scheduled to pitch again in the ALCS, the maelstrom created by the news was hardly helpful to the Indians, who found themselves fending off more questions about HGH than about the Red Sox.

Next thing anybody knew, the Tribe had dropped three straight, rendering moot any question about whether Byrd would be allowed to pitch in the World Series that got under way at Fenway Park last night.

While *l'affaire* Byrd undoubtedly proved a distraction to the Cleveland players and management, the timing of the bombshell report also served to place Mitchell squarely in the crosshairs of the media debate. Indians fans, as well as several newspapers around the country (including the *New York Times*), suggested that the man heading up Major League Baseball's in-house probe into performance-enhancing drugs also had a vested interest in the fortunes of the Boston Red Sox, and that he might have had a hand in leaking word of Byrd's past transgressions at what, from a Cleveland perspective, could not have come at a more inappropriate time.

Mitchell, the former US Senator who gained worldwide respect as the chairman

Senator George Mitchell who headed up the drug probe.

of the Northern Ireland peace accords, was given a brief in April 2006 to head up the probe into baseball and performance-enhancing drugs. His committee's report is scheduled to be released in the coming weeks, but since the investigation has been repeatedly stonewalled by a lack of cooperation from the players' association over privacy issues, it is expected to be less damning than it probably should have been.

Here's the problem: Mitchell also sits on the board of directors of the Red Sox. While he does not, as some have erroneously suggested, own stock in the team, the terms of his arrangement with the Boston club would give him an equity position in the (extremely unlikely) event the Red Sox were sold. Sceptics seized upon this apparent conflict of interest to lay the timing of the news about Byrd squarely at his feet.

Mitchell was forced to issue a statement insisting: "Neither I nor any member of my investigative staff had anything whatsoever to do with the publication of the allegations about Mr Byrd. We had no prior knowledge of those allegations, and we first learned of them, along with the rest of the public, through news accounts. Any information obtained in my investigation will not be made public until the report is released in the near future."

We believe him on this count. Not only is Mitchell a man of unquestioned integrity, but last weekend's news about Byrd was unearthed by Lance Williams and Mark Fainaru-Wada of the *San Francisco Chronicle*. The authors of *Game of Shadows* didn't need any help from George Mitchell. If anything, their investigative resources are probably better than his.

Although HGH has been included on the list of baseball's banned substances since January 2005, it cannot be detected by urinalysis, which is the only testing procedure allowed under the agreement between MLB and the players' union.

Byrd, in a hastily-convened press conference beneath Fenway Park in Boston last weekend, acknowledged having purchased the drugs in question, but maintained that they were obtained and used under medical supervision.

"I have not taken any hormone apart from under a doctor's care and supervision," said Byrd on the eve of his team's elimination. "The Indians, my coaches and MLB have known that I have had a pituitary gland issue for some time and have assisted me in getting blood tests in different states."

His statement seemed to acknowledge that he was still using HGH.

"That's a private matter, but I still have a pituitary issue," he maintained. "But I haven't tried to do anything behind anyone's back."

Cleveland pitcher, Paul Byrd. Just what the dentist ordered.

But Byrd also seemed to acknowledge that what he described as a "pituitary tumour" was of comparatively recent vintage. Such pituitary abnormalities are a known by-product of protracted HGH use.

If he expected his employers or Major League Baseball to support his alibi, Byrd reckoned wrong. Cleveland general manager Mark Shapiro said that the first he'd heard about Byrd and HGH was when he was contacted by the *Chronicle* reporters last Friday night.

Another big-league official found Byrd's rationale laughable.

"He has access to the best medical care in the world," said the official, "and he goes to a *dentist?*"

A defrocked dentist, at that.

MLB vice president Rob Manfred heatedly denied that Byrd had been given a "Theraputic Use Exemption" permitting him to use the drug.

"If he's saying that to create the impression that he was authorized or had permission, we have never granted a therapeutic use exemption for human growth hormone, ever."

October 25, 2007

PART II

HOOTERS GIRLS, HOOTIE'S GIRLS, AND OTHER MAJOR CONSIDERATIONS

Hooters girls strut their stuff in the absence of one of their keenest fans, former British Open winner and PGA champion John Daly.

Wild Ryder pair meet The Members

BROOKLINE

Ben Crenshaw and Mark James have, between them, participated in 11 Ryder Cups, but their only head-to-head competition came in 1981 at Walton Heath, where James partnered Sandy Lyle to a 3 and 2 four-ball victory over Crenshaw and Jerry Pate. Somewhat ironically, given the eminence of their accomplishments, the Ryder Cup playing careers of the two 1999 captains will be largely remembered for episodes both would just as soon forget.

In 1987, at Muirfield Village in Ohio, Crenshaw's fabled putter, "Little Ben," was misbehaving. Following a three-putt green that put him two down to Eamonn Darcy in their singles match, Gentle Ben and Little Ben repaired to the woods, where ensued a violent altercation which Little Ben lost. Putting with his one-iron and the blade of his sand wedge thereafter, Crenshaw lost his match to Darcy and Europe won, 15-13, for their first triumph on American soil.

For his part, James may be forever stigmatised by his comportment at the 1979 matches at the Greenbrier in While Sulphur Springs, West Virginia. The behaviour of James and his running-mate Ken Brown (who will, along with Sam Torrance, serve as James' deputy at the Country Club next year) was so abominable that they were nearly sent home in disgrace. Two months after returning home, James was fined £1,500, while Brown, whose behaviour in the four-balls was deemed uncivil and unpardonable, was fined £1,000 and suspended from international team competition for a year.

"I don't want to comment on the specifics, but I don't think it would have been important today," said James. "A lot of things have changed since then. The tournament committee has changed, and I've worked very hard at changing my own image. I'll admit I was something of a rebel back in the Seventies, but what happened back then was really more about personalities than about misdemeanours."

The question was put it him: would Mark James the 1999 captain have tolerated Mark James the 1979 player?

"Oh, he'd have tolerated him, all right," replied James. "We're expected to deal with personalities in this job."

In an event still celebrated as a benchmark in American golf, the 1913 US Open saw Francis Ouimet, a 20-year-old caddie who had grown up in a house abutting the fairway at The Country Club in Brookline, Massachusetts, find himself tied at the conclusion of regulation play with two of the most renowned golfers of their day, British professionals Ted Ray and Harry Vardon.

The next day, Ouimet defeated his more famous adversaries in an 18-hole play-off. Not only was his legend firmly established, but so, to its occasional chagrin, was that of the venue.

While most golf clubs unabashedly lobby for the opportunity to host Major championships, the staid, blue-blooded membership of The Country Club has deigned to permit professionals to tread its hallowed fairways only twice since, commemorating the 50th and 75th anniversaries of Ouimet's triumph by playing host to the 1963 and 1988 US Opens. (Ironically, each of these also resulted in a Monday play-off; in 1963, Julius Boros defeated Arnold Palmer and Jackie Cupit, and in 1988 Curtis Strange routed Nick Faldo.)

It is a measure, then, of the status the modern-day Ryder Cup has achieved that The Country Club coveted the 1999 matches so enthusiastically that the membership acceded to the unthinkable, a devil's bargain in which the Brookline club agreed to stage the 2005 US PGA Championship as tribute for getting next year's Ryder Cup.

If ever there existed a real-life instance of being dragged, kicking and screaming, into the 21st Century, this was most assuredly it.

Two days ago the captains of the respective sides were on hand for breakfast at the Country Club. It was an opportunity to get together under more amiable circumstances than are likely to obtain 10 months from now (Crenshaw and his wife, Julie, had taken Mark and Jane James to dinner in downtown Boston the previous evening.) It was also a chance for James to explore firsthand a golf course he had not seen.

"I can't imagine a better place to have the matches than here at The Country Club," said Crenshaw, an accomplished historian of his sport. "A lot of wonderful things have taken place here. The terrain, I think, reflects beautifully its New England setting. It's a natural, rustic course, one that requires a great deal of thought, both off the tee and going to the greens."

James said this week that "before the event, picking the wild card players will be the most important duty, because if you get that wrong, you've got a serious problem with your team."

All of which may be more easily said than done. Consider: of the following roster of players who have been part of a European resurgence that has resulted in two straight Ryder Cup triumphs — Faldo, Torrance, Ian Woosnam, Jose-Maria Olazabal, Seve Ballesteros, Bernhard Langer, Costantino Rocca, Jesper Parnevik, PerUlrik Johannson and Philip Walton — not one would be among the 10 automatic qualifiers if James had to select his squad today.

"With more tournaments from this side of the Atlantic counting towards our Ryder Cup points, the list will be more representative (by next) year," said James. "Specifically, Parnevik and Faldo have both rejoined our tour on a full-time basis and they'll be playing enough tournaments to qualify for our money list. The two wild cards will be truly wild, but I think everyone who has a chance of making the team will have had their chance."

Given the economic explosion that has accompanied the Ryder Cup in recent years, it's no surprise that some greedy players on both sides of the ocean have begun to wail that they should be sharing in the booty. The would-be dissidents will not find a sympathetic ear in either Crenshaw or James.

"I feel very strongly about keeping things the way they are," said Crenshaw. "I'm just old enough to feel than any deviation would be an affront to the players who have come before us since 1927, and who have made it possible for Mark and myself to enjoy the life we've enjoyed in professional golf. That supersedes any other viewpoint I can possibly come up with. People know we're out there playing as hard as we can for what we represent. I think any deviation would be something I'm against."

"I couldn't agree more," said James, the one-time rebel. "For the ordinary person on the street to look at how much the players have won over the past 12 months just to get into the team, they're going to wonder where reality has disappeared to. A lot of players would give their right arm to have played in a Ryder Cup, let alone want to be paid for the privilege of doing it."
November 26, 1998

A golfing character retires to 19th hole

It hardly seems appropriate to describe a man's passing as "tragic" when he had lived for nearly a century, encompassing a life as rich and rewarding as had the man christened Eugenio Saraceni, who died at 97 last week, but like a few other people I know, I'd been praying that the old man would make it through September.

Four months from now the 1999 renewal of the Ryder Cup will be played at The Country Club in Brookline, Massachusetts, roughly 50 miles from Worcester, where the first Ryder Cup was contested 72 years earlier. Gene Sarazen was the event's last surviving competitor.

In the process of researching the 1927 matches at the Worcester Country Club earlier this year, I'd tracked down Sarazen at his winter home in Naples, Florida, and left a message on his answering machine. A few days later, his daughter Mary Ann phoned back. She explained that her Dad had his good days and bad days. I was welcome to keep phoning in the hope of catching him on one of the former, she said, or, alternatively, I could fax her a list of specific questions which she would put to Sarazen at what she deemed appropriate times. This is what I did.

There were, of course, no esoteric tabulations of 'Ryder Cup points' in those early days. The make-up of the visiting team was determined by Harry Vardon, James

Braid, and J.H. Taylor, who had been appointed as selectors by the British PGA. The American selection process was more informal. Walter Hagen had been named to captain the American side and had recalled Sarazen, "Hagen just picked the team from among his golfing buddies.

"I suppose I'd have been automatically qualified," said Sarazen. "I'd already won a US Open and a PGA, but most of us who played on the team that first year were friends and continued to be friends on and off the course."

Although Sarazen was the last surviving player, eyewitnesses remain. Fred Hill, now 88, caddied for The Squire that week. Frank Hickey, 87, caddied for Ted Ray, who replaced Abe Mitchell as captain when the latter, suffering from appendicitis, was left behind in England.

"He and Hagen were both former caddies themselves," said Hill. "They were such rivals for the spotlight they'd sometimes push each other off the tees if there was a camera around."

Gene Sarazen: sportingly three putted the final green.

On the eve of the matches, it became clear that while the Americans wanted to be good hosts, they had no intention of becoming the first country to lose the Ryder Cup.

A delegation from the US PGA met with Ray and British team manager George Philpot with four proposals to amend the rules of competition. The original understanding of the rules, as formulated by Ryder, had called for the matches to precisely follow the format of the Walker Cup, which had been launched five years earlier. The Americans, however, wanted to substitute four-ball matches for foursomes, a form of the game rarely played in the host country even then.

The Americans also proposed that any match finishing all-square continue to sudden-death result, that two points instead of one be awarded for victories in two-man team events, and that both teams should be allowed to substitute a player in singles on the second day.

The British conceded only on the last point, for both captains had reason to anticipate that some line-up-juggling might be in order. George Gadd had become so violently seasick on the crossing that he had never fully recovered his form. He had played so poorly in practice rounds that at his own suggestion he was held out of competition, and ultimately did not participate in a match at Worcester. The Americans feared that Al Watrous, who was nursing what the local newspaper described as "a split finger," might be similarly indisposed.

"It is doubtful that Watrous will be able to play tomorrow," predicted the June

3rd Worcester *Gazette*, but as it turned out, he not only played but won in both the foursomes and the singles. It was Gene Sarazen who teamed with the ailing Watrous to win their foursomes match with Arthur Havers and Herbert Jolly, 3 and 2.

"One of the chief reasons for our failure was the superior putting of the American team," Ray told the Worcester *Telegram* after the first day's play. "They holed out much better than we did."

Hickey says that that was an understatement. "The British players were almost all better strikers of the ball than the Americans were," recalled Hickey. "Their short game just wasn't there."

Ted Ray's professed hopes for a big comeback in singles were dashed almost from the outset, as the Americans won going away.

Fred Whitcombe halved the day's last match with Sarazen to salvage half a point for the visitors, but even that outcome should probably be marked with an asterisk. Down five with nine to play, Sarazen had charged from behind to draw level on the penultimate hole. Aware that the competition had already become a rout, he sportingly (and intentionally, insists caddie Hill) three-putted the last to produce the tied result. The final result was a 9½–2½ triumph for the home side in the first-ever Ryder Cup, even though its benefactor never saw those matches.

"It was a few years later that I finally met Samuel Ryder himself," recalled Sarazen. "He was a great gentleman and a great lover of golf."

As was Gene Sarazen. The obituaries and tributes which have rolled off the presses for the past week ably chronicled his exploits — the double-eagle 'two' on the 15th at Augusta that not only won him the 1935 tournament but put the Masters itself on the golfing map, the fact that he was one of four players (Hogan, Player, and Nicklaus being the others) to have won each of the modern 'Grand Slam' events, his two eagles on the same hole in winning the 1932 British Open at Princes, his hole-in-one at Troon in the 1973 Open — but every golfer who has ever safely escaped a bunker should stop and pay him homage as well.

The way Sarazen told the story to my *Boston Herald* colleague Joe Gordon was that he had been taking flying lessons from Howard Hughes, the legendary billionaire playboy, movie magnate, and aviation pioneer. He was practising on Long Island when he mentally began to assimilate a correlation between the aerodynamic principle of lift, which Hughes had taught him, and what had up until then been his own poor bunker play.

"So I sent someone to the hardware store to buy all the solder they could get," Sarazen told Gordon. "I stayed in the bunker all day, adding solder and filing it off."

Sarazen unveiled the club that emerged as the product of that day's experimentation at the Prince's course that summer, and won the Open using it. For want of a better name, he called it a "sand wedge." No golfer today could live without one.

May 20, 1999

US sorry, but not too sorry

BROOKLINE

Jeff Maggert may have set the stage for all of this earlier in the week when he proclaimed the US Ryder Cup team "the 12 best golfers in the world." Whether they upheld that claim with Sunday's comeback performance may be open to some debate, but there is no disputing that the US golfers showed themselves to be the world's 12 biggest assholes.

The infantile celebration which accompanied Justin Leonard's improbable 45-footer that all but iced the Cup was a thoughtlessly appalling breach of sportsmanship. While Jose Maria Olazabal stood forlornly by, awaiting his turn to attempt a putt that could have halved the hole and kept Europe's hopes alive, members of the American team were stomping all over the green, exchanging high-fives, bear-hugs, and war-whoops.

"I would like to think," Mark James later reflected on the episode, "that wouldn't happen with my players."

Off to one side, Olazabal's young protege Sergio Garcia and Spanish countryman Miguel Angel Jimenez protested in vain to the match referee, but between the celebrating players and the rowdy crowd, many of whom were by now behaving like ice hockey fans who'd gotten lost on their way to the FleetCenter, there was to be no abating.

Although US Captain Ben Crenshaw later apologised, the damage had been done — and that Tom Lehman was one of the principal culprits is particularly inexcusable, since on the same green not minutes earlier he had done precisely the same thing.

When Mark O'Meara holed an eight-footer to ensure at least a halved hole in his gripping match with Padraig Harrington, Lehman had charged onto the green to hug O'Meara, trampling all over Harrington's line in the process.

O'Meara then graciously conceded Harrington's two-foot par putt. The Irish golfer felt it might have been conceded anyway, and that O'Meara had only made him mark the ball in the first place for, as they say, negotiating purposes.

"I was going to hole it anyway," said Harrington. "I wasn't putting very well, but I certainly wasn't going to miss from 18 inches. Mark was just being a gentleman."

Be that as it may, Lehman surely should have learned his lesson there.

Instead, moments later, there he was leading another stampede out onto the green.

"You know, what happened on 17 was unfortunate, but in the excitement of the moment, Justin making a 50 (actually, it was more like 45) foot putt to probably clinch the Ryder Cup, we all got excited," said Lehman. "There was never any ill intent on anyone's part in any way whatsoever. Obviously, in retrospect, we probably wish we all would have jumped up and down in place instead of running down the side of the green.

"But I'm not going to apologise for being excited," said the defiant Lehman. "It was a great day for the American team."

In other words, he was sorry, but not too sorry.

Nor does Leonard's subsequent recollection of the incident — "As far as I know, I was never on the green when we were all going nuts" — wash. They were *all over* the green, and if Leonard didn't know that, he is an even bigger idiot than Tom Lehman.

That Crenshaw might have done the gentlemanly thing and ordered Leonard to concede Olazabal's putt seems to have occurred to no one.

From where she was seated beside the right greenside bunker, in fact, Julie Crenshaw, the American Captain's wife, leaned over and whispered to Jarmo Sandelin "I'm sorry they got on the green."

"That's too much," replied a glowering Sandelin.

Well, it *was* too much, but it was very much in keeping with what went on all week. Both Crenshaw and James thought they had put a lid on all of this stuff going into the matches. Moments after he stepped off the Concorde on Monday, in fact, James had described 1991's Kiawah Island "War at the Shore" as a low-water mark in Ryder Cup annals, and said that he and Crenshaw had taken steps to ensure that proper decorum would obtain during the 1999 staging of golf's premier international event.

Just what those steps might have been is anybody's guess, but the American players evidently didn't pay much attention.

In the first match on the first day, Phil Mickelson missed a putt from the apron, leaving Paul Lawrie-Colin Montgomerie two for the match from a distance of less than five feet. After consultation with partner David Duval, Mickelson made the British Open champion putt the first one before conceding.

A day later, as Montgomerie stood over a 10-foot birdie putt on the sixth, a voice from the audience bellowed out a familiar refrain — *"Mrs Doubtfire!!"*- causing Monty to back away from the putt as most of the audience then heckled the heckler.

Montgomerie and Lawrie correctly accused the American duo of Hal Sutton and Maggert of "geeing up" the crowd with their impromptu celebrations on the green on Saturday, and the audience was riding Montgomerie hard enough on Sunday that opponent Payne Stewart took Monty aside five holes into the match and said "if it happens again, let me handle it."

All told, it was, as Olazabal described it, "a pretty ugly picture," and ascribing it to the emotion of the moment or blaming Valderrama simply isn't good enough.

Instead of basking in the limelight of what they never stopped describing as "the greatest comeback in Ryder Cup history," the American players ought to be

ashamed of themselves. That they are not makes it all the more disturbing.
September 28, 1999

No time for men behaving badly

BOSTON

It may have taken nearly a month for history to explain itself, but at least we now know what all those rowdy fans at The Country Club were up to. Turns out those people who taunted Colin Montgomerie, spat at Mark James's wife and beat up Sergio Garcia's caddie when they weren't chanting "USA! USA!" were merely warming up for the baseball play-offs.

The New York Yankees needed just five games in the best-of-seven series to oust the Red Sox, but if it appears that the Boston team went quietly, the same could not be said of the hometown crowd. Monday night's finale was contested under a heavy police presence after the Boston fans interrupted Sunday night's loss by throwing bottles and other debris onto the field in such profusion that chief umpire Al Clark suspended play and evacuated the field.

The displeasure of the Boston supporters stemmed not only from eight decades of frustration in which New York teams have frequently been the principal antag- onists, but from a couple of blatant gaffes on the part of the umpiring crew. In both cases, the respective umpires took the extraordinary step of publicly acknowledging after the games that they had blown the calls in question, which in the end only served to exacerbate the persecuted feelings of the frustrated Boston audience.

In the wake of Sunday night's mini-riot at Fenway Park, Boston Mayor Tommy Menino issued a public apology Monday morning "to the baseball fans of America, citing "inappropriate behaviour" which was "an embarrassment to the city of Boston."

Before the day was over, talkshow hosts were ripping the Mayor over the airwaves for having apologised at all, the presumption being that the fans' behav- iour was somehow justified and that even if it weren't, the Yankees and the umpires sort of had it coming.

New York's 6-1 win that night was decisive enough for Game Five to be completed without incident. The Yankees move on to Sunday's World Series, while the Red Sox, for the 82nd consecutive time, are left to re-group for next year.

If that episode seems destined to recede into the background, the same cannot be said of the 1999 Ryder Cup and its unseemly aftermath. Last week, I heard from a couple of interested parties – Mrs. Frances Hickey of Shrewsbury, Massachusetts, whose late husband Frank served as caddie to British captain Ted Ray in the first Ryder Cup at Worcester Country Club 72 years ago, and Mrs. Melissa Lehman of

Scottsdale, Arizona, whose husband Tom was a member of the victorious American side at Brookline last month.

"I was saddened when Frank passed away on June 17th, knowing that he would not be able to watch the Ryder Cup matches," wrote Mrs, Hickey. "He would have admired the ability of the American golfers, but would have abhorred their lack of manners and golf etiquette.

"He always referred to golf as a gentleman's game. It seems that the 1999 Ryder Cup matches were anything but that."

Mrs. Lehman, on the other hand, feels that I unfairly targeted her husband as the ringleader of the rancorous behaviour of the American team on the 17th green following Justin Leonard's decisive putt there on Sunday afternoon.

"Tom didn't 'lead the charge," pointed out his wife. "If you'll look at the picture in Sports Illustrated you can see that he and I were still off the green when several other players and caddies were already on it."

Mrs Lehman, in fact, made several points, some of them more valid than others. For one thing, she noted that the "USA!" chants weren't the only noise on the course that day.

"Everywhere I went I kept hearing people singing *"Ole! OleOleOle!"* she said. "That certainly wasn't an *American* chant."

True enough. But to the best of my knowledge, the *"Ole"* people never did it in the middle of Tiger Woods's backswing, or when an American player was lining up a crucial putt.

Another of Melissa Lehman's claims — that when Garcia sat down in the middle of a fairway during a Saturday four-ball match he did so to put off his American opponents — strikes me as a bit silly, if not downright paranoid. It seemed clear to me at the time that Garcia's was a spontaneous and good-natured gesture in response to the taunts of the crowd, and had nothing to do with gamesmanship or devious match strategy.

Mrs Lehman also took issue with my characterisation of her husband's subsequent expression of contrition as "sorry, but not too sorry."

"Tom was just as sorry as could be," she insisted. "If you look up the dictionary definition of 'contrite,' that was Tom after the Ryder Cup. The minute he got home he hand-wrote three letters of apology, one to Jose Maria Olazabal, one to Sam Torrance, and one to Mark James."

I also heard from Mrs. Lehman's husband. "If you want to write a column calling me an 'asshole' and an 'idiot' that's your right," said Lehman in a phone call, "but you have a responsibility to get your facts straight. I didn't set foot on the 17th green when I hugged Mark O'Meara after his putt, and I certainly didn't step on Padraig Harrington's line. Ask Padraig if I stepped on his line."

It appeared to me that he had, although my vantage point wasn't the best.

Several people who had a better view claimed that Lehman had, and O'Meara's body language just before he conceded Harrington's putt appeared to confirm it.

"I thought Mark had already conceded the putt to Padraig," is Lehman's recollection. "It was definitely an embarrassing moment when I realised he hadn't."

Okay, if Tom Lehman swears he didn't set foot on the green following O'Meara's putt, I've got to believe him. But in accepting his version of the episode I think he also has to accept my contention that having been a participant in one premature celebration at the 17th makes him doubly culpable for engaging in another only moments later.

Call me a curmudgeonly traditionalist if you will, but to my mind end-zone gyrations, sack-dances and congratulatory chest-bumping have no place in the world of sport. I don't like it when a soccer player whose goal has just cut a 3-0 deficit to 3-1 pulls his shirt over his head and comports himself as if he's just single-handedly won the World Cup, and I am particularly disgusted when golfers behave that way.

But if I'm going to criticise people for surrendering their manners to hot-headed emotion I suppose I must be consistent. If Walter Hagen and Ted Ray, the original Ryder Cup captains, would never have tolerated this sort of behaviour on the part of their players, neither would Grantland Rice or Bernard Darwin have called them "assholes" and for that I should apologise.
October 21, 1999

Pin flag that has become priceless

Many heartfelt words will by now have been written in tribute to the deep and abiding kinship harboured by the late Payne Stewart for Ireland, for Irish golf and for the Irish people, but a brief episode earlier this summer remains unchronicled. Of this I am confident, because there were only two witnesses, and one of them is no longer with us.

For the past four years I have chaired a golf tournament at my home club outside Boston to benefit Our Lady's Hospital for Sick Children in Crumlin, Dublin. The proceeds of this event are substantially augmented by an auction conducted in conjunction with the awards dinner. Over the years, a pin flag from a Major championship, signed by the winner, has been demonstrated to be a consistently popular item, and since I am the one with presumed access to said champions, it has fallen unto my lot to secure the signatures.

I had two Pinehurst flags — one for our event, another to be donated to the golf classic Eamonn Coghlan runs at Luttrellstown Castle each June to benefit the same hospital — in my possession at the conclusion of this year's US Open, but in the clamour that reigned following Stewart's third Major win, the opportunity for a private moment never presented itself, and the flags went for the moment unsigned. Not a big deal, I thought. I've got nearly nine months to take care of this.

After the Luttrellstown Castle event the following week, however, the matter acquired some urgency. Undeterred by my failure to secure the signatures, Eamonn Coghlan auctioned off a Pinehurst flag signed by Payne Stewart for, I believe, £1,000 — on the promise that it would be delivered immediately after the British Open.

Payne Stewart: three-time major winner and gentleman.

Under normal circumstances this would have presented no problem, but the events surrounding the baseball All Star game delayed my arrival in Carnoustie until the morning the championship began, and, by the time I got to the course on Thursday, Stewart had already finished his round, completed his interviews, and helicoptered his way back to St Andrews, where he was staying.

On Friday afternoon, I was waiting near the 18th green as Payne completed his round. Circumstances did not augur well for my mission. Having bogeyed the last two holes, the US Open champion was not only likely to be in ill humour, but it momentarily appeared that he might be in danger of missing the cut. Under these grim circumstances almost any other golfer would have been unapproachable.

After putting out, Stewart first visited the scorer's cabin to sign his card, and then endured a couple of television interviews after he emerged. When he had finished, he saw me there waiting.

"What do you want?" he asked in mock disgust.

I told him that I needed a favour and did my best to briefly explain the situation.

"Where are the flags now?" he asked.

"Right here in my briefcase," I told him.

"Come on," he said, casting a nervous eye toward the dozens of autograph-seekers lining the path to the clubhouse. "Bring them down to the locker-room and let's do it right now."

Given the circumstances, many a golfer might at that moment have been smashing clubs against the wall, and others would have sought refuge in the physio's trailer or the players' lounge, which are off-limits to the press. But as Payne Stewart spread the flags on a table in the Carnoustie locker-room and signed his name, he wanted to know about the hospital and the charity tournament.

"How have you done so far?" he asked.

I told him that we'd managed to donate over $100,000 to Our Lady's Hospital over the four years.

"Wow," he smiled. "That's great."

William Payne Stewart was never what you'd call a hell-raiser, but earlier in his career, prior to the spiritual phase which accompanied his later successes, he indulged his fondness for both cigars and cigarettes.

Later on, he became a spokesman warning kids off tobacco, but those of us in this business knew that he hadn't really quit smoking, he'd merely stopped buying. If you chose to follow him out of the press tent at the conclusion of a post-round interview session hoping for a more private chat, he was usually amenable, but at a price: he'd want to bum a cigarette.

He won two US Opens and one PGA Championship, but, to my mind, it is his comportment throughout last month's Ryder Cup which will remain his lasting legacy. At one point during his final-day match against Colin Montgomerie, one of the Brookline hecklers bellowed in the midst of Monty's backswing. Stewart, who was waiting to play his own shot, came racing across the fairway and stood at the edge of the ropes.

"Who said that?" he demanded, and after several members of the gallery pointed out the offender, Stewart told the fellow: *"Get out of here! We don't need your kind around here."*

He stood there until he was satisfied that the marshals had taken the miscreant into custody.

On several other occasions that day Stewart implored the crowd for civility in its treatment of Montgomerie. At the final hole, he probably could have halved his match with the European Number One, or even won it had Monty three-putted, but instead he conceded a 30-foot putt and went into the record books as a loser in the singles match. In fact, he was the biggest winner of the day.

"I looked at Mike (Hicks, his caddie) and said, 'I'm not going to make him putt this'," Stewart recalled later that day. "My individual statistics don't mean crap out here, and we'd already won the Ryder Cup. I wasn't going to put him through that. It wasn't necessary."

The gesture was very much in keeping with the tradition of the event. In the first Ryder Cup at Worcester, in 1927, with the matches safely in hand, Gene Sarazen intentionally three-putted the final hole to halve his singles game against Charles Whitcombe, and of course at Birkdale in 1969 Jack Nicklaus famously conceded Tony Jacklin's missable putt to produce a drawn result.

A self-described "rah-rah guy," Payne Stewart was probably more responsible than anyone for instilling the patriotic unity which brought the Americans back from the brink of defeat at Brookline, but no one was more embarrassed than he when that team spirit spilled over into runaway emotionalism and the disrespectful demonstrations that ensued that afternoon.

"That," he sighed, "is not what this event is about."

Eamonn Coghlan, by the way, got his Pinehurst flag, and delivered it to its new owner the week after the British Open. I still have the other. It is now priceless.
Thursday, Oct 28, 1999

Is Tiger about his father's work?

ST. ANDREWS

Comparisons, said the Buddha, are odious. Wonder what he would have said about comparisons *to* the Buddha?

Look, we've been as impressed as the next guy by what Tiger Woods hath wrought over the past year, but some people are getting a bit carried away with themselves.

Since Tiger tamed St Andrews and demolished the British Open field over the weekend to claim his third Major title in his last four attempts, the inevitable yardsticks have been trotted out: Ben Hogan, the last to accomplish this approximate feat, and Jack Nicklaus, whose prodigious collection of 18 professional Major titles will remain the standard until and unless Tiger overtakes it.

Comparing the 24-year-old Woods to Hogan and Nicklaus may not be fair, but it is at least understandable. Other people, including some in this business who ought to know better, seem to have gone completely over the top.

A day after Woods' Open win, one Scottish tabloid ran a spread placing Tiger squarely in the company of Ali, Pete Sampras, Pele, Mark Spitz, and Carl Lewis, suggesting that Woods might be "the Greatest Sportsman of All Time".

Michael Wilbon, writing in the *Washington Post*, suggested the time had come for Tiger to take his place alongside Babe Ruth, Joe Louis, Muhammad Ali, and Michael Jordan in the pantheon of American heroes who not only influenced their sports but "helped shape history".

As if that's not all a bit overwhelming, consider the estimate of Tiger's father (who was notably absent at the Old Course, but then, come to think of it, so was Mike Wilbon) of his son.

Speaking with *Sports Illustrated's* Rick Reilly, Earl Woods likened young Eldrick, who he likes to describe as "the Chosen One," to Gandhi. (You remember him. Short hitter, deadly putter, that Gandhi fellow. Crowds loved him.)

The Scottish *Sun* and the *Washington Post* weren't alone in making the Tiger-Ali analogy. Earl did it too, managing to backhand Ali in the process.

"Tiger will be a more important figure outside of golf than in it. He will make his mark on world history . . . He'll impact nations. Do you recall the impact Muhammad Ali had, even with his lack of education and lack of communication skills?"

"Lack of communication skills?" We might suggest that Woods dig up some video clips of the pre-Parkinsons Ali. Nor can one help but *pere* wonder what the opinion of Earl Woods the Green Beret might have been toward Muhammad Ali the anti-war activist 35 years or so ago, but anyway . . .

You find yourself left wondering, why did he stop with Gandhi? Why didn't Earl liken his son to Moses, or even to that other fellow?

The spectacle of Tiger leading his followers from the 18th tee and into the Promised Land on Sunday afternoon would be a powerful argument. Literally thousands of them surged forward, leaping like steeplechasers across the Swilcan Burn. For every one who miscalculated the jump (or worse, made it over only to be shoved back in by one of Pharaoh's men, who were disguised as R&A stewards), a hundred more made it to the land of milk and honey.

Earl Woods: likening Tiger to Gandhi.

Once he reached the 18th, Tiger blew another chance to fulfill his father's vision. He was, you will recall, preceded there by a prancing Edinburgh stripper named Jacqui Salmond, who cavorted about on the green wearing only a pair of spectacles until the stewards wrestled her to the ground and hauled her away.

Had he had his wits about him, instead of complaining that his "special moment" had been "interrupted," Tiger might have ordered the centu-rions to unbound the woman. He could then have reached into his bag and covered her nakedness with a Nike rain-suit, after which he could have held up his hand and admonished the crowd, "Let he who is without sin cast the first stone."

And then, while he was at it, he could have marched in and, brandishing a 60-degree wedge, driven the Scribes and Pharisees from the R&A clubhouse bar.

Well, maybe not the scribes. For the most part they were hammering away on deadline over in the press tent.

While unwavering in his conviction that his son is "The Chosen One," by the way, Earl Woods voiced a bit of disappointment in Tiger's sometimes worldly ways.

"His humanity and his compassion need work," lamented the father. "They have to counterbalance his striving for superiority. Nicklaus had his wife and kids for balance. Tiger has only me and his mother. Girlfriends don't do it. Girlfriends are here today and gone tomorrow. Without the proper balance, the individual becomes pompous and domineering."

Wonder what Tiger's girlfriend, Joanna Jagoda, thought when she read that? On the other hand, Eldrick probably has it in better perspective than does his dad. When it comes to matters like this, the old Boston Red Sox pitcher-cum-philosopher, Luis Tiant, once summed it up with his personal credo: "There's no such thing as an ugly white woman."

Three weeks from this morning Woods will tee it up at Valhalla in Louisville in search of his third Major title of the new millennium, but if you add the PGA title he won at Medinah last August to his US Open at Pebble Beach last month and last week's conquest at St Andrews, he has already won three within 12 months.

At St Andrews last week Tiger lamented the fact that he is sometimes held to a different standard than that reserved for mere mortals.

"I think that's been the case for awhile," said Woods. "I've had to do things other players don't have to do. Then again, I've gotten slammed for things that players do out there."

Could Eldrick possibly have meant throwing clubs on the Old Course, or was it a reference to the inventive stream of rich profanity accompanying a mis-hit shot at Pebble that was caught by a live television microphone?

"That's part of being in the spotlight more than others," said Woods. "When you have the camera on you and people look at you a little more intensely, then you're going to find sometimes that I am human, too."

Perhaps we should all back off and attempt to understand that sentiment.

Perhaps The Chosen One's father should as well.

July 27, 2000

The ins and outs of august Augusta

AUGUSTA

Monday at Augusta could have been Bargain Day at K-Mart. The queue started at the front door, snaked around the wooden porch which encircles the forest-green building, stretched across the bounds of the tarmac, out through the pines, and on nearly to the boundary of the first fairway. This was, mind you, three days before the 2001 Masters tournament would even start, and these people weren't waiting in line for liquid refreshment, the public toilets, or even Tiger Woods' autograph.

Rather, having ponied up several hundred dollars for a $26 practice-day badge, they were now queueing to enter the merchandise shop so they could spend hundreds more. The members of the semi-orderly procession were prodded along their way into the building, quickly relieved of their money, and ushered out another door, bearing their new swag — logoed Masters caps, shirts, jumpers and jackets — in green-and-white Augusta National carrier bags.

You might suppose that the staid officials of Augusta National would be above such blatantly manipulative marketing ploys, but you'd be wrong.

The face value of a four-day badge for the Masters Tournament is laughably priced at $100. The same badge will fetch 50 times that on the street outside, more when it represents the centerpiece of one of those $10,000 corporate packages. In the midst of all this unseemly money-changing on Washington Road, it is conveniently overlooked that the original suppliers of most of these black market badges are the Augusta National members themselves.

As a former Masters champion once put it: "They're whores for one week a year, and then they spend the other 51 weeks pretending they're *not* whores."

One cannot enter the grounds of Augusta National without feeling he has passed through a time warp of some sort. From the antebellum architecture and ambiance of the clubhouse to the stunning beauty of the spring magnolias and azaleas, the genteel and courtly charm of the hosts, the dignified deference of doting waiters and fawning clubhouse servants, the whole place is straight out of *Gone With the Wind.*

In January of 1933, the carefully-selected membership of an exclusive new golf club convened in Augusta. Following a lavish dinner at the Bon Air Hotel, Grantland Rice, the most celebrated sportswriter of his day and a charter member, rose to make a toast.

Prefacing his remarks by explaining that he had previously been a member of several nascent clubs, none of which had made it out of infancy, Rice opined that the other ventures had for the most part died from self-strangulation brought about by an overabundance of conflicting committees and meetings. Rice proposed a resolution that meetings should be dispensed with and that cofounders Bobby Jones and Clifford Roberts be authorised to operate the club at their discretion.

His audience, well-fortified with bootleg corn whiskey, to a man shouted *"Aye!"*

Jones and Roberts are no longer with us, but 68 years later, the guiding principles at Augusta National remain essentially undisturbed: it remains a virtual fiefdom, answerable to no laws but its own. Its practices are every bit as shrouded in secrecy as those of a Klan chapter.

Publicly discussing club business is itself grounds for expulsion, but then an Augusta member is never expelled as such. He just doesn't get a bill for the following year.

There is no membership list and no published dues structure. Indeed, one does not apply to become a member at Augusta National at all. Rather, one waits to be invited. Microsoft founder Bill Gates, at the time the world's richest man, once made the mistake of inquiring about membership, and is as a result still cooling his heels.

Another wealthy self-made American, the founder of a national hamburger chain, reputedly asked about joining Augusta National. Initially rebuffed, he sent word back that if he were accepted for membership, "I'll build them a new clubhouse," thereby ensuring that he would *never* get in.

A decade ago the Augusta membership recognised the potential threat posed by the furor at Shoal Creek. That Alabama country club, scheduled to play host to the 1990 US PGA, was forced to integrate, at risk of losing the tournament. Augusta National hastily recruited Ronald Townsend, its first (and only) black member, and in a radical departure from its traditional practices announced his nomination with great fanfare.

To this day, Ron Townsend's station during Masters week is the press centre, thereby ensuring that the media can't miss him in his green member's jacket, a daily reminder that the wheels of progress have turned.

In the absence of a published membership list, we have no idea how many Jewish or Catholic members Augusta National might have, but the probable answer is: not many.

Clifford Roberts' recorded views on the subject suggest that his disdain for the former faith bordered on anti-Semitism. As for the latter, we know this much: Roberts was childless by choice through two marriages, and left a substantial portion of his estate to Planned Parenthood.

Indeed, the story is told of a prospective nominee who had been warmly embraced by the membership, but who was ultimately blackballed by Roberts, who offered one simple (and unchallenged) justification for his veto:

Any man, said Roberts, "who is stupid enough to have five children isn't smart enough to belong to Augusta National."
April 05, 2001

Ben won his stripes before Tiger era

'It is the greatest achievement in golf — in the modern era.' William (Hootie) Johnson. *AUGUSTA*

Talk about left-handed compliments. On the other hand, what did you expect the esteemed chairman of the Augusta National Golf Club to say? Even as historians debate the issue of whether Tiger Woods's accomplishments over the past 10 months constitute a Grand Slam or merely a clean sweep of the sport's four major championships, the revisionists are already at work.

Not that anybody really expected the purists at Augusta to accept Woods's feat as the equal of Bobby Jones's 1930 run, when he won the US and British Amateur Championships and the US and British Opens — but as the vanquished Masters runner-up David Duval said in another connection on Sunday evening: "It's not even comparing apples and oranges. It's more like comparing apples and peanuts."

Duval was actually replying to an interrogator who had asked him to liken Woods's feat to Joe DiMaggio's 56-game hitting streak, but the observation is appropriate when it comes to Jones as well.

You wouldn't want to say it very loud on the hallowed grounds of the botanical cathedral Jones (with a little help from Alister McKenzie) carved out of a fruit orchard in Augusta, but what Jones did in 1930 hardly compares with what Eldrick Woods has accomplished since last June — and the fact that Woods's four majors didn't all come in the same calendar year should have absolutely no bearing on the argument.

"If it's not a slam," said David Feherty when we discussed the subject earlier in the week, "it's only because it's even *better* than a slam."

Comparisons between Tiger's achievement and Jones's 1930 run are entirely misplaced, and here's why: professionals could not even compete in two of the four "majors" (the British and US Amateurs) Jones won. Not only did he not have to face the likes of Gene Sarazen, Walter Hagen and Henry Cotton in winning those two events, but the field he beat consisted of a bunch of doctors and lawyers like himself.

Jones circa 1930 shouldn't be the standard at all. No one has matched Tiger's run of four straight modern majors, but if you're looking for valid comparisons, what Ben Hogan did almost half a century ago is at least worthy of mention in the same breath. In 1953, Hogan won the Masters, US Open and British Open in an era when it was logistically impossible to play all four events. The USPGA, a matchplay tournament in those days, finished the day before the British Open began, and since Hogan was obliged to qualify at Carnoustie, he was playing a qualifying round on the day the PGA semi-final was taking place in Birmingham, Michigan.

As it happened, following his near-fatal car accident in 1949, Hogan forever eschewed the PGA Championship, but he couldn't have played in it that year even if he'd wanted to.

In any event, having, like Tiger, won three majors the year before, Hogan came to Augusta in 1954 gunning for another, and very nearly pulled it off, losing the championship in a play-off when Sam Snead chipped in for a birdie on the 10th.

"It never occurred to me, and it certainly never occurred to Ben, that that would have constituted a Grand Slam or even for his fourth straight major," says Hogan's Boswell (and pallbearer) Dan Jenkins. "It wasn't in the same calendar year."

As awe-inspiring as Tiger's run since last June has been, Jenkins believes a case can be made for Hogan's post-recuperative achievements having been comparable.

"After the accident, Ben played a very limited schedule, but he still won six majors — the US Open in 1950, the Masters and the US Open in '51, and the only three he played in '53 — in four years," says Jenkins. "Tiger has now won six in five years."

Hogan had won 11 of the 25 tournaments he played in 1948, the year before the

Ben Hogan, watched by his partner Sam Snead (arms folded), during the 1956 Canada Cup, at Wentworth which the United States won.

accident, and in fact had two wins in four tries in 1949 before the head-on collision with a Greyhound bus which broke virtually every bone in his body.

The foremost medical specialists of his day predicted that, even if he did live, he would never play golf again. But in 1950 Hogan played four tournaments, and won two of them — including the US Open at Merion.

He played four events in 1951, and won three of them, including the Masters and the US Open at Oakland Hills. He had an off-year in 1952 with just one win in four tries, that in the Colonial in Texas, but bounced back the next year to set the standard that would go unrivalled for 47 years until Woods matched it last year.

In short, from the beginning of 1950 through the fall of 1953, Hogan entered just 18 tournaments, and won 11 of them — including six majors.

Whether Woods's achievement at Augusta last Sunday constitutes a *bona fide* Grand Slam may be debated by golfing purists for years to come; but then again, by the time he gets through, there may be no room for debate at all. Unlike Hogan, Tiger's streak isn't necessarily over yet. He could have *seven* in a row by the time the year is out.

April 12, 2001

Captains resolved to healing wounds

PORTSMOUTH, RHODE ISLAND

Relations between the two superpowers have been somewhat strained of late, but the leaders of the respective sides got together this week for a bit of civil gamesmanship that appears, at least for the moment, to have produced a cordial detente.

No, not George W Bush and Vladimir Putin. We're talking about Curtis Strange and Sam Torrance.

For this particular summit meeting, the 2001 Ryder Cup captains engaged in a friendly match over Peter de Savary's spectacular new Carnegie Abbey links on the shores of Rhode Island's Narragansett Bay last Tuesday afternoon. For drama and excitement, the made-for-television event had all the drama of a US Open play-off, as Strange led from wire to wire to win 74-76 in a medal-play game taped for inclusion on Shell's *Wonderful World of Golf* series later this fall.

Strange pocketed $100,000 for his day's work, (double what Torrance earned), but any attempt to view the outcome as a harbinger of things to come at The Belfry this September would be misplaced. The last time two sitting Ryder Cup captains played one another on the Shell series was back in 1997, when Tom Kite kicked the living spit out of Severiano Ballesteros (65-74 — on Seve's home course in Spain), but it didn't help much when the teams got to Valderrama later that year.

The convivial atmosphere stood in marked contrast to the last time the Americans and Europeans faced off on a golf course, less than 100 miles removed from Tuesday's venue. Torrance, in his role as Mark James' vice-captain at the 1999 Ryder Cup, had been among the more vocal critics of the war-dance the American players performed across the 17th green at The Country Club following Justin Leonard's dramatic putt (while Jose Maria Olazabal stood forlornly awaiting his chance to equalise), but two days ago the Scotsman declined a chance to restate his objections.

"Brookline is over," he said. "I don't want to go back to it."

Strange, by contrast, came as close to an apology for the 1999 episode as has yet been uttered by an official US Ryder Cup representative. Although he was not present (he was home in Virginia, watching on television) for the appalling breach of sportsmanship, Strange said this week: "I'll admit it. In the pure sense of golf etiquette, we crossed the line." In the hope of blunting the pugnacious attitudes that have characterised recent Ryder Cups, Strange and Torrance have decided to revive an abandoned tradition — the Sunday night post-match "victory dinner," attended by both teams.

"We're going to have all 24 players sit down and eat and have a few drinks together when it's over," said Strange. "When I mentioned reviving the Sunday night dinner to Sam, he told me he'd been thinking the same thing. It's going to be a little more informal than it used to be."

Strange represented the United States in six Ryder Cups, while Torrance played in eight, in addition to his role at The Country Club two years ago. Both men know that their toughest task may be blunting the lingering bad feelings on both sides following the emotional displays that attended the last event. The fact that the two adversaries are old friends may help.

"We're good mates, and we've been good mates a long time," said Torrance. "And we'll carry that through the teams."

"Everybody knows how well Sam and I get along," added Strange. "Twenty-six years ago when I went to Europe for the first time at the age of 20 or 21. I had dinner with Sam the first week I was there."

"That was only because I liked your missus," Torrance interrupted with a smile. "I still do."

Of more concern to the two captains may be the selections of their respective sides. Given their propensity for wholesale collapses on Sunday afternoons this year, Strange was asked if he was concerned about the recent form of Phil Mickelson and David Duval.

"Where are they ranked in the world?" asked Strange by way of reply. (Second and seventh, actually.) "There's your answer."

And while the last thing Strange needs is one more shaky putter on his team, Stewart Cink's third-place finish in last weekend's US Open vaulted him to eighth place in the US points table.

Torrance forthrightly admitted that he may have an even bigger problem. The European skipper noted that while the current top five European players (Pierre Fulke, Padraig Harrington, Lee Westwood, Darren Clarke, and Thomas Bjorn) all appeared to be on solid ground, "the next six or seven could all change in the next few months."

And Torrance, for one, hopes that they will, if only to alleviate a looming nightmare in selecting his captain's picks.

"If it were done right now I'd have a major headache," said Torrance, "because Sergio Garcia, Colin Montgomerie, Jesper Parnevik and Bernhard Langer would all be out."

At the same time, asked about the attendant pressures of captaining in a Ryder Cup, Torrance said "It's a hell of a lot easier than playing in one."

Tuesday's match was a light-hearted affair, with Peter Allis and Jack Whitaker roaming the fairways alongside Strange and Torrance.

Now, you might assume that the contest would provide a perfect lead-up to September's confrontation at the Belfry, but in actuality the telecast won't be shown until October 2nd — a week after the Ryder Cup has been played. Asked if he wished it could air before the matches, Torrance had a quick reply.

"No!" The European captain shook his head. "Jesus, he *won!* Do you think I'm stupid?"
June 21, 2001

Mickelson insists he has no major cause for regret

GULLANE SCOTLAND

The title is now, by consensus and by acclamation, his alone: Best Player Never To Have Won A Major. "I don't mind," said Phil Mickelson. "As a matter of fact, I feel kind of honoured when people say that. But make no mistake about it, it's a club I'd like to resign from at the soonest possible moment."

Officials at St Andrews' Old Course have become accustomed to visiting Americans arriving at the first tee, hoping to bluster their way onto the course in the absence of a tee time, but when Lefty showed up with his fourball Monday afternoon, an accommodation was made. Mickelson and his gang were slotted in just before our 3:40 game, meaning we followed the life-and-death match between Lefty and his caddie Jim (Bones) Mackay (with a couple of their higher-handicap buddies filling in).

After 16 holes the servant was on the verge of bludgeoning the master, but Bones sent an errant drive into the Old Course hotel off the 17th tee, Mickelson birdied the last, and the match finished level.

At the same time, it speaks volumes about Mickelson's renewed dedication that he had driven the two-and-a-half hours from Muirfield to St Andrews after 54 holes' worth of practice time on the former over the previous two days.

Although he has come close in the other three majors, Mickelson's British Open record has been spotty at best. In nine attempts he has missed two cuts, and finished 11th in his only Top 20 performance.

A couple of years ago, recognising that his game was ill-suited to links play, he began to work on it in earnest on both sides of the Atlantic. Titleist, his club sponsor, even built a links-style hole at its California testing facility so he could practise run-up shots.

Last year he prepared for the Open at Lytham with a stop-over in Ireland, and was made an honorary member at Lahinch. This year he arrived early in Scotland, and has been touring the East Lothian links when he hasn't been playing Muirfield and St Andrews.

"The biggest motivating factor is I want to win events, and the most elite events are the four majors. Winning the British Open would give me the greatest satisfaction, given the degree of alteration I've had to go through to accommodate playing here," said Mickelson on the eve of the 131st Open Championship.

Phil Mickelson: "I didn't have the control over the ball..."

"It was about a year and a half ago that I realised my style of play was not going to be conducive to doing well in this event, and I wanted to change that, because not only did I want to compete here, I wanted to compete more regularly. Every time I'd come (to Scotland) I felt I had a chance to win, but as the wind would pick up and the greens would dry out and firm up, I found I didn't have the control over the ball I needed. I was putting the ball in horrendous spots, and having a tough time scoring.

"My golf swing had to take on a number of changes," he explained. "My ball flight had to take on a number of changes. My visualisation of shots had to change to accommodate the ball landing 30 yards short of the pin, being able to turn the ball around the bunkers, as opposed to just flying over them.

"I'm ready to go. I'm just coming here with a variety of shots I didn't have before."

Mickelson turned professional just a month before the Open was last played at Muirfield in 1992. He flew to Scotland and attempted to qualify at North Berwick that year, but came up short. So he turned around and flew home again.

By his own estimate, Lefty is playing the best golf of his career.

In the year's two earlier majors, he finished outright third at the Masters, and was runner-up to Tiger Woods in last month's US Open at Bethpage. A week later (with Woods taking the week off), he won the Canon Greater Hartford Open. He has already pocketed nearly $4 million this year alone.

"I've been fortunate, on and off the course, to put myself and my family in a position where we don't have to worry about finances," said Mickelson. "All I care about is winning golf tournaments."

Whether he is destined to go down in golf history as one of the game's great unfulfilled talents or merely as a very good player whose career happened to coincide with Tiger Woods' remains unlearned, but we do know this much: Phil Mickelson isn't complaining.

"It's a great opportunity and a great challenge to play against a man who's arguably the best player of all time," said Mickelson. "What a great way for me to try to compete, try to get better, and bring out my best golf.

"Had Tiger not been in the field, and not been doing as well as he had and not challenged me to get better, I don't think I would have played to the same level for the past year or two, so it's been a huge benefit. The fact is, he's driven television ratings, driven the purses up, driven the fan interest and the spectator interest."

Given all of that, someone asked Mickelson yesterday whether his "dream" would be coming down the stretch neck-and-neck with Woods on Sunday and pulling ahead to win.

"Dream?" asked Mickelson. "It's something I work for, yes. It's a motivating factor for me to try to get better, to make that a reality. But '*dream?*'

"I don't lie in bed thinking about it, if that's what you mean."
July 18, 2002

Tiger puts his paw in his mouth again

SANDWICH

Tiger Woods has at times displayed an uncanny propensity for uttering inappropriate things at inopportune moments, witness last year's impetuous observation that he had "a million reasons" why a win at Mount Juliet would be more important to him than a Ryder Cup victory. And on the eve of the 132nd British Open Championship he did it again.

Enter the Ugly American.

Given what we know of Tigermania and the British media, the surprising thing is that the story didn't acquire more legs than it did, but as one who bore witness to Tuesday's *faux pas* at Sandwich, I believe it's safe to say that it was never Tiger's intent to disrespect Paul Lawrie, but once the words were out of his mouth it required a contorted bit of logic to interpret his remarks any other way.

Ironically, Tiger's gaffe followed an uncharacteristically revealing bit of introspection in which he had explained his guarded stance toward the press.

"It's one of those things where no matter what you do, you're going to get ripped," he had sighed. "If you show too much, you're going to get criticised for that. If you don't show enough, you get criticised for that . . . I think I've shown more of myself of late, the last few years, than I did when I first turned pro, because obviously I wasn't comfortable at all."

The next question, while not particularly elegantly phrased, had to do with "quirky golf courses" producing quirky champions. It looked like a fastball down the middle, and Tiger couldn't resist swinging.

"I don't think so," he said. "I don't think so at all, because if that was true, then '99 in Carnoustie, one of the best golf courses in the world, if not the best golf course in the world, the most difficult. I think the winner says it all right there."

Never mind that it doesn't parse. That's what he said, verbatim. No sooner had the words escaped his lips than I saw the heads of three Scotsmen huddled together, asking one another, no doubt, "Did he just say what I *think* he said?"

In short order the sound bite was circulating over the BBC, and the Scots formed a posse and chased Tiger down in the car park. Of course Tiger hadn't meant to insult Lawrie, he explained; in fact he had meant to compliment him.

That the Scottish scribes decided to accept his explanation and, at Tiger's request, to downplay the episode can mean only one of two things: they are either extremely gullible or extremely polite.

Whether Tiger meant to diss Lawrie or not, the fact of the matter is that Lawrie was the world's 178th-ranked golfer on the Sunday in question, and what Woods was clearly saying was that if a Paul Lawrie could win the Open Championship on that course that day, then *anybody* could have. Twist it any way you like, but it's hard to see how he could have meant anything else.

But then Woods can sometimes be given to speaking elliptically, inviting us to draw our own conclusions. "My knee is fine," he tells us, but in almost the same breath allows that he wishes his legs would allow him to practice for five and six hours a day the way he'd really like.

Whether the fault is his or ours, the impression lingers that all is not well in Tigerland. For the first time since 1999, not one of golfdom's major trophies resides at his home in Isleworth, and not even last weekend's victory in Chicago has managed to dull the perception that Eldrick is in the throes of a slump.

Some slump, this one. Woods has gone to the post 11 times this year and come home a winner in four of them. If he fails to win at Sandwich this week he will have gone five straight majors without a win. But since he won the 2002 US Open at

Bethpage, Tiger has earned $8,500,000.

It probably also bears noting that between his first major — the 1997 Masters — and his next, Woods played 10 majors without winning one, and we don't recall hearing the word "slump" then.

Part of the problem lies in our unrealistic expectations. When Woods won four grand slam events in a row he encouraged debate over the legitimacy of the "Tiger Slam," but concomitantly set himself up for a fall: for a while it became bigger news when Tiger *didn't* win a major than when he did.

By placing an avowed premium on grand slam events, and by tailoring his schedule to attack them, of course, Woods played his own part in this little psychodrama.

On the other hand, it's not just that Tiger's been losing majors, it's how he's been losing them. He began this year's Masters with a 76 and closed it out with a 75. He shot 75 in the third round of the US Open. And his 81 on Saturday in last year's Open Championship was his worst round ever.

At Tuesday's *tête-à-tête* with the press at Sandwich, Tiger pointed out that while the Muirfield nightmare represented his highest score in a professional event, it was not by a long shot his highest on a golf course. Moreover, he noted, "I shot 65 the next day."

Which was true enough. And that was good enough for a piece of 28th place.
Jul 17, 2003

Hootie hogs limelight as Martha misses cut

AUGUSTA

Less than a half-mile from the front gate of Augusta National, the local constabulary had set aside a vacant lot for last Saturday morning's protests. Several dozen squad cars and over 100 Augusta policemen, sheriff's deputies, and Georgia Highway Patrolmen were on hand to keep Martha Burk's minions and the pro-Hootie Johnson counter-demonstrators from the Ku Klux Klan from setting upon one another.

They needn't have worried. J J Harper, the self-proclaimed Grand Imperial Wizard of the American Knights of the Ku Klux Klan, had even worse luck marshalling his troops than Martha did hers. In fact, when we came upon the Grand Imperial Wizard and his lone deputy the two of them were in mufti (apart from a Confederate hat the junior wizard was wearing) as they attempted to erect a sign bearing a hate message.

"When are you guys going to suit up?" we asked them, but Harper's hoods and sheets must have still been at the cleaners.

One suspects that the memberships of the Royal & Ancient Golf Club, Royal St George's, and, for that matter, Portmarnock, watched last weekend's events in Augusta with more than cursory interest. One also suspects that along about Sunday afternoon they were breathing the same sigh of relief Hootie did after Martha missed the cut.

The Burk bandwagon, which had threatened to cast a pall over the 2003 Masters, barely caused a ripple. Trepidation over a potentially embarrassing demonstration by Burk and her followers from the National Council of Women's Organizations evaporated the moment the coach emptied out just before noon on Saturday, disgorging 16 demonstrators who'd been bussed down from Atlanta. Burk lamely attempted to claim that she had deliberately "negotiated" an undersized demonstration, but clearly, she was the one who'd been embarrassed.

"They couldn't even fill a bus," marvelled one onlooker.

Although a scattering of sympathetic onlookers pitched in to join the NCWO group, Martha's demonstration never exceeded three score. Craig Stadler, the last-place finisher in the Masters, had bigger galleries than that.

The day before the Masters began, the Augusta National chairman had said: "I don't tell Tiger how to play golf, and he won't tell us how to run our private club."

Perhaps Hootie *should* have told Tiger Woods how to play golf. Sunday's events conspired to ensure that the first commercial-free Masters telecast was also Eldrick-free, as the two-time defending champion double-bogeyed the third hole and was never heard from again.

On the other hand, anyone who spent much time around the 2003 Masters is going to be seeing pigs in his sleep.

Hootie Johnson: "There never will be a female member..."

Once the mud dries, the enduring image of the event isn't going to be Mike Weir trying on his green jacket, Len Mattiace hockeying putts back and forth across the 10th green, or Jeff Maggert under attack from his own golf ball.

Rather, it's going to be a pig.

At her demonstration on Saturday, Burk addressed her platoon while standing before a gigantic pink pig balloon festooned with the logos of the Augusta National's corporate sponsors.

Just down the road vendors were doing a brisk business peddling "Root for Hootie" t-shirts which coupled a caricature of the chairman posed alongside a centaur-like creature combining Martha Burk's head and a porcine torso.

At Saturday's rally, Burk's NCWO minions were also distributing cute little buttons reading: "Women Pay while CEOs Play," depicting several green-jacketed pigs playing golf.

Let's put this in perspective, though. Hootie Johnson was clearly responsible for escalating the battle with his overreactive response to Burk's interrogative, but Burk's strident rhetoric has often made her seem downright puerile. Her suggestion early on in the debate that the Masters should be moved to another golf course painted her as golf-ignorant, and many found last month's attempt to link the women's membership issue to the war against Iraq nothing short of disgusting.

When he responded to Burk's first letter Johnson said that "there well may come a day when women will be invited to join, but that timetable will be ours and not at the point of a bayonet." After last week's activities, Hootie, sounding like George W Bush gloating about Saddam Hussein, had revised his posture.

"There never will be a female member, six months after the Masters, a year, 10 years, or ever," he promised a sympathetic Atlanta columnist. "There never has been, at any time, any consideration of Augusta National taking in women members."

In other words, the sum effect of Ms Burk's protest coupled with its evident lack of support may actually have emboldened Hootie and strengthened the club's resolve.

Meanwhile, at his pre-Masters address, Johnson had said: "The club's position on our membership is very comfortable with our present status.

"It's not my issue alone," he insisted. "I promise you what I'm saying: If I drop dead this second, our position will not change."

Sixty-two of Augusta's 300 members showed up at Hootie's news conference, pushing many legitimate reporters out of the room and giving at least the illusion of solidarity.

But just because Hootie says he speaks for all of them doesn't make it true. Nearly a year's worth of moral debate resulted in just two resignations this time around, but if Martha can successfully persuade her followers to, as she vowed last weekend, "vote with their pocketbooks," she will be speaking a language the boys in green jackets understand.

Martha Burk may have been the clear-cut loser last weekend, but we may not have heard the last of her.

While the laws of the land, and, more importantly, the US Constitution support Hootie's side of this issue, the moral imperative and the tide of history could still be on Martha's.

Meanwhile, spare a thought for the poor pig, who never asked to be dragged into any of this.

April 17, 2003

This Ben Curtis pots the famous Claret Jug

SANDWICH

Since the British Open was first played at Royal St George's 109 years ago, the locals had been waiting for a man from Kent to win, and when one finally did, he turned out to be from Kent, Ohio.

Ben Curtis played his college golf at Kent State University, but he wasn't born until 1977, fully seven years after that institution of higher learning came to world-wide attention when the Ohio National Guardsmen turned their guns on student protesters and killed four of them.

Prior to last Sunday's stunning developments at Royal St George's, the nearest Curtis had come to full-scale media interrogation had come last February, when Ben Curtis was busted for pot.

Ben Curtis: last minute qualifier and unlikely winner.

We should hasten to explain that until late last weekend Ben Curtis the golfer wasn't even the United States' most prominent Ben Curtis. Ben Curtis also happens to be the name of the actor who portrays "Steven," the "Dell guy" in an irksome series of television commercials inundating American living rooms, and when Ben the Actor was arrested for criminal possession of marijuana earlier this year after making an ill-advised decision to purchase a bag of high-grade grass from a street dealer on New York's Lower East Side, Ben the Golfer found himself answering a lot of annoying questions.

American headline writers could not restrain themselves from gleefully capitalizing on the TV computer pitchman's most quotable line: "Hey, dude, you're getting a *cell!*"

Along about the time he got to five-under par in the final round and it became apparent Curtis might not disappear back from whence he had come, British journalists began flocking to their American colleagues in the press tent in search of background information on the upstart leader.

"Are you kidding?" *Boston Herald* golf correspondent Joe Gordon replied to one. "I've only written two words about him all week, and those were 'Ben' and 'Curtis'."

Curtis may well have been the most unlikely winner in the 132 year-history of the championship. His only previous win as a professional had been pretty small potatoes indeed, at the Myrtle Beach stop on the Hooters Tour last year, and the most significant titles of his golfing life had been back-to-back wins in the Ohio Amateur.

Half an hour spent with the new champion in the media centre did little to illuminate the picture. He'd grown up in Ohio, on a public golf course in Ostrander, outside Columbus, which his grandfather owned and operated.

He'd qualified for the 2003 Open on 10 days' notice, when his best-ever PGA Tour finish, a 13th-place tie at the Western Open, got him in under the "top eight finishers not otherwise exempt" clause, and prior to arriving in Sandwich for his practice rounds, Curtis said the sum of his links golf experience consisted of two rounds in Germany during the 2000 Amateur World Team competition.

If the 26-year-old seemed unfazed by his lofty place among the leaders going into the final day, you could probably chalk that up to innocence.

"I've been playing a lot better the last three weeks and this kind of golf suits me the best. It's not going to take 10, 15 or 20 under par to win. If you stay around par, you're going to be right in the hunt," he said late on Saturday, and you just wanted to pat him on the head.

"Even if you are like two or three back going into the back nine, you never know what can happen," he said. "If I shoot like I did today, like four-under, you never know. You get a couple of putts to go in and anything can happen. There are a lot of heavy guys out there and I'll just do the best I can."

At one point on the back nine young Curtis became dizzy atop the leaderboard and carded four bogeys in a six-hole stretch, but in the end his game held up where those of Thomas Bjorn, Vijay Singh, Davis Love, and Tiger Woods did not, and even while being grilled under the hot lights and microphones an hour later, Curtis seemed blissfully undaunted: No, he hadn't been surprised. He'd always had confidence he would win a tournament sooner or later. He described the experience as "a dream come true," but it was stunningly apparent it seemed of small consequence to him.

And when he finally took his leave of the press tent, R & A officials had to chase him down to remind him to take his newly acquired hardware along with him. Having just won the most coveted trophy in golf, Ben Curtis tried to walk out of the press tent without the Claret Jug.

Whether Curtis goes on to take his place in the pantheon of great champions or proves to be a flash-in-the-pan on the order of Bill Rogers, another postwar St George's Open winner, it would seem improbable that he will ever win another in Sandwich.

Although R & A officials heatedly denied that a decision had already been taken to drop St George's from the Open rotation, it seems more likely than not the Sandwich club may join its immediately abutting neighbours, Prince's and Royal Cinque Ports, on the historical roster of courses which have previously hosted Opens but no longer do.

Ben Curtis may miss it, but it's a safe bet most of the professionals will not.

While he wasn't exactly rancorous about it, Tiger Woods reminded people all week long that St George's could be a penally unfair track, one which could reward a perfect drive (though God knows Tiger didn't hit many of those last week) with a flukish kick into almost unplayably tangled rough.

Jack Nicklaus may have won three Opens, but he never won at Sandwich, and when he last played in a championship there, Nicklaus found himself fending off accusations that he had described Royal St George's as "the worst golf course" on the British Open rotation.

"I never said that," explained Nicklaus. "What I did say was that as a rule you could rank the British Open venues from north to south. Sandwich just happens to be the furthest south."

July 24, 2003

Arnie and Army set to quit field with pride

AUGUSTA

Every man who has ever played the Masters tournament recalls his first trip down Magnolia Lane, but for Arnold Palmer it was particularly memorable. Palmer won $695 for finishing 10th in that 1955 Masters, but it was the first cheque he was ever allowed to cash.

After opting to join the professional ranks in the fall of 1954, Palmer had played what was then known as the "Winter Tour,' but PGA regulations of that era mandated a six-month probationary status in which an apprentice pro could compete in tour events but was not allowed to keep his winnings.

"It was a relief to get here," said Palmer as he reflected on his first visit to Augusta, "because I knew that if I won any money, I'd get it, and that was important."

The weekend before the Masters four years later, Palmer had tied for the lead after 72 holes of the Azalea Open, a now-defunct event which was played in Wilmington, North Carolina. Most tournaments weren't televised back then, so there was no need for "sudden death" play-offs, and in this instance the issue would be resolved by a 36-hole play-off.

That Monday, under brutal conditions, Palmer shot 75-78 to defeat Howie Johnson, and then raced across two states to Augusta, where he registered for the Masters that night.

The next morning The Man Who Would Be King was paired with Dow Finsterwald against Ben Hogan and Jack Burke in a not-so-friendly practice-round Nassau at Augusta National.

A fatigued Palmer struggled so badly that at one point he overheard Hogan sneer in a stage-whisper to Burke, "How the hell did Palmer get an invitation to this tournament, anyway?" Stung by the criticism, Palmer used it for motivation as he went on to win the tournament. His score of 284 left him a stroke ahead of Doug Ford and Fred Hawkins.

At 28, he was the youngest Masters winner since 25-year-old Byron Nelson had taken the green jacket in 1937.

"Things back then were so different it's hard to explain," Palmer recalled on the eve of his 50th and final Masters. "In '58, the total money on the Tour, counting the Masters and everything, was less than $1 million. First place here that year was $14,000, and I'd never seen $14,000 in my life. That's a fact."

After being fitted for his green jacket, Palmer slipped his cheque book to his late wife, Winnie, with instructions to pay his caddie, Nathaniel (Ironman) Avery.

"I said, 'Here, write Ironman a cheque and give him 10 per cent'," remembered Palmer.

So Winnie made out a cheque for fourteen *thousand* dollars and presented it to the caddie.

"It's funny now, but it wasn't funny at the time," said Arnie after the laughter had subsided yesterday. "By the time we realised what she'd done, old Ironman was headed out the gate, because he knew no one would cash it for him here. The good news was we caught up with him and gave him a cheque for $1,400."

Good news for Palmer, anyway. Ironman's reaction remains unrecorded.

On the Tuesday night before the Masters a year later Palmer found himself hosting his first Champion's Dinner.

"Maybe I was just sort of a green kid and didn't know a hell of a lot about it, but I had great respect for the guys that played golf, like Hogan and Nelson and Snead and Sarazen and that gang that were in there," he recalled.

"To be in that room with them and Bobby Jones and Cliff Roberts, the whole scene was one that you could never duplicate. You couldn't put a room of characters together like we had when I first won the Masters."

Arnold would become the Tiger Woods of his own special era. He was the King before Elvis, and no one ever questioned whether Arnold Palmer belonged after that 1958 win. As either the champion or defending champion, he was a participant in every green jacket ceremony for the next eight years, winning in 1958, 1960, 1962, and 1964.

"How many could I have won? A lot more than four," said Palmer.

"There were a couple of obvious ones, and there were others that weren't so obvious. In '57 I had a shot with nine holes to go and didn't perform very well, but from '58, oh, God, almost up till 1970, with a few exceptions I would have had a shot every year."

In those early years Augusta National used to provide free passes to the soldiers

Arnold Palmer (right) and Jack Nicklaus during practice for the 1965 Open Championship.

from nearby Camp Gordon, and the GIs in their fatigues became the earliest recruits in what would grow into a worldwide movement known as Arnie's Army.

Arnie's Army will stage its final march this weekend. The 74-year-old Palmer reiterated on Tuesday what the golfing world had known for months when he said: "This will be my last Masters."

Today's playing partners will include Bob Estes and Nathan Smith, the US Mid-Amateur Champion with whom he played a Tuesday practice round.

Asked what advice he might impart to the 25-year-old Smith, Palmer replied: "I've seen a lot of them, from Tiger back to Nicklaus and others, and if I can teach them to leave the game better when they leave than when they found it, then I've been successful."

Arnie hasn't made the cut at the Masters since 1983, but when he was asked how he'd like his final walk up the 18th fairway to unfold tomorrow he had a defiantly predictable answer.

"I know exactly how I want Friday to unfold," replied Palmer. "At the end of the day I want to be asking, *'What's my starting time on Saturday?'*"
April 08, 2004

Hooters on a Daly basis

AUGUSTA

At six o'clock on Tuesday evening a score of green-jacketed Masters legends were convening in the Augusta National clubhouse for the traditional Champions Dinner. (The *piece de resistance*, as chosen by this year's host Phil Mickelson, was lobster ravioli.)

At just about the same time half a mile up Washington Road another press conference involving a two-time Major winner was about to get underway at the local chapter of Hooters.

In what must be considered a marriage made in heaven, the restaurant chain specialising in beer, wings, and scantily-clad waitresses was about to take the wraps off its one-man golf stable.

And surrounded by Hooters girls, Hooters executives, and noisy, beer-swilling Hooters customers, John Daly was plainly in his element.

Spotting a familiar face in the crowd, he smiled, shrugged his shoulders, and delivered his one-word summation of the ongoing proceedings: "Chaos."

Chaos would better describe Daly's working garb these days, but then, a man with three ex-wives and a backlog of casino markers probably needs a lot of sponsors.

It is believed that when Daly tees up in the 2005 Masters today he will set an all-time PGA Tour record for most logos, one shirt.

Let's see: The right collar is embroidered with the name of "Mark Christopher Chevrolet," a California automobile dealership. The left collar advertises Daly's "Red Neck Putters".

The right sleeve says "Dunlop," and the left is emblazoned with the logo of Daly's clothing line, Lion merchandise.

Centred squarely in the middle of the back of his shirt is the logo for Loco, a low-rent ball Daly endorses (but does not play), while on the right front of his shirt he wears an advertisement for "Lumber 84," a company which also sponsors Vijay Singh.

The left front of the shirt bears the title of Daly's latest sponsor, Hooters.

His status as a walking billboard might strain the bounds of good taste, but it apparently does not bring him into conflict with PGA Tour regulations.

"There's no limit," said Daly. "You can wear as many logos as you want."

Daly will not only wear the Hooters logo on his golf shirts, outerwear, and bag, but will participate in advertising campaigns for the restaurant chain and its affiliates, including Myrtle Beach-based Hooters Air, and the soon-to-be-opened Hooters Casino in Vegas.

He will also serve as "honorary chairman" of the Hooters Tour, a minor league circuit which functions as a feeder system for the PGA-affiliated Nationwide Tour.

Flanked by a bevy of young blondes in orange hot pants, Bob Brooks, the 72-year-old chairman of Hooters International, said his company had been approached about sponsorships by several tour players, "But John Daly is what we've always wanted, and John is the guy we got."

"He's absolutely the perfect guy to represent Hooters," said marketing director Mike McNeil. "He is, in fact, a lot like Hooters."

Which is true enough: there's always been a lot of cross-pollination between Daly's gallery and a Hooters clientele, and it's no accident that Daly has been setting up his merchandise trailer in the parking lot of the Augusta Hooters during Masters week for the past several years. That, after all, is where his fans are.

A sign outside the Lion Trailer warns "John Daly Will Sign Autographs on Lion Merchandise Only," but that didn't seem to be exactly accurate. In an hour of watching, the best we could tell, John Daly will sign *anything*.

At least a hundred people were queued up before the trailer in the Hooters parking lot. The Lion Trailer won't threaten the business of the public merchandise shop at Augusta National, but Daly did have on sale shirts, T-shirts, sweat-shirts, towels, balls, flags, Red Neck putters, and assorted golf clubs.

In commemoration of the sponsorship deal, Brooks presented Daly with what he called "the most coveted card in America," a Hooters VIP card, entitling him to free food and beverages at any of the chain's 400-plus worldwide establishments.

Hooters' one-man golf stable, John Daly, being measured for bra size during the 2008 Bob Hope Classic.

"Use it wisely and carefully," warned Brooks.

"Giving me this card was bad timing on your part," said the former PGA and British Open champion, "because I just made a hole-in-one on 16 yesterday."

With that, the golfer turned to the bartender and set up the house by ordering one hundred bottles of beer.

Although Hooters describes itself as "a family restaurant," its own marketing surveys suggest something like 90 per cent of its clientele to be male and between the ages of 21 and 52.

And while the chain has its roots in the old Confederacy, there are now Hooters "stores" in 46 of the 50 States, as well as several countries around the globe. There are two of them in Guatemala City. Earlier this year Brooks opened a Hooters in Croatia.

Any Hooters opening north of the Mason-Dixon line can expect to be picketed by feminists, who deride the Hooters Girls as "one step above strippers." The company line is that Hooters Girls are "All-American cheerleaders."

And how does Mrs Daly feel about her husband's arrangement with the orange hot-pants and breast-implants crowd? "She's not very happy about it," admitted the golfer. "But it's such a great deal."

"It's going to be a great deal and a great relationship," said Daly of his new sponsorship arrangement. "I can't wait 'til the casino gets built."

Daly also has a fledgling golf course design business. His first, Wicked Stick, is up and running in Myrtle Beach. Another called Thundering Water is under development in Canada, as is another Daly course in Blarney.

"We broke ground on the one in Ireland last year and had hoped to open this summer, but the weather wouldn't cooperate. Now it looks like next year," said Daly, who plans to fly to Cork the day after the 2005 British Open at St Andrews in July.

"But there aren't any Hooters in Ireland," he was reminded.

"I know," he said. "Maybe I could be the one to start it there."

Apr 07, 2005

Lefty and Vijay get a little spiky

AUGUSTA

Coming as it did on what had been a dreadfully slow news day — in a rain-spattered 69th Masters, no contending player had completed his second round on Friday — news of a tiff between Phil Mickelson and Vijay Singh was music to the ears of the scribes.

The first inkling had come earlier when Will Nicholson, the chairman of the

Masters competition committee, convened a press briefing in which he assessed the condition of the course and explained the reasons (possible lightning in the area, mainly) for the early suspension of play.

Almost parenthetically, Nicholson volunteered the information that an unnamed player had complained that Mickelson was leaving spike marks on the damp greens and had asked to have his shoes inspected. The spikes had been checked by a member of the rules committee and found to be in compliance.

"(Mickelson) very generously, as you know he would, said he would change them when he got in if there was a problem," said Nicholson, who added: "There wasn't."

This was interesting, but hardly stop-the-presses stuff. Then about an hour later, Lefty's publicist T. R. Reinman distributed a statement with Mickelson's version of the afternoon's events.

Mickelson not only identified Singh as the player who had accused him of doing the elephant walk all over the Augusta National greens wearing possibly illegal footwear, but volunteered details of the subsequent confrontation in the Champions locker-room, which had been inspired when he heard Singh mouthing off to another former Masters winner.

"On the 13th hole, two officials approached me at two different times," said Mickelson in his version of the events.

"They were sent by Vijay to check my spikes, because he felt they were unduly damaging the greens. If that is the case, I am very apologetic and will make every effort to tap down what spike marks I make in the future.

"However," continued Lefty, "I was extremely distracted and would have appreciated if it would have been handled differently or after the round."

Mickelson said that after he heard Singh complaining in the locker-room, "I confronted him. He expressed his concerns. I expressed my disappointment with the way it was handled. I believe everything is fine now."

All over the press room, early copy was quickly shredded, and the war of words between two members of the Fab Four became the most significant story emanating from Augusta that day.

And as the field completed its second round on Saturday morning, all eyes were on the scoreboard. Dozens of reporters were literally praying for a convergence of scorecards that would pair the two combatants in that afternoon's play.

Alas, the dream match-up didn't come until Sunday, by which time most eyes had been diverted to the dramatic Tiger Woods-Chris DiMarco battle.

While no one who's ever played on a spiked-up green would have been entirely dismissive of Singh's complaint, there's no question that in this instance most of the sympathy lay with Mickelson.

Even those journalists who have decided to forgive the Fijian his past misdemeanors haven't forgiven Singh's persistently churlish attitude toward the press.

In the age of soft spikes, fewer than 30 per cent of the tour pros wear metal spikes these days, although the wet conditions which obtained over the first two days may have swelled that number. Tour pros are allowed to wear spikes, but limited to 8mm. Mickelson's were 6mm.

Singh, if he was truly bothered, had ample opportunities to discreetly say something to Mickelson over the course of two days, and that he waited until a critical moment to 'sic' the rules committee on Lefty, smacked of gamesmanship.

It also occurred to me that at least one other option had been available.

When similarly damp conditions hit the 1996 Irish Open at Druids Glen, Pat Ruddy, who had designed the course, approached European Tour officials with a simple remedy. Since Ruddy reckoned that it would be a downright shame for the championship to turn on a missed putt deflected by a spike mark, he suggested that after each group putted out, the grounds crew make emergency repairs to any spike marks left on the green. The advice was taken and there were no complaints.

By the time they were paired for Sunday's final round, Mickelson and Singh were out of contention and battling for third place at best, but they still drew a substantial gallery, at least a few of whom were hoping for some fireworks.

The pairing of the defending Masters champion and the world's number one-ranked golfer (for a few more hours, anyway) was the first time this year members of the Fab Four had been paired in a final round, and the memory of Friday's confrontation — Lefty's word, not mine — was still fresh in the memory of everyone save Mickelson and, apparently, Singh.

When the pair hit the fairways together on Sunday, a uniformed security guard told the *Augusta Chronicle*, "Everybody came here wanting to see a little golf and a little something else," but the "something" else never materialised. Mickelson and Singh are mature enough to realise little would be served by prolonging the feud, and they even attempted to make nice as they marched up the final fairway.

Fair enough, but then after signing his scorecard, Mickelson not only attempted to revise history but to place the blame squarely on the press for reporting it.

On his way from the 18th green to the Butler Cabin to present a green jacket to the winner of the 69th Masters, the winner of the 68th paused to chat with a CBS reporter, who asked him whether any residual bad blood from Friday's confrontation in the locker-room had spilled over into his final-round *mano-a-mano* duel with Singh.

"There was nothing there," Mickelson smiled disarmingly. "I don't know where you guys come up with this stuff. We had a great day."

Now, it's one thing to downplay the controversy, another entirely to pretend that it was a fiction cooked up by an irresponsible media.

As we have seen, it's not difficult to figure out where we guys came up with "this stuff". While the media might have been willing (and even grateful) accomplices, nobody made "this stuff" up. Mickelson's fingerprints were all over it, and his lame attempt to distance himself from it was nothing short of disgraceful.

Simply put, you can't have it both ways.

Apr 14, 2005

Tiger left musing on Slaughter in Straffan

Hours before Woosie rolled over and reached for the aspirin bottle on Monday morning, Tiger Woods was already in London and engaged in one of his least-favourite pursuits: speaking to reporters on the telephone.

Under normal circumstances Woods would be one of the hardest guys in the world to find on the morning after another Ryder Cup ass-kicking, but the conversation had long been pre-arranged, and Tiger had a vested interest in beating the drums for his personal favourite on the December golfing calendar: an invitation-only event at Sherwood Country Club in Thousand Oaks, California, whose proceeds will benefit the Tiger Woods Foundation.

Although the tournament's date places it squarely in the middle of the silly season, the numbers bandied about this week are certain to make people sit up and take notice.

The overall purse will be $5.75 million, with $1.35 million of that going to the winner. The last-place finisher in the field will earn $170,000, which ought to be good for a few Christmas presents.

After rounding up as many of the top-dozen rated golfers in the world as he could muster, the field was filled with four special exemptions. One of them went to Darren Clarke, to whom Tiger personally extended the invitation. (That the others went to John Daly, Fred Couples, and Davis Love III may have been Tiger's way of telling Tom Lehman what he thought of his captain's picks for The K Club.) Clarke's addition means there will be 11 members of the respective Ryder Cup sides represented at Tiger's Target tournament.

Team-mates Padraig Harrington, Colin Montgomerie, Paul Casey, David Howell, Luke Donald, Henrik Stenson, and Jose Maria Olazabal will join Clarke in California, while the losing team at The K Club will be represented by Woods, Chris DiMarco, and David Toms.

Tiger was still licking his wounds.

"It still hurts, no matter what, even more when you get dusted by nine points," he said Monday. "It didn't feel good at Oakland Hills and it certainly doesn't feel good now."

Having had a night to sleep on it, he had pondered possible explanations for the Americans' implosion in Kildare.

Some aspects of the Slaughter in Straffan defy explanation. Woods, for example, was asked why the likes of Montgomerie, Clarke, and Sergio Garcia can raise their games for the Ryder Cup but can't win a major tournament, while major winners like Phil Mickelson and Jim Furyk get to the Ryder Cup and fall flat on their faces.

Tiger's one-word response spoke volumes.

"Interesting," he said.

Woods did offer up one possible explanation for the recent European dominance, which is that the organisers on both sides of the Atlantic haven't done the Americans any favours with their choice of venues.

Europe were always going to have the crowd last weekend, but the Palmer Course, as American a course as one is apt to find in Europe, should have suited the visiting squad as well — at least until the rain started falling and the winds began to howl.

But, Tiger pointed out, the US team's familiarity with the venue was limited to August's reconnaissance mission, while most of Team Europe plays it at least once a year. The same, he noted, is true of recent host sites in Europe such as the Belfry and Valderrama.

On the other hand, American Ryder Cup host courses have tended to be as unfamiliar to the US players as they are to their opponents.

"The ones we've chosen are fantastic venues and difficult golf courses, but they're courses we don't play," at least not regularly, noted Woods.

The tour pros hadn't seen the Country Club in Brookline between the 1988 US Open and the 1999 Ryder Cup. Oakland Hills went even longer between visits — the 1985 US Open and the 2004 Ryder Cup.

Six years have elapsed since Tiger won the 2000 PGA at Valhalla, the site of the next Ryder Cup, and by the time the matches roll around it will have been eight.

"And on top of that, I heard Jack (Nicklaus) is going in there and redoing all the greens," said Woods, noting any nuances retained in his meticulously-taken notes from 2000 will have been rendered useless. "You'll have to relearn all the greens," said Tiger.

Before he hung up the phone to head over to The Grove, Tiger had another interesting observation, one that hardly bodes well for the competitive nature of the Ryder Cup in the immediate future: of the team the Americans brought to Ireland last week, only Zach Johnson and Vaughn Taylor — and they each by a matter of months — are younger than Tiger himself.

"They have Luke (Donald) and Sergio (Garcia) and Paul Casey, who are all in their 20s, and those three have won tournaments all over the world," pointed Woods. "When our youngest player is 30 years old, that's not a positive thing."
September 28, 2006

Darren Clarke clearly displaying his emotion at the conclusion of his singles match against Zach Johnson in the 2006 Ryder Cup which Clarke won 3 and 2.

PART III

Referee Lane Mills steps in to stop the World Boxing Heavyweight championship fight between Mike Tyson (left) and Evander Holyfield. Tyson was disqualified for biting his opponent's ear in the third round.

BIG GEORGE, IRON MIKE, AND OTHER SWEET SCIENTISTS

Tyson over the edge again

LAS VEGAS

Mike Tyson, who just a few days ago was lamenting that he sometimes felt everyone in the world was against him, may soon discover that he was right. As the snarling two-time heavyweight champion left the MGM Grand Garden Arena in disgrace following Saturday night's disqualification loss to Evander Holyfield, his once adoring fans pelted him with invective, rubbish and stale beer. Tyson responded by angrily shaking his fist at the crowd.

Given his own shaky medical history and Tyson's fearsome reputation, it should not have been startling that Holyfield would wind up in hospital following the fight, but who could have guessed he would be there as plastic surgeons worked feverishly to reattach a segment of his right ear, which Tyson had bitten off and spat into the ring?

Holyfield successfully defended his World Boxing Association title when referee Mills Lane disqualified Tyson after the challenger had twice deliberately bitten Holyfield during the third round.

Somewhere along the line, what had been billed as a morality play pitting good against evil was transformed into a cautionary tale which had more to do with civilised and uncivilised behaviour.

Tyson's $30 million purse was withheld by the Nevada State Athletic Commission, which will act to suspend his boxing licence at an emergency meeting tomorrow.

While it is doubtful that the commission had the authority to keep the entire amount barring exceptional circumstances, the maximum fine allowable by statute would be $300,000, a piddling one per cent of Saturday's earnings — that could represent a drop in the bucket compared to the other penalties Tyson might face.

Beyond losing his right to practice his trade, he could also face civil action on Holyfield's part. There is also the possibility that Tyson's action could be construed as criminal in nature, in which case it could in turn constitute a parole violation that might even send him back to prison.

Suffice it to say that the least surprised person in the whole world was probably Desiree Washington, the young Rhode Island woman Tyson raped six years ago.

Saturday night's rematch began in much the manner of its predecessor, last November's fight in which Holyfield engineered his monumental upset. In an effort to smother Tyson's rapid charges and neutralise his lightning like combinations, Holyfield was quick to wrap Tyson into what looked like complicated wrestling holds at every opportunity. At times it looked as if Lane would need a crowbar to separate the two.

When a fight is engaged at such close quarters, there is the ever present danger of a clash of heads, and this one wasn't long in coming. Early in the second round, Tyson came straight ahead just as Holyfield, bending low from the waist, rose to embrace him yet again, Holyfield's forehead caught Tyson on the side of his right eye, opening a cut which immediately spurted blood.

Lane immediately signalled that the damage had come as the result of an unintentional head butt," meaning that had the fight subsequently been stopped as a result of Tyson's wound it would have been either ruled a technical draw (in the first three rounds) or the result would have gone to the judges' scorecards.

Tyson, apparently dissatisfied with the interpretation, decided to take matters into his own hands, settling it the same way such matters used to be resolved back at the Indiana Youth Facility.

Jun 30, 1997

Tyson off the moral menu at Alice's

Almost 35 years ago, a young folksinger named Arlo Guthrie wrote what became a minor antiwar anthem, an account of his personal travails before his local Draft Board, which had decreed that Guthrie's status as a convicted litterbug rendered him morally unfit to be sent to Vietnam to kill women and children.

Without attempting to trivialise the past transgressions of Mike Tyson, it might be noted that the former heavyweight champion was due to face his own *Alice's Restaurant Massacree* this morning when he was scheduled to appear before the New Jersey Athletic Control Board for their decision on whether to grant the disgraced boxer a licence to fight in the state. Less than 14 months after he tried to gnaw Evander Holyfield's ear off, Tyson is looking to go back to work, although the recent heavy betting was that his request wouldn't be granted.

"I've been around this game for a long time, and the way things went, I just don't think they're going to give him a licence," said Pennsylvania boxing commissioner Greg Sirb, who is also the president of the Association of Boxing Commissions.

The speculators also suggested that the NJACB would take the easy way out by claiming that it lacks proper jurisdiction to overrule a suspension originally handed down in Nevada. Now, though, this is all moot. The heavy betting must have for once persuaded the normally financially inept Tyson that discretion was the better part of valour and he has withdrawn his licence request.

This, of course, does not mean that Iron Mike has seen the error of his ways. He has merely decided to have his errors debated in another state.

Tyson will eventually be allowed to fight again, he just has to find a licensing body lacking the moral fibre of the New Jersey committee. After all, in a sport where savagery is commonly considered a virtue, what is the proper punishment for excessive *savagery*? Tyson wasn't by a long shot the first boxer to bite an opponent; in fact, Andrew Golota did it just a couple of years ago, even before he was twice disqualified for low blows in fights against Riddick Bowe, and nobody even suggested suspending The Foul Pole.

If, and when, Tyson does return it will be to a heavyweight landscape vastly different from the one he departed last July. The generally acknowledged champions of a division Tyson once ruled without dispute (Holyfield, who holds the World Boxing Association and International Boxing Federation belts, and World Boxing Council titleholder Lennox Lewis) are no closer to fighting each other now than they were then, and in fact both face `mandatory' defences next month, each against a top-rated but virtually anonymous challenger.

Holyfield, whose June defence against the WBA's Number One Henry Akinwande was scrapped when Akinwande tested positive for Hepatitis B on the eve of the bout, is scheduled to face something called Vaughn Bean in Atlanta's Georgia Dome on September 19th.

Bean is rated the top heavyweight on the IBF's list of contenders, although as someone pointed out, he may not even be among the world's 10 best Beans.

Eager to box before his hometown crowd, Holyfield and promoter Don King (who just last month was acquitted on federal insurance fraud charges) had hastily arranged the contest on the condition local business interests underwrite the $3 million `site fee' a fight like this would normally command from Las Vegas casinos.

After it developed that not even Georgia businessmen were that stupid, Holyfield bit the bullet and agreed to underwrite the expenses himself, banking on a sell-out in the 40,000-seat arena. At a press conference officially announcing Holyfield-Bean in Atlanta this past Tuesday, King tried to boast that seats were "selling briskly," until a man tugging on his coat sleeve reminded The World's Greatest Promoter that the tickets wouldn't go on sale until the following morning.

A week after Holyfield fights Bean, Lewis will defend against the WBC's number one, Zelkjo Mavrovic, an anonymous heavyweight from Croatia.

Of Lewis' last four title fights, two ended in disqualification (Akinwande for excessive holding and Oliver McCall for excessive crying) and, in the other, he knocked out a man (Golota) who allegedly suffered a Ronaldo-like seizure in the dressing room. In the last, against `linear' champion Shannon Briggs, he was nearly knocked out himself before reviving to stop the young New Yorker.

Briggs is supposed to return to the ring himself in September, or was, until he was charged with aggravated assault following a late-night brawl outside the House of Blues in New Orleans early on Wednesday morning. And, in the meantime,

George Foreman, the man Briggs allegedly `beat' for the linear title, isn't done either. The two-time heavyweight champion, who will turn 50 next January, is scheduled to fight another one-time champion, Larry Holmes, who turns 49 in November, and rest assured that some boxing board, somewhere, will license both of them.

Tyson's decision to withdraw his application won't mean the end of his career, but it is a small shame that he did not give the New Jersey Athletic Board of Control an opportunity to reflect on all of this as a basis for a decision on his suitability for a legitimate place in the heavyweight division's ever more ludicrous three-ring circus.

August 14, 1998

New Tyson returns to basics

PHOENIX

At the conclusion of Mike Tyson's workout, the entourage sets to work transforming a dingy gym in Phoenix into Santa's Workshop. While three of them dismantle the ropes, half a dozen others, aided by a group of volunteers from an Arizona bank, begin trundling in the toys and packages from the car park and stacking them in the ring. There are Beanie Babies and Barbie Dolls, basketballs, soccer balls, footballs, baseballs, video games, and toy aeroplanes.

Tyson split the cost of underwriting the Christmas party with Jamal Anderson, the Atlanta Falcons running back who is the son of his chief bodyguard. To his credit, it appears to have been a genuinely selfless gesture, at least to the extent that not even the local television stations were notified. Somehow the word has gotten out, and children from Phoenix's poorer neighbourhoods — black, white, Mexican and Native American, some accompanied by their parents — soon form a queue that stretches out of the gym and through the car park to the footpath outside, where it snakes around the tin-roofed *Hermosillo Taqueria* next door and extends down the block as far as the eye can see.

"This isn't a charitable thing," insists Tyson. "You've just got to take care of people."

At the same time, he probably wouldn't mind if word of his largesse crept back to the proper authorities. Tyson fights South Africa's Francois Botha at the MGM Grand in Las Vegas on January 16th. Barely three weeks later he faces sentencing in Montgomery County, Maryland, over an assault charge to which he has already pleaded "no contest". (The former heavyweight champion was accused of kicking one man and punching another following a multi-car fender-bender in August.)

A jail term is one possible outcome, but that may be the least of his worries. Tyson is still on probation for an earlier rape conviction in Indiana, and authorities there, including the Hon. Patricia Gifford, the judge who originally sentenced him, have let it be known that the disposition of the Maryland case will have a substantial effect on their decision on whether to send him back to prison in their state.

In other words, Tyson could earn almost $30 million in the first month of 1999 and be behind bars for the second.

Two months have passed since Tyson's boxing licence, revoked after he disgracefully bit Evander Holyfield's ears in their June 1997 title fight in Las Vegas, was restored. Gone are promoter Don King, co-managers John Horne and Rory Holloway, and other hangers-on who made Tyson's post-prison entourage one of the more loathsome collections of human beings ever assembled under one roof.

Tommy Brooks has been engaged as Tyson's new trainer. Since dismissing the respected Kevin Rooney a decade ago, Tyson had gone through a collection of sycophants and yes-men patently more afraid of the boxer than his opponents were.

"*He* was training *them*," says Brooks (44) of his predecessors. "That's not the way it's supposed to operate."

On his first day in the gym with Tyson, Brooks put the boxer through an exercise in which he attacked a slip-bag in 30-second spurts. Sweating, heaving, and gasping for air, Tyson finally vomited on the spot.

"Most trainers would have let him off the hook there, but I said, `Look, Mike, if you throw up in a fight, you got to keep fighting! Get back to work!' "

"*Kill me, man! Kill me!*" responded Tyson, who wearily re-attacked the elusive bag.

"He wants somebody to push him," said Brooks, who is given to interrupting Tyson's workouts whenever he spots a mistake (which, these days, is often) and pointing it out on the spot.

There is some irony in watching a two-time heavyweight champion return to the boxing equivalent of Sesame Street, but Brooks says: "We've gone all the way back to basics in this camp. If he doesn't learn something new every day, we're just wasting our time."

Tyson says Brooks has him doing things in the gym "I haven't done since I was a kid," but he appears to be a willing pupil. Moreover, he seems genuinely relaxed and content to be back in the milieu he understands — a dank and sweat-stained inner-city gym.

"Mike is a good person," said Brooks. "He just needs guidance. He doesn't want `yes' men around him anymore. I don't think he ever lost confidence in himself as a fighter, but I do think he lost confidence in his corner. He was allowed to go his own way for so long that he forgot many of the things that made him great in the first place.

"You've also got to take into consideration," added Brooks, "that opponents just aren't going to be intimidated by him the way they used to be. The bully syndrome won't work anymore. Now he has to *fight*."

"Nobody likes taking orders, but that's part of being a fighter," said Tyson. "And maybe being able to fight takes a load off my mind. I'm just happy to be fighting again."

Both times Tyson fought Evander Holyfield, Brooks was in the opposing corner. ("I thought Mills Lane should have disqualified Mike after the first bite," he opines.)

"This was strictly a business decision," Brooks says of his departure as Holyfield's assistant trainer to become the head man on the latest version of Team Tyson.

It is also a decision which could backfire if Tyson goes away in February.

Tyson seems almost serenely prepared for whatever destiny may bring him. While he insists that he is not attempting to remake his image (by playing Santa Claus to the children of Phoenix, for instance), he is only too aware of how badly that image is in need of repair.

At one point he compared himself to the embattled American president, noting that: "We knew what he was before he got in office. We all get in those situations. We're just hoping we don't get caught!"

(Asked whether he had voted for Bill Clinton, Tyson reminded you: "I'm a felon. They don't let me vote!")

When it was delicately put to him that "much of the public still considers him some sort of . . ." it was Tyson who gleefully interrupted to finish the sentence.

"An *animal!*" He clapped his hands.

"I just hope I'm a *good* animal," he said. "I hope I'm, you know, *domesticated.*"

It was Tyson who recalled an episode in a Phoenix hotel room several weeks ago. When the room-service waiter who had delivered his breakfast addressed him as "Mr Tyson," the boxer replied: "Please, not *Mister* Tyson. Call me Mike."

"Oh, sir, I wouldn't do that," said the waiter, who went on to tell Tyson how much he admired him and that he wished he could be "just like you".

"No, you don't," Tyson told him. "In fact, I'd rather be *you.*"

"No, you don't," said the waiter. "I'm trying to raise six kids — on one check."

"Yeah?" replied Tyson. "Well, I've got millions of dollars — and no friends!"

December 24, 1998

Holyfield can do the right thing

NEW YORK

With the Internal Revenue Service's April 15th filing deadline just a few weeks away, I've already decided who I want to do my taxes: Eugenia (Jean) Williams.

Ms Williams is an accountant by trade, and if she can bring the same creativity to my income tax returns that she did to scoring Saturday night's Lewis-Holyfield fight, I can probably count on a substantial refund.

Lennox Lewis (right) won a comfortable points decision over Evander Holyfield to claim the undisputed heavyweight title in their 1999 rematch, somewhat correcting the controversial outcome – a draw – of their New York encounter earlier in the year.

On the other hand, if her calculations include anything half so egregious as her scoring of last Saturday's fifth round — which she scored for Evander Holyfield, even though Lennox Lewis out-punched him 43-11 and knocked his head clean through the ropes in those three minutes — we could both go to jail.

Which, come to think of it, wouldn't be a bad place for her at all.

The outrage over the decision at Madison Square Garden has already sparked three separate investigations by New York authorities alone: the state legislature, Attorney General Eliot Spitzer and Governor George Pataki have all vowed inquiries into how and why this travesty of justice occurred.

The expectation here is that the investigations of the aforementioned will unearth not corruption (well, no more corruption than usual; this is boxing, after all) but gross incompetence on the part of at least one of the judges.

While Ms Williams obviously deserves to be singled out, it should be noted that the scoring of British judge Larry O'Connell wasn't much better. Even World Boxing Council president Jose Sulaiman, who appointed him, "respectfully disagreed" with his 115-115 draw verdict.

"Mr O'Connell is one of the most prestigious and experienced officials in the world, and is known for his integrity, competency, and impartiality," said Sulaiman in a statement on Tuesday, "and we must assume he went overboard to prove it."

Somewhat surprisingly, O'Connell subsequently (and somewhat sheepishly) acknowledged that he believed Lewis had won the fight, and that he was surprised to hear the totals of his scorecards when they were announced. Nonetheless, O'Connell didn't give Lewis a round between the end of the fifth and the final round.

It is the rare instance that we find ourselves in agreement with *Senor* Sulaiman, but fairness requires that we point out here that, had he had his way, neither Williams nor O'Connell would have been working on Saturday night.

With the undisputed heavyweight championship at stake, each of the sport's three sanctioning bodies was allowed to appoint one judge, subject to the approval of the New York State Athletic Commission. It was Sulaiman's position, as well as that of the World Boxing Association (WBA), that the judges should all come from neutral countries.

Thus the WBA appointed South Africa's Stan Christodoulou and the WBC Belgium's Daniel Van de Weile. It was the International Boxing Federation (IBF) which muddied the waters by insisting upon Williams.

The other two strenuously objected, not because Jean Williams is an incompetent boob (which she is), but because they felt it inappropriate to have a referee and one judge from Holyfield's country and none from Lewis'. O'Connell was duly summoned to fly in from England to stand by as an alternate in case IBF president

Bob Lee proved to be intransigent on the matter, which, of course, he did.

If the objections to Williams centered around her lack of experience and potential home-country bias, it should be pointed out that, as a New Jersey official, she is a product of what *New York Post* columnist Wallace Matthews described as "the same scummy pipeline that gave us Calvin Claxton and Lawrence Layton".

Claxton and Layton were the judges who scored the 1997 George Foreman-Shannon Briggs fight for Briggs, a decision every bit as ludicrous as was Saturday night's "draw". Clayton, Layton and now Williams all spring from a rich tradition of home-grown ineptitude nurtured in New Jersey by present commissioner Larry Hazzard and his predecessor, who happened to be Bob Lee.

Promoter Don King, who began beating the drums for a rematch the moment the verdict was announced, defended the officials — Ms Williams included.

"Judge not lest ye be judged," bellowed King at the post-fight press conference. "Shall we castigate the judges just because you don't have the same eyeballs?"

New York mayor Rudolph Giuliani, who was seated at ringside, echoed the disgust of most witnesses to the Lewis-Holyfield larceny.

"There were a lot of people here from England," said Giuliani, "and they have to be going home thinking that we're a bunch of cheats."

Grateful for the decision, Holyfield shrugged and said: "I don't judge fights."

Only once during post-fight questioning did Evander slip up. In recalling his wrong-headed strategy, he concluded one string of excuse-making by saying: ". . . but I don't want to take nothing away from a man's victory."

On Monday, Lewis and Holyfield sat down in a midtown HBO studio and watched the fight together. Their comments were taped for the network's home telecast of the bout, which will be shown, free of charge, to the nation tomorrow night.

Lewis reiterated his contention that he had been robbed. Holyfield said just what you would have expected him to say, that the fight was a draw.

Before they met in the ring, Lewis had suggested that Holyfield was a "hypocrite" for espousing his spirituality while fathering five out-of-wedlock children. The devout Evander would seem to have further jeopardised his place in Heaven, standing in violation of at least one and possibly two more commandments: "The Shalt Not Bear False Witness Against Thy Neighbour" and, maybe, "Thou Shalt Not Steal".

All three sanctioning bodies, both fighters, and, of course, King are already beating the drums for a mandatory rematch — although as we have pointed out, given the contractual realities of the situation, it is by no means certain that Lewis-Holyfield II will even be economically viable.

Evander, a proud man, still has a chance to do the right thing. He could announce his retirement right now, and hand the belts over to Lennox Lewis. To

do otherwise, in fact, is to risk having his reputation forever tarnished by what happened in New York last weekend.
March 18, 1999

Politicians must accept blame for boxing tragedy

Stephan Johnson might die this morning. If he doesn't die today, he could die tomorrow, and if he doesn't die at all, some say he may be worse off than if he had. Comatose since he was knocked out by Paul Vaden in the 10th round of a November 20th light-middleweight match in Atlantic City, the New York boxer developed pneumonia and a 104-degree fever earlier this week.

Doctors performed an emergency tracheotomy yesterday to help him breathe, but breathing is literally the only sign of life Johnson has evinced in the past 12 days.

Boxing is a dangerous and sometimes brutal sport. Ring fatalities aren't common, but they do happen. The most tragic thing about this one, if and when Johnson expires, is that it was eminently preventable. Stephan Johnson should not have been fighting at all. If the "Muhammad Ali Boxing Reform Act," which the US Senate allowed to die on the vine that same week, had been in effect, he would not have been permitted to enter the ring.

Back in April, Johnson travelled to Toronto, where he was knocked out by a right hand delivered by Fitzroy Vanderpool, an outcome that eerily foreshadowed the denouement of his Atlantic City fight on November 20th.

Following the Vanderpool loss, Johnson was suspended for 60 days and ordered to undergo a battery of medical tests. When he failed to complete two tests ordered by the Ontario Commission, he remained under medical suspension.

This did not prevent Johnson from being approved for subsequent fights in South Carolina and Georgia, where the administration of boxing is decidedly informal and virtually unregulated.

Following the Vanderpool loss, Johnson outpointed journeyman Otilio Villareal in South Carolina, and then in Georgia won another decision over Sam Garr. In October he registered a third-round knockout over Calvin Moody, who had gone into the fight with a 9-60 record.

In researching the 31-year-old Johnson's credentials for the Vaden fight, New Jersey officials never checked with the Commission in Ontario to see if he had been reinstated.

Matched against Vaden, a former world champion, but hardly known as a fearsome puncher, for a 12-round United States Boxing Association title fight on the undercard of that evening's Michael Grant-Andrew Golota heavyweight showdown, Johnson acquitted himself well. He was actually ahead on points on the cards of two of the ringside judges going into the fateful tenth.

Vaden sent him staggering backward with a jab. Vaden then missed a right hand but caught him with a left to the head that sent Johnson toppling over backward. The back of his head hit the lower ring rope before his body hit the canvas, and although referee Earl Morton began a count, he was interrupted by the time he got to "four," as ringside physician Rick Snepar and three other doctors raced to the boxer's side.

Johnson had gone into a Grand Mal seizure. Oxygen was administered in the ring, and he was taken from the arena and transported by ambulance to the Atlantic City Medical Centre, where he remains today, in critical condition with what was diagnosed as a subdural hematoma — blood collected between the brain and skill, causing swelling and pressure.

Even as the physicians were attending to the unconscious boxer, his trainer and manager Ken Woods was heard to marvel: "This was just like the one in Canada."

HBO, which was televising the card from the Trump Taj Mahal, didn't even show the Vaden-Johnson bout.

As a prelude to Grant-Golota (won by Grant), the network instead showed a replay of the previous Saturday's Lennox Lewis-Evander Holyfield championship match.

Here's the kicker: The fight never should have happened, and had Senator John McCain's boxing reform law been in effect, it would not have.

Although other issues — the recent indictments of several officials, dubious scoring in several title fights this year, and charges of corruption throughout the sport — have been more visible, one of the major tenets of the proposed legislation involves enhanced vigilance to protect boxers themselves through federal regulation. But for the third year in a row Congress adjourned without passing McCain's bill.

Once, the bill was passed by the Senate but not by the House of Representatives. On another occasion both houses passed it, but in differing versions, and Congress adjourned before a conference committee could come up with a compromise. This year the House passed the measure, but the Senate failed to act before the bell sounded.

The fact that McCain is an announced presidential candidate whose campaign would doubtless have gotten some mileage out of the Ali bill is, of course, purely coincidental.

When Johnson dies, his blood will be on their hands. And if he doesn't, the politicians who helped kill the boxing bill should be dragged to the hospital to view first-hand a tragedy they might have averted.

December 02, 1999

Deluded Prince proclaimed pretender

LONDON

A week ago this morning Al Valenti was on the phone to me at my London hotel. "Do you know anyone who plays the Irish pipes?" he asked. Of course I did. "Why?"

There would only be £100 in it, Irish Micky Ward's Boston-based promoter told me, but the perks would include a ringside seat and television exposure in over 100 countries. All that would be required of Finbar Furey, or a suitable replacement, would be to march into the Kensington Olympia's Grand Hall ahead of Ward, leading him into the ring with an appropriate battle hymn.

"I don't think so," I told Al.

Why not? Maybe he could stretch it to £150.

"That's not the problem," I told him. "Have you ever *seen* a set of uilleann pipes? You can't exactly 'march' while you're playing them."

In the end, Irish Micky settled on more generic rock-and-roll entrance music. His adversary, WBU light welterweight champion Shea ("The Shamrock Express") Neary, came in to the strains of Shane McGowan and Ronnie Drew alternating choruses in their rendition of *The Irish Rover.*

With last Saturday's Prince Naseem Hamed-Vuyani Bungu featherweight title fight taking place six days in advance of St Patrick's Day it had been determined, both for domestic consumption and for the convenience of HBO, which was televising the show to the US, to provide an "all-Irish" match-up as the co-feature.

That Irish Micky hailed from the French-Canadian mill-town of Lowell, Massachusetts, and that "The Shamrock Express" was a former infantryman in the King's Regiment from Liverpool seemed of small consequence to the promoters.

When Micky Ward embarked on his professional career 15 years ago he was shortly hailed by Teddy Brenner, the legendary Madison Square Garden matchmaker who died early this year, as "the best fighter to come out of New England since Marvin Hagler," and Ward did little to diminish that high praise when he won his first 14 fights, 11 of them inside the distance.

Irish Micky's birthplace, which was also the hometown of one-time *Lowell Sun* sportswriter Jack Kerouac, has traditionally spawned useful boxers, among them Ward's brother Dickie Ecklund, who in 1978 became first man to knock down Sugar Ray Leonard, and who a year later travelled to London, where he narrowly lost a decision to Commonwealth champion Dave (Boy) Green.

The win earned Green a 1980 shot at Leonard, who had by then won the welterweight title, while Ecklund's career disintegrated into a life of booze, drugs, and crime. For the past 15 years he has spent more time in the sneezer than on the street, and was only released two months ago from a Massachusetts halfway house after serving a sentence for armed robbery.

Since his release on parole, Ecklund has become his brother's trainer, chief second, and principal sparring partner, but early on in Mickey's career, Dickie had nearly ended it.

The way I've always heard the story, Ecklund got into one of his traditional beefs with the local constabulary outside a Lowell pub when Micky attempted to pull his brother from the fray. An overzealous cop threw Ward over a squad car and used a nightstick to break his left hand.

Despite numerous surgeries, Ward refractured the hand nearly every time he fought, and in 1991, having gone 7-7 in his next 14 fights, he retired. He spent three years working as a prison guard and as a labourer before making a comeback six years ago at the age of 28.

He had lost only twice since — once when he was stopped on cuts in a challenge for Vince Phillips' IBF junior welterweight title, and a points decision to Zab Judah, the current holder of the same belt.

It was a crowd-pleasing scrap from the outset. According to CompuBox statistics, Ward and Neary were on a world-record pace, having exchanged over 1,200 punches in the eight rounds it lasted, and while Neary had the advantage in the early going, he was always taking a lot of punishment from Ward's pulverising left hook.

The cumulative effect took its toll by attrition. In the eighth round Ward unleashed a devastating combination — a left hook to the body followed by a crushing left uppercut — that sent Neary tumbling down. The Shamrock Express struggled to his feet the first time, but when Ward leapt upon him he tagged him with a left to the chin. Neary spun furiously backward across the ring before landing flat on his back. Mickey Vann, the referee from Leeds, immediately ended the bout.

Irish Micky, now 35-9, was paid a career-high $100,000 for the performance, and, along with the dubious WBU belt, earned himself another payday, most likely against former champion Arturo Gatti on HBO later this year. Neary is now 22-1, but having been thoroughly unmasked, is reportedly considering retirement.

As for the other featured bout on last weekend's London card, God knows there are enough arrogant and snotty little show-offs boxing on our own side of the Atlantic. Why HBO wanted to go and spend millions signing Naseem Hamed to a multi-year contract remains one of the great mysteries of our time.

It has, in any case, been widely proclaimed that the boxer formerly known as The Prince silenced his critics with his perfunctory knockout of Bungu. Suffice it to say that he has not silenced this one. This was a mismatch from the moment the match was made. Bungu had never before fought as a featherweight and had not fought at all in 13 months.

Hamed toyed with Bungu for two rounds and then, appearing to have become bored with the exercise, stood him up with a right-handed jab and then put his lights out with a straight left. Although Bungu rolled over while Joe Cortez was counting to 10, there was never any danger he might regain his feet. Naseem was borne from the ring on a sea of his wildly cheering supporters.

Shea Neary. Prince Naseem. My, these Brits are easily deluded.

March 16, 2000

The brains behind the White Buffalo

LONDON

The author Nelson Algren enunciated his credo of life in dispensing his immortal advice: "Never eat at a place called Mom's. Never play cards with a man named Doc. And never sleep with a woman who has more problems than you do."

To which he might have added: "Never back a heavyweight named Francois."

Although the Fleet Street press seems determined to whip up the fervour for Lennox Lewis' first London fight in half-a-dozen years, the plain truth is that Francois "The White Buffalo" Botha, who challenges the heavyweight champion at the Docklands Arena Saturday night, has even less chance against Lewis than Lou Savarese had of upending Mike Tyson in Glasgow three weeks back.

That said, his manager Sterling McPherson ought to be named Boxing Executive of the Year.

They are strange bedfellows, a white South African and a streetwise black American; but in the past two years McPherson has shrewdly managed to manoeuvre Botha into big-money fights against Tyson, Shannon Briggs and now Lewis. Botha, who by almost any standard should by now reside in boxing's scrap heap, is being paid a reported £1.5 million sterling for what figures to be a brief exercise.

McPherson himself had a fling as a lightweight. He came up in an era when Don King was signing almost anyone who could properly lace on a pair of gloves, mainly to keep them out of the clutches of his rival promoters. McPherson languished for several years, seldom fighting but building up a record of 11-0.

Although he never enjoyed life inside the ring, McPherson was a clever lad, and obviously paid attention to what was going on around him. He was able to cut through the obfuscating and often contradictory details to understand the complex machinations of how the boxing world really worked, and when he announced his decision to retire, King welcomed him into the fold — although in retrospect it might have been a case of inviting the fox into the henhouse.

McPherson's first job entailed serving as a straw manager for several of King's fighters. Most US states have laws against collecting both a promoter's fee and a manager's share from a boxer's purse. It was thus handy to have a loyal employee like McPherson around to put his name on the managerial papers.

McPherson eventually showed himself to be a shrewd fellow. During the 1990s, when it appeared Don King might be headed for prison, his name arose as a possible regent to run the empire while King was behind bars, but when the promoter was acquitted in his federal insurance fraud case, McPherson quietly dropped back into the shadows.

It was McPherson who played Ribbentrop to broker the uneasy alliance between King and Frank Warren, and when that arrangement inevitably fell apart, he threw in with Warren. If he is not a full partner, McPherson is clearly the British promoter's American representative.

In the meantime, McPherson had maintained his role as Botha's manager. King, recognising the fiscal importance of a white heavyweight who could fight just a little bit, had invested several years in building up the man he christened "The White Buffalo," feeding him a steady diet of anonymous stumblebums.

Prior to one such meeting, it should be noted, Botha was to face a tomato can named Brian Sargent on a St Patrick's Day card in Massachusetts. In the principal attraction that night, Peter McNeeley was meeting another inept heavyweight, Danny Wofford, in the grooming process for McNeeley's role as Mike Tyson's get-out-of-jail present.

The White Buffalo: South African Francois Botha.

At a press conference a few days before the bout, Botha said something that annoyed McNeeley, and McNeeley, who had not yet become a national laugh-ingstock, responded by belting him, with an open hand, in front of a hundred witnesses. It is difficult to imagine a more humiliating experience for a would-be boxer than being bitch-slapped by Peter McNeeley, but Botha just stood there, blinking back tears, as his cheek reddened.

We concluded on that day that in addition to lacking boxing skills, Botha also lacked the stones to go very far in this business. We were marginally off the mark in the first assumption, and dead wrong in the second.

All right, Botha proved more courageous than previously suspected when he lasted into the 12th round before being stopped by Michael Moorer in their 1996 IBF title fight. A year earlier, in a fight that didn't prove much, Botha had outpointed an undistinguished German named Axel Schulz to win the vacant title. The German crowd was so displeased with the verdict, a split decision for Botha, that they showered the ring with empty beer bottles and full glasses, which led one leading scribe to describe the occasion as *"Kristallnacht"*.

Botha, who subsequently tested positive for steroids, didn't have the title long, but he did get the role as Tyson's foil in his first fight back after the ban for eating Evander Holyfield's ears, and gave a good account of himself right up until the moment he was knocked out and left for dead in the fifth round.

McPherson's head bobbles energetically from an elongated neck, and engaging him in conversation could give one the illusion he could be talking to Kermit the Frog. Botha, who affects a wispy goatee and closely-cropped fair hair, has the appearance of a well-fed storm trooper.

The Las Vegas sports books make Lewis a 13 to 1 on favourite, and the odds should probably be longer than that. Botha's slim chances rest on two far-fetched hopes: the possibility that Lennox may have been distracted by all the Tyson talk which has dominated the run-up to Saturday night's homecoming, and the memory of Lewis' last London fight six years ago, when Oliver McCall caught the heavyweight champion napping at Wembley and knocked him silly.

The suspicion here is Lewis could knock out Botha even if Tyson were in the ring with them, and apparently enough British fans agree that barely half the 12,000 tickets had been sold by yesterday morning. Still, one must give credit where credit is due here, and when McPherson and the White Buffalo leave for America after the bout, they can gleefully count their money all the way across the Atlantic.

What more could a man ask of his manager than that?

July 13, 2000

Hands-on work of the Rope Burns

'I'm not the one who decides when to stop the fight, and I don't stitch up cuts once the fight's over. And it's not my job to hospitalise a boy for brain damage. My job is to stop blood so the fighter can see enough to keep on fighting. I do that, maybe I save a boy's title. I do that one little thing, and I'm worth every cent they pay me. I stop the blood and save the fight, the boy loves me more than he loves his daddy.'

— F.X. Toole, *Rope Burns*

There is something about boxing that the best of them have always found intoxicatingly alluring. In the first half of the 20th Century Jack London, Ernest Hemingway, and Paul Gallico took their turns probing the mindset of the fighter; and everyone from Budd Schulberg and Norman Mailer to George Plimpton, Hunter S. Thompson, and Joyce Carol Oates has, at one time or another, felt obliged to have a go at the Sweet Science.

Over the past several weeks the world of the literati appears to have gone gaga over *Rope Burns,* which represents F.X. Toole's maiden voyage into the world of fiction, turning its 70-year-old author into a most unlikely celebrity.

I won't pretend to have "discovered" *Rope Burns*, but I did stumble upon it in a roundabout fashion before most of my boxing acquaintances did. Several months ago a friend had written, asking my opinion of Toole's work.

This question was phrased in the offhand manner of "what do you think of Lewis' jab?" or "how about De La Hoya's corner?" although I must confess that, at the time, I'd never heard of F.X. Toole. Reluctant to display my ignorance, I determined that it might be prudent to investigate this Toole fellow before replying.

I managed to track down a short story called "The Cut Man," which had been published last year in a London-based literary magazine called *The Richmond Review*.

The story was a knockout. Not only could the man write, his command of the language was exceeded only by the uncommon accuracy of his knowledge of the inner workings of the fight game. This wasn't some dilettante poet's stab at romanticising the fight game, but a guy who knew his stuff.

And, I must confess, I found this oddly troubling. Like a lot of other boxing people I was smelling a rat. The contributor's note, after all, claimed that "F.X. Toole has spent his entire career in the world of professional boxing. He has been both a trainer and a cut man, and still is."

Impossible. I'd never heard of him. And neither had anyone else I asked. "And I thought I knew everybody in the business out here," said Freddie Roach, Steve Collins' former trainer who works with boxers in the same ratty California gyms in which this Toole fellow would supposedly be a familiar face.

The answer to this bewildering mystery has unfolded with the publication of *Rope Burns*, and the concomitant acclaim which has been heaped upon its author. Finding himself splashed across the pages of the *New York Times* and the *Wall Street Journal*, as well as on television programs here and there didn't do much for Toole's attempt at anonymity.

Turns out, its author is indeed a *bona fide* gym rat and vagabond California cornerman, only his name isn't F.X. Toole, it's Jerry Boyd, and he hasn't spent his whole life immersed in boxing, just the last 20 years of it.

Which is a lot longer than he's been writing, or at least publishing, his work. While he was working the mostly minor-league California circuit so memorably described in Leonard Gardner's *Fat City* a quarter-century ago, Boyd/Toole quietly moonlighted as a closet writer, accumulating an impressive collection of rejection slips along the way.

Three years ago, a San Francisco literary magazine called *Zyzzyva* published one of his short stories called "The Monkey Look." (The same story which turned up in England, retitled "The Cut Man," it comprises the lead piece in *Rope Burns*, a collection of five stories and a novella.) Nat Sobel, the New York literary agent, read "The Monkey Look," tracked down its author, and asked him if he had any more like it.

Jerry Boyd, of course, had several desk drawers full of them. Sobel proceeded to get a reported $100,000 advance for the book. HBO paid at least as much to option the movie rights. Boyd, whose biggest career payday in the corner was $1,260 was, suddenly, for the first time in his life, solvent.

Rope Burns has been universally praised, and the most frequent comparisons have been to early Hemingway. In truth, Toole's prose and milieu owe more to Gardner than Hemingway, but that the latter was a profound influence on how Jerry Boyd has lived his life is undeniable: Married three times, he has been at various times a bootblack, cab driver, bartender, and even a bullfighter.

Always fascinated by the fight game, he didn't take it up until he was 50, and no, he didn't jump straight into the corner with a spit bucket. Rather, he showed up at the gym, learned the ropes, and finally summoned the courage to engage a trainer, who did his best to discourage Boyd by regularly bloodying his nose. Instead, he only whetted his appetite for — and his understanding of — the Sweet Science.

Jerry Boyd has spent the past two decades as a white man in a milieu dominated by blacks and Hispanics, and FX Toole manages to recreate the dialogue of ethnicity as accurately as he does the smell of the gym itself.

Although the narrators of his stories are sometimes black and sometimes white, the stories have one thread in common: Somewhere in them, a major character, whether he's a trainer or a cutman or a gym owner, is a wise old Irish (or Irish-American) fellow, and you can take it to the bank that whether he is named Frankie Dunn or Mac McGee or Pats Moran or Con Flutey, he is every bit as much Jerry Boyd as is his other alter ego, F.X. Toole.

"Boxing is an unnatural act," whispered the voice. 'Understand me on this, kid. Everything in boxing is backwards to life. You want to move to the left, you don't step left, you push off the right toe, like this. To move right, you use the left toe, see?' The old white man didn't look into your eyes, he looked clear through your eyes, and straight to the inside of the back of your head."
September 28, 2000

People's Republic takes on King

In the course of his whirlwind Asian tour, the US Secretary of State Colin Powell visited Beijing last Saturday, and while the American government had earlier negotiated the return of the US spy plane and its crew, Powell was evidently unable to arrange for the release of another prominent hostage, the boxing promoter Don King.

One suspects he didn't try very hard.

I had just been issued my Chinese visa and was supposed to land in Beijing myself yesterday morning, and I suppose I should count myself fortunate that I didn't get on the plane. Six days after the John Ruiz-Evander Holyfield fight, scheduled for August 5th, was called off (sorry, "postponed"), King is still there, and while The World's Greatest Promoter denies that he is being held for ransom, there seems little doubt that the Chinese are looking for $2 million or so before they'll allow him to leave the country.

Yesterday King's matchmaker Bobby Goodman told American boxing scribe Michael (Wolf Man) Katz that the frazzle-haired promoter was still in China because "he likes it here," but there were also unconfirmed reports of fractious shouting matches between King and his Chinese partners from Great Wall International Sports Media.

For official consumption, the World Boxing Association heavyweight championship bout was scratched when Ruiz, the Boston-based champion, sustained a neck injury that left him, in King's words, "almost paralysed."

Three doctors — one of them Australian, the other two Chinese — were trotted out to attest to Ruiz's infirmity, one we'd find a bit more credible had we not been forewarned two days ahead of the announcement that the China card was in serious financial difficulty and that one of the participants would imminently come down with "a bad back."

It is possible, of course, that all of this was a timely coincidence, that Ruiz is genuinely injured, and that King and the Chinese actually plan to go through with their new rescheduled date of October 6th, but even King spokesman Alan Hopper warned that this was only "a working date."

Generally speaking, "working date" is a boxing code word meaning that one has no confirmed date, no site, and no television deal. (Even the Chinese promoters conceded that the 18,000-seat Capital Gymnasium would probably not be the venue for the rescheduled match.)

Since the Beijing fight was first proposed back in March it had been widely accepted that the Chinese government, after decades of banning boxing in any form, had suddenly become enthusiastic about staging a heavyweight championship fight because they thought it would boost their chances of landing the 2008 Olympics, and had originally asked for Ruiz-Holyfield to take place in June. Once the Olympic bid was rendered *fait accompli*, the government's ardour cooled noticeably.

In fact, the day after the "postponement" announcement, the state-backed People's Daily voiced scepticism over the entire affair, and on ESPN's weekly "Friday Night Fights" show last week, analyst Teddy Atlas suggested that Great Wall may have attempted to renege on as much as $10 million of the $17 million site fee it had promised King.

One could also, one supposes, look at it from the perspective of the Great Wall people. King had promised that this glorious championship fight — actually, the

A giant amongst kings: legendary promoter Don King with one of his trademark cigars.

third instalment of a comparatively tedious trilogy between the two — would bring worldwide boxing fans and media flocking to Beijing.

In reality, while the tickets had sold well, most of them were purchased by curious locals. Only a few hundred Americans had committed to make the journey, and most of those were blue-collar boxing fans, as opposed to the high-rolling Vegas crowd the Chinese expected.

After Ruiz-Holyfield III had been spurned by both HBO and Showtime, King had planed to produce the pay-per-view telecast himself. We have no way of knowing what the advance sale for the pay-per-view telecast might have been, but we can probably surmise that it was also underwhelming.

When Ruiz knocked down Holyfield on the way to an upset decision in Las Vegas last March, Great Wall chairman Niu Lixin was waiting in the wings, and shared in King's breathless post-fight announcement that the rematch would take place in China.

It was apparent from their enthusiasm as the Chinese kept babbling about Holyfield that they were only dimly aware that he'd lost his title that night. Only over the next few months did it begin to dawn on them that they'd been sold a bill of goods, that Ruiz, not Holyfield, was the new champion, and that, moreover, while his WBA belt was genuine enough, most of the boxing world continued to regard the other two-thirds of the title (held by Lennox Lewis and then, shortly thereafter, by Hasim Rahman) as substantially more consequential.

King attempted to mollify the Chinese, first by purloining Rahman away from rival promoter Cedric Kushner, and then by announcing that Rahman would also appear on the Beijing card, but he was stripped of that trump card when an American court ruled that Rahman's first title defence had to be a rematch with Lewis.

It had been an open secret that ticket sales for the fight were nearly as slow as the pay-per-view buys. Last week a Beijing-based Western producer, speaking under cloak of anonymity, told London's *Independent* that Chinese executives had informed him the show was in trouble, and that Great Wall may have "overcommitted itself" in the generous terms of its arrangement with King.

Great Wall apparently now wants King to post a $2 million bond to cover what it has already laid out in airfares and promotional expenses before he is allowed to leave the country.

It could be that we've got it all wrong, but one day after the postponement was announced, the *Peoples Daily* suggested that financial problems on the part of the Chinese promoters meant that "the fight might not take place at all."

If that indeed proves to be the case, you can look for the *"Free Don King!"* rallies to commence in Tiananmen Square any day now.

August 02, 2001

Hopkins scratches beneath surface

NEW YORK

Alec Harvey's name may not ring a bell, because his annual moment of fame is fleeting indeed. Harvey is the master jeweller employed by the R&A to inscribe the name of the winner of the British Open Championship on the Claret Jug, and once a year on a Sunday afternoon in July he turns up in the living-rooms of television viewers around the world as he painstakingly performs his expert handiwork.

As a rule, Harvey's touch is so deft that he can have the new champion's name on the trophy before he leaves the scorer's cabin. On occasion, when the winner has a lead he deems safe, Harvey has even been known to jump the gun a bit: at St Andrews last year he had Tiger Woods' name on the jug before Eldrick had finished putting out on the last, and one can't help but wonder how close he came to actually etching Jean Van de Velde's name at Carnoustie the year before.

One couldn't help but think of Alec Harvey in light of certain developments in New York a week and a half ago. While the "Sugar Ray Robinson Trophy" might not enjoy the cachet or the history of the Claret Jug, it was every bit as expensive: a handsome, 125-pound sculpture commissioned by promoter Don King from Tiffany & Co, it was created to be awarded to the winner of the exercise modestly known as the Middleweight World Championship Series.

With an eye toward unifying the 160lb title for the first time since Marvelous Marvin Hagler ruled the middleweight world 14 years earlier, King had gathered the three principal claimants — World Boxing Association (WBA) champion William Joppy, World Boxing Council title-holder Keith Holmes and International Boxing Federation champ Bernard Hopkins — along with Felix Trinidad, the undefeated Puerto Rican who began the series the holder of the WBA's 154lb light-middleweight title, under his promotional umbrella for a knockout tournament to produce an undisputed champion.

That the winner was supposed to be Trinidad, the centerpiece of King's promotional empire, there can be little doubt. All three fights were set in Madison Square Garden, to take advantage of the popular boxer's avid Puerto Rican fan base. Once Hopkins disposed of Holmes and Trinidad stopped Joppy, the stage was set for a grand finale originally scheduled for September 15th.

The terrorist attacks on the World Trade Centre had pushed the fight back two weeks, but the Garden was sold out, with over 19,000 on hand, when Trinidad, a 3-1 favourite, finally met Hopkins a week ago Saturday.

In a stunning upset, Hopkins thoroughly dominated Trinidad to claim all three belts, but when he (and King) materialised at the post-fight press conference in the wee hours of Sunday morning, Sugar Ray Robinson had gone missing.

It might be noted at this point that the trophy in question had proudly been displayed at every press conference before and after the previous two bouts, and at another that took place at the Garden Theatre three days before the September 29th finale.Moreover, it wasn't something you'd likely just stick in a corner and forget about. At 125 lb, the likeness of the great Sugar Ray Robinson wasn't life-sized, but it was bigger than at least six boxers who fought on that evening's undercard.

King explained to bleary-eyed reporters that the trophy had been locked away for safekeeping in a Garden storeroom and that the employee charged with the duty had gone home for the night and taken the key with him.

He promised to present Hopkins with the trophy the next day.

"It was locked in the Garden's Box Office and the alarms had been set," confirmed MSG official Eric Gelfand. "The post-fight press conference went off so late we couldn't get it out."

"If Trinidad had won, they would've had it here," grumbled Hopkins.

The next day came and went, but still no trophy. Finally, on Monday afternoon at a luncheon at Gallagher's Steak House in Manhattan, one of King's minions showed up and gave the statue to Hopkins.

By the time it was handed over to the new champion, the name plaque on the trophy had obviously been altered and re-engraved with Hopkins' name.

"You could tell by the scratches on it that they changed the nameplate," said Hopkins. "They told everyone that the trophy was locked in an office and no one had the keys to get it out. But the real reason was they were so sure Trinidad was going to win that they already had his name engraved on the plate."

Enter Gelfand with an amended story.

"The truth is, the plaque originally was mistakenly engraved by the sculptor to Don King," went Gelfand's latest explanation.That remains the official alibi, although it seems highly dubious.

Not even the dumbest craftsman in Tiffany history is likely to have supposed that Don King was the middleweight champion of the world.

Put it this way: Alec Harvey wouldn't have made that mistake.

"My gut feeling," said Hopkins, "tells me Felix Trinidad's name was on that trophy."

October 11, 2001

Shadowy figure emerges from past

MEMPHIS

Mike Tyson might be a convicted rapist and mugger who in the past half dozen years has punched a referee and bitten at least two opponents, but he isn't even the most despicable character in his own camp.

Lewis is. And we're not talking Lennox here.

The run-up to Saturday night's fight at the Pyramid in Memphis took an ugly turn on Monday when Carlos (Panama) Lewis turned up in Tyson's training camp, ostensibly at the invitation of the challenger. If the mention of this Lewis' name rings a bell, then you're dating yourself. Suffice it to say that for all his transgressions, Mike Tyson still found a jurisdiction willing to issue him a boxing licence.

What does that say about Panama Lewis, who has been permanently banned from the sport throughout the world for nearly two decades? A fringe player on the boxing stage a quarter-century ago, Lewis first came to prominence working the corners of world champions Roberto Duran, Vito Antuofermo, and Aaron Pryor. During a rough patch in Pryor's epic, 1982 fight against Alexis Arguello, the television cameras caught Lewis admonishing a cornerman who attempted to give the boxer a swig from the water bottle.

"No, not that one, give him the special bottle, the one I mixed myself," Lewis was heard to say. After partaking of the "special" mixture, Pryor went on to stop Arguello. By the time the word got around and the authorities viewed the videotape, the evidence had disappeared.

That wasn't what got Panama kicked out of boxing, though. That came in a comparatively minor undercard fight between Luis Resto and Irish Billy Collins, a supporting act on the night in 1983 when Duran beat Davey Moore to claim his third world title.

Collins, a youngster from Tennessee who brought an undefeated record and a promising career to Madison Square Garden that night, absorbed a fearful beating from the light-punching Resto, under circumstances so suspicious that the New York State Athletic Commission, at the behest of Collins' father and trainer, impounded Resto's gloves.

Laboratory testing conclusively proved that the gloves had been tampered with. Three-quarters of the horsehide padding had been squeezed out through a small perforation on the side, meaning that Resto might as well have been using a blackjack on Collins' face.

Collins was badly disfigured. He came out of the fight with two fractured orbital bones and his career was ended. In his despair, he had within a matter of months abandoned his wife and baby son, taken to drink, and eventually he drove his car into a cliff. Officially it was termed an accident. His father said it might as well have been suicide, but also pointed out that his son had died, for all intents and purposes, that night in the ring.

They couldn't charge Panama Lewis with murder, but both he and Resto eventually stood trial and were convicted of conspiring to fix the outcome of a sporting event. Resto was never allowed to box again. Lewis did less than a year of a five-year prison sentence, but he was permanently exiled from the sport, and remains *persona non grata* to this day.

This hasn't kept him out of the gyms, where his shadowy and mysterious presence is beyond the jurisdictions of most boxing commissions.

He has continued to "advise" and "motivate" boxers from afar, and sometimes, from very near, serving as a *de facto* cornerman, shouting instructions from a ringside seat. When one of his charges, Francois Botha, fought Tyson, the Nevada Commission did its best to disrupt communication by ordering Panama removed from his ringside seat and placed well back in the audience.

Now he has emerged from the shadows as an "adviser" to Tyson here in Memphis, and apparently he has Iron Mike's ear. If Ronnie Shields, the trainer who took over the duties after Tyson split with Tommy Brooks, had an ounce of self-respect he would have quit this week, but the trainer's share of Tyson's $17.5 million purse is apparently too compelling.

When Shields agreed to train Tyson it was with two stipulations: first, that he would be in charge, with no second-guessing; and second, that Tyson purge his gym sessions of all the leeches, sycophants, and hangers-on who had been cluttering up the scene for years.

The most prominent leech exiled under this edict was the loathsome Steve (Crocodile) Fitch, the self-proclaimed "motivator" who envisions himself the 21st century version of Bundini Brown to Tyson's Ali. So far as anyone has ever been able to determine, the gravel-voiced Crocodile's function is to strut about the gym, dressed in combat boots and desert camouflage, periodically bellowing out *"Gorilla Warfare!"*

Nobody else missed him much, but apparently Tyson did. After setting up shop at a fitness centre in nearby Cordova last week, Tyson remarked that it was entirely too quiet and asked someone to phone up Fitch. Now not only is Crocodile back, so is Panama Lewis.

Tyson missed a scheduled press conference in Tunica on Tuesday, but did show up at a local hotel gym long enough to hit the speed bag for 10 or 15 minutes before disappearing and leaving the press in the hands of Shields and his assistant, Stacey McKinley.

"I want him to break ribs and break jaws," McKinley told reporters. "I want them to take Lennox Lewis out on a stretcher."

It turned out later that Tyson left early because of a bomb scare at the hotel.

Shields and McKinley were apparently asked to keep the press (which had been locked, *en masse,* inside the gym) busy while the constabulary investigated.

After listening to Shields and McKinley (and Crocodile) for half an hour, Michael (Wolf Man) Katz, the dean of American boxing writers, was moved to conclude: "I'd rather have been bombed."

June 06, 2002

Mississippi river bank hustle

MEMPHIS

This old slave-trading centre on the banks of the Mississippi might be a comparative neophyte when it comes to professional boxing, but it would be inaccurate to say Memphis has no history or tradition of memorable fights.

On October 18th, 1956, a sometime guitar player named Elvis Aaron Presley pulled his Lincoln Mark II into a Gulf station on Second Street for repairs. His presence soon attracted a crowd, and an attendant named Ed Hopper ordered him to move the vehicle.

When Presley didn't respond quickly enough for Hopper's liking, the attendant, according to testimony of the day, took a shot at Elvis, belting him in the chops through the open driver's side window, at which point Presley stepped out of the car and belted him back.

"Both men were charged with assault and disorderly conduct," reads the Memphis Commercial Appeal's account of the fracas. "When asked for his name, Presley told police: 'Maybe you'd better put down Carl Perkins'."

The winner: Presley, by decision. He was let off the next day. Hopper was fined $26. A witness said Hopper's eye "looked like a travelling bag."

Apart from the night when the present mayor, the Honourable Willie Herenton, scored a one-punch knockout over a circuit court judge in a downtown saloon, Presley's TKO of Hopper stood as the most famous fight in Memphis history.

That is about to change tonight, when heavyweight champion Lennox Lewis and Mike Tyson, the self-proclaimed "baddest man on the planet," meet for a scheduled 12 rounds at the Pyramid, the 19,000-seat home of the NBA Memphis Grizzlies.

* * *

When Tyson was greeted by gay-rights pickets at his Cordova training site last week, he leapt out of his car and hugged a startled protester, assuring the fellow: "I'm not homophobic." When he showed up the next day and the pickets were gone, Tyson asked: "Where are all my homosexual friends?" So when Iron Mike arrived for Thursday's weigh-in at the Memphis Convention Centre, it was to find a swarm of *pro*-Tyson gay demonstrators.

"THANKS, MIKE, FOR SAYING GAY IS OK," read one placard. "TYSON OPPOSES HOMOPHOBIA. THANKS, MIKE!" read another, while a third proclaimed: "WE SUPPORT TYSON'S STEP UP TO TOLERANCE."

Tonight's adversaries even took different routes to and from the venue lest they run into each other going and coming. The last time Lewis and Tyson had been in the same room together, back in January, a melee had broken out and Tyson took a bite out of Lewis' thigh.

The pro-Tyson demonstrators weren't the only ones espousing their cause in

Memphis on the day of the weigh-in. Some religious zealots marched outside the media centre wearing T-shirts that read: "JESUS CHRIST IS THE REAL HEAVY-WEIGHT CHAMPION OF THE WORLD." They found themselves competing for space with a crowd of travelling Lewis supporters assembled outside the convention centre for the first weigh-in.

When the English fans showed their backsides, they had letters printed on the backs of their red-on-black T-shirts spelling out F*** TYSON.

On the same day that Lewis, a celebrated chess buff, played a match against a 13-year-old member of a local chess club, Tyson's PR minions did their best to salvage their own photo op by having Tyson, who had disdainfully hit the speed bag for 15 minutes and then departed without speaking to reporters a day earlier, invite a group of grade school students to meet the former champion after his workout.

Most of the children were, reportedly, timid, but one of them, 10-year-old Jamal Cornes, marched up to the ring and asked Tyson: "Why did you bite off Evander Holyfield's ear?"

The startled Tyson chuckled uneasily and replied: "That was a long time ago."

* * *

Not even the locals seemed to know what to call tonight's encounter: *The River Bout. The Rumble on the River. The Showdown in M-Town. The Clinch in the Pinch. The Fight of the Century.* Promoters eventually opted for the understated "Lewis-Tyson Is On," and placards bearing that slogan line the streets of Memphis, to say nothing of the 40-mile stretch of Highway 61 from here to the Mississippi casino enclaves.

One-hundred-and-thirteen years have elapsed since Mississippi played host to its first and only heavyweight championship fight. When John L Sullivan, Jake Kilrain, their respective entourages, and a medium-sized regiment of paying customers departed New Orleans at midnight on July 8th, 1889, most of the party didn't even know their final destination — which turned out to be a ring set up on the banks of the Mississippi River a hundred miles upstream.

The match-up of heavyweight champion and challenger had been banned from most respectable venues, and the location of the site had to be kept secret lest the authorities intervene.

Back then, it was the notoriety of the sport itself, and not that of one of the participants, that made the fight a pariah in the eyes of civilised society, but a scribe of the day, writing for the *New York World*, might have been talking about Tyson when he assessed Sullivan's chances: *"According to all such drunkards as he, his legs ought to fail him after 20 minutes of fighting."*

Tonight, Lewis (39-2-1 with 30 KOs) and Tyson (49-3, with two no-contests and 43 KOs) will properly be fighting across the state line in Tennessee, but for the past week Mississippi loomed large in the proceedings, and the epicentre didn't really shift to Memphis until Thursday afternoon's weigh-ins. It was money from the

Tunica casinos which eventually pushed the Pyramid backers over the top in the dwindling bidding to stage the fight nobody else wanted, and both champion and challenger were headquartered in Mississippi — Lewis at Sam's Town, where Jerry Lee Lewis (unrelated to Lennox, but a cousin of Elvis) headlined last night, while Tyson was officially assigned accommodation at Fitzgerald's Hotel & Casino, though he showed his face there only briefly last week.

Both contestants flew into Memphis a week ahead of time. Lewis was feted with a parade down Beale Street, while Tyson arrived by private jet and was whisked away to the house he had rented for the week. Promoters carefully orchestrated the week's events, right down to the separate-but-equal weigh-ins, to ensure there wasn't even a chance encounter before the two step into the ring.

The thankless task of refereeing tonight's fight has fallen to Eddie Cotton of New Jersey, the lone American included on a multinational slate of officials. Bob Logist of Belgium, Anek Hongtongkam of Thailand, and Alfred Bukwana of Soweto will be the ringside judges.

The suspicion here is that their services may not be required. If Lewis dominates Tyson as handily as we suspect he might, it wouldn't be surprising to see Tyson do something to get himself disqualified before the fight reaches its midpoint. Put it this way: when was the last fight you saw the bookies post odds of 4-1 on a disqualification?

* * *

With the likes of Jack Nicholson and Denzel Washington, Mel Gibson and Britney Spears, Wesley Snipes and Johnnie Cochran already due in town for the fight, you could hardly blame the hotel executives down at Sam's Town Hotel & Casino for their excitement when they learnt that Prince William and his entourage would be staying at their hostelry over the weekend.

The Tunica hotel spent the better part of last Tuesday making security arrangements for their new special guest. With Lewis and a small army of his English supporters already in residence there, the hotel had thoughtfully added shepherd's pie and lamp chops to the menu, and were prepared to roll out the red carpet for the royal party when they learned that the Prince William in question wasn't the heir to the British throne after all, but rather the potentate of a principality in Africa so tiny that "I can't even remember the name of it," said hotel general manager Maunty Collins.

* * *

Although Lewis and Tyson have managed to avoid one another through an aggregate 94 previous professional bouts, they are not exactly strangers. In 1983, Lewis recalled the other day, in a search for quality sparring as he prepared for the World Junior Championships in Santo Domingo, his trainer drove him to the Catskill, New York, gym of the late, legendary trainer Cus D'Amato.

Winner ok: Lennox Lewis celebrates after knocking out Mike Tyson in the eighth round during their heavyweight championship bout in 2002.

Accounts of those sparring sessions between the teenaged Lewis and the teenaged Tyson vary widely. Tyson trainer Stacy McKinley boasted the other day that Tyson "knocked out Lewis wearing 18-ounce gloves". McKinley, who was certainly not there 18 years ago, said he was in possession of photographs establishing the veracity of his claim. That was three days ago and he still hasn't produced them.

Lewis' recollection is that "we went at it pretty good for four days. Mike Tyson never knocked me out in those four days. He gave me a fat lip. I gave him a bloody mouth, so we were pretty even on that exchange."

What effect the memory of that long-forgotten sparring session 18 years ago might have when Lewis and Tyson climb into the ring at the Pyramid tonight for the richest match in boxing history remains to be determined, but as he held court at Sam's Town casino yesterday, Lewis revealed that at the conclusion of hostilities between the two youthful boxers, Tyson's wise old trainer took him aside and ventured a prediction.

"One day," D'Amato told Lewis, "you and Mike Tyson will meet in the ring for the heavyweight championship of the world."

* * *

"This is a very important fight for me," Lewis reflected this week. "It would have been unfortunate for me if I didn't box the best boxers of my era. Tyson is the best out there right now. This is what the world wants to see: me and Mike Tyson in the ring. I'm glad it's finally come about. I've been waiting for this fight for a long time.

"This fight," sighed Lewis, "is my legacy. I'm getting rid of the last misfit in boxing."

Tyson has studiously avoided the press throughout the week, but following Thursday's weigh-in he did pause to offer one reflection on tonight's bout.

"I just hope," muttered Tyson, "he doesn't have a heart attack between now and Saturday night."

June 08, 2002

Savage beating by Lewis ends Tyson's claims as a pretender

MEMPHIS

Once Lennox Lewis took over the fight in Saturday night's second round, it became apparent what a mismatch was unfolding. The heavyweight champion at work was a disciplined master beating the rage out of an unruly pet, and did such a good job of domesticating him that when the end came, a surprisingly civil Mike Tyson appeared dangerously close to having been housebroken.

When closure arrived with Tyson, bleeding from both eyes and his nostrils, stretched out on the canvas being counted out by referee Eddie Cotton, Lewis strutted about the ring, pounding on his chest with his left glove.

"This is my defining fight," he proclaimed. "It's what the whole world wanted."

Perhaps not the whole world, but at least that portion of it which had decided that Saturday night's match-up constituted a morality play.

Lewis had promised to "rid boxing of its last misfit," and he may have done just that. Although the contracts Lewis and Tyson signed for Saturday night's heavy-weight championship fight at the Pyramid provided for a rematch, Lewis' performance was so decisive and Tyson's so, well, toothless, that there are few compelling reasons for them to stage a reprise, or for the rest of us to watch it.

Saturday night's fight may not only have ended Tyson's championship pretensions, it may have signalled the end of his career as a useful boxer.

After battering and pulverizing Tyson over the last seven rounds of the eight it lasted, Lewis waved an extended left arm in Tyson's face and crushed him with a roundhouse overhand right, and the onetime "Baddest Man on the Planet" was counted out at 2:25 of the eighth.

From the second round on it was apparent that Tyson was but a shell of the dangerous fighter who burst onto the heavyweight scene 17 years ago.

Lewis, in registering his 40th professional win against two losses and a draw (all three of which were avenged in subsequent rematches) completely dominated Tyson, landing 109 jabs and 84 power punches, most of them right uppercuts which Tyson was unable to avoid.

The upset, if there was one, was that Tyson, in Lewis' words, "took it like a man" and did not resort to the foul tactics many among the announced crowd of 15,327 had come half-expecting to witness. There were no bites, no scratches, no arm-breaking attempts in the clinches, and by the time Tyson aimed a couple of punches at Lewis' scrotum late in the fight, he was too spent to do any damage to even that tender spot.

The one-sided beating may have pleased the more sadistic among Lewis's army of supporters, but it did little to whet the appetite of the public for another fight between the two.

Lewis is next obligated to defend the IBF portion of his championship against that organisation's top-rated contender Chris Byrd, and assuming he gets past that mandatory defence would then theoretically be free to fight Tyson again. But selling the reprise as a competitive match would tax the imagination of showman PT Barnum.

For nearly a dozen years now, Tyson has been more sideshow freak than legitimate threat, and even those who clung to that delusion will by now have been disabused.

Finding a site for Lewis-Tyson II wouldn't be a problem. Some boxing backwater will always be willing to follow Memphis' example and risk bankrupting its fortunes by underwriting the fight as a civic endeavour, although it is unlikely any venue would match the $12.5 million site fee Memphis posted for this one.

If all else failed, one could always take the fight to Lewis's native Britain, where the boxing public is so gullible they'll believe almost anything as long as it involves one of their own. (See Naseem Hamed, *et al.*)

The larger problem would lie in selling a rematch to the living-room consumers who pay the freight in the world of contemporary boxing economics.

The pay-per-view telecast of Lewis-Tyson was priced at a world-record $54.95, and while Saturday night's sales were brisk, most viewers grudgingly shelled out to watch what they had been persuaded was a once-in-a-lifetime opportunity.

Fooling them again would take some doing, and the notion of persuading Lewis (who contractually would earn the better end of a 60/40 split in any rematch) to fight Tyson at a reduced price seems fancifully unlikely.

There is no earthly reason to suppose that the outcome would be any different the second time around, but that having been said, in a very odd sense, Tyson, on the strength of bravery alone, probably deserves a second fight more than he deserved the first one.

If his number one ranking (by the World Boxing Council) was demonstrated to be a sham illustrative of boxing politics at its worst, he is at the same time probably no worse than many among today's poor crop of heavyweights likely to come knocking at Lewis's door.

"Anything is possible," allowed Lewis when asked about the possibility of Tyson II. "If the public demands it, we should do it."

If the public demands it, the public should have its collective heads examined.
June 10, 2002

Morrison is taking his right to the wrong place

Top Rank chairman Bob Arum was all smiles when he arrived in Tulsa, Oklahoma, that October evening 10 years ago.

He had just negotiated an agreement for his white heavyweight Tommy Morrison to fight Riddick Bowe for the championship of the world two months later. All Morrison had to do was get past an English-born journeyman named Michael Bentt that night and the multi-million dollar deal was done.

Boxing folk have learned to expect the unexpected, but few could have been prepared for what happened that night. Bentt pole-axed Morrison, knocking him out in the first round.

Arum had another show featuring light-flyweight champion Michael Carbajal and up-and-comer Oscar De La Hoya in Phoenix the following evening, and had chartered a private airplane to take him from Oklahoma to Arizona after the fight. In the midst of a bumpy flight Mike Malitz, then Top Rank's president, found himself obliged to heed the call of nature.

A few minutes later Maltiz's voice could be heard behind the paper-thin walls separating the small cabin from the even smaller toilet.

"*Dammit!*"

"What's the matter?" asked Arum.

"No toilet paper," replied Malitz.

Barely missing a beat, Arum fished around in his briefcase.

"Here," he said glumly as he passed the pages of the already obsolete Bowe-Morrison contract into the stall.

Tommy Morrison: a devout and serial hetrosexual.

With the possible exception of a chin, Tommy Morrison seemed to have it all. A distant relative of the late John Wayne (whose nickname, Duke, he adopted as his *nom de guerre*), he co-starred with Sylvester Stallone in *Rocky V*, defeated some of the best heavyweights of his day, including George Foreman, Razor Ruddock, Pinklon Thomas, and Joe Hipp, and even briefly held the fringe World Boxing Organization title.

Then, hours before he was scheduled to fight in Las Vegas in February of 1996, Morrison's whole world came crashing down. The Nevada Commission had just begun testing boxers for HIV, and Morrison's sample came up positive.

Needless to say, Lennox Lewis was almost as nervous over this news as was Morrison. A few months earlier Lewis had stopped Morrison in the fifth-round of a blood-spattered bout in Atlantic City. Lennox wasted little time in getting himself tested. He came up clean.

Morrison was a devout heterosexual and had not at the time used injectable drugs, but acknowledged having prodigiously engaged in unprotected sex.

"Wilt Chamberlain (the late basketball great who boasted of having slept with 20,000 women) had nothing on me," said Morrison in an admission which was undoubtedly of small comfort to his recent partners.

Morrison fought once more. In October of 1996 he managed to find the combination of a rogue commission (in Japan) and a willing opponent (Marcus Rhode), allowing him to collect one last payday in the ring, but his world continued to crumble.

Neither his boxing nor his Hollywood "friends" would return his phone calls. When he returned to his home in Jay, Oklahoma, the signs proclaiming the sleepy little town the "Home of Tommy Morrison" had all been torn down. His marriage ended.

"My best friends," he recalled, "wouldn't even wave at me." Already on probation for more minor transgressions, he was arrested on drugs and weapons charges. He eventually plea-bargained his way to a two-year sentence and spent the next two Christmases behind bars.

He and his wife, Dawn, had one child by artificial insemination. Now, having discovered a scientific process which will allegedly "wash" his sperm, the couple are expecting another child.

And, oh yes, Tommy wants to box again.

As absurd as it seems, Morrison recently floated the idea on his website.

"I think it's completely possible for me to fight again," wrote The Duke. "I've been encouraged by several political friends of mine that I should reapply for a boxing license and when, not if, I'm turned down that I should sue the Athletic Commission under the American Disabilities Act for discrimination."

Although he has evinced no movement toward full-blown AIDS, Morrison's HIV-positive status bars him from boxing in the United States and in most recognized jurisdictions elsewhere in the world. And though he's been away from the ring for seven years now, he's still only 34 — younger than Lewis and Mike Tyson, and only two weeks older than Roy Jones Jr.

The Americans with Disabilities Act was used by, among others, the golfer Casey Martin, who successfully sued to be allowed to use a golf cart in professional events. It was under threat of an ADA suit that, two years ago, Marvelous Marvin Hagler's erstwhile attorney Stephen Wainwright managed to procure a Massachusetts boxing license for Tim Welch, a boxer with an artificial leg. (It was something of a pyrrhic victory; the $30,000 prosthesis shattered in Welch's first pro bout.) But that it could serve as the basis for licensing an HIV-positive boxer seems unlikely.

If boxers who are brain-damaged (or, for that matter, pregnant) can be denied licenses, how could anyone reasonably countenance licensing a man who could endanger an opponent in a sport in which blood often flows copiously?

"The fact that there's never been a single documented case in the history of this planet of anyone ever contracting HIV in the ring seems to me like a leg perfectly strong enough to stand on in terms of a lawsuit," Morrison answers on his web page.

That HIV-positive boxers aren't allowed to compete in the first place would be a pretty good explanation for that bit of fuzzy logic.

We're all for protecting the rights of the downtrodden, but this is a bad idea whose time has not come.

June 12, 2003

Foreman gets ready to rumble once more

HOUSTON

Most of my sportswriting brethren were still in bed nursing hangovers a week ago Sunday when I hailed a cab and drove across Houston to the Church of Our Lord Jesus Christ, where the Rev George Foreman was presiding over the morning services.

The Rev Foreman had chosen the Book of Samuel, Chapter 17, for his homily on Super Bowl Sunday. He would read a few verses and then pause to draw out a life's lesson, expounding on points suggested along the way by the tale of one of fistic history's greatest upsets, David's first-round knockout of Goliath, a bout in which King Saul (as opposed to Don King) was cast in the role of the unscrupulous promoter.

This aspect of the morning worship had been preceded by a substantial round of lovely, hand-clapping music, and George was already well into the second hour of the proceedings when he abruptly snapped the Good Book shut and declared the lesson ended.

"When people start falling asleep, it's time to stop reading the Bible," he thundered in a voice loud enough to awaken the aged parishioner who had been snoring from a front-row pew. He then smiled gently at the man, suggesting the preacher wasn't nearly as cross as he had pretended to be.

"That was like watching an old fight on ESPN Classic," I told George when he greeted me on my way out of the church. "It was interesting, even though we knew who was going to win that fight."

I reminded him later he'd probably picked a good place to stop. The children had just been returned to the congregation after Sunday School and retaken their places alongside their families. Had the Rev Foreman read on for just a few more verses he'd have gotten to the part about David decapitating the deceased Goliath and parading into the city with the head held aloft on a stick, an image which might have produced more than a few nightmares.

That morning George had seemed to be hammering home the message — that however daunting the odds might seem, nothing is impossible — to his flock.

Who could have guessed he was actually steeling himself for another comeback? At a press conference in Humble, Texas, yesterday, the 55-year-old Foreman announced his intention to return to the boxing ring.

Reaction to this news has ranged from shock and indignation to fears for his safety to abject ridicule.

"Right," said the Showtime network's vice-president for sports, Jay Larkin. "Who's he going to fight, Muhammad Ali or Laila Ali?"

It has been seven years since Foreman's last fight, and seven months since he was inducted into the International Boxing Hall of Fame. Election to this body requires that a boxer have been retired for five years, but in point of fact Foreman never did formally announce his retirement. He just didn't fight again after the controversial 1997 split-decision loss to Shannon Briggs in which he lost his claim to the linear heavyweight championship.

Seventeen years have passed since Foreman ended a 10-year retirement to resume the comeback which culminated in his 1994 10th-round knockout of Michael Moorer to reclaim the title he had lost in the jungles of Zaire two decades earlier. His motivation in 1987 was much clearer. His church was in tatters and his Youth Centre in Houston was teetering on the brink of bankruptcy. He needed the money then, but he certainly doesn't now.

He earned $5 million a year for the HBO commentator's role he resigned two months ago, and a few years ago he sold his interest in the George Foreman Grilling Machines for $137 million, retaining "consultant's" role which currently nets him a million dollars a month in residuals. His family has been well provided for, and the Youth Centre and the church are fully endowed. He has given freely to charitable causes — including the tens of thousands of dollars he spread around Father Joe Young's Southill parish when he and I visited Limerick together five years ago.

No, Foreman is apparently coming back this time just to prove it can be done. He has been quietly training for the past two months, and says he has already shed 25 pounds. He won't fight, he says, unless he can get himself down to 225, which would be nearly two stone lighter than he was when he fought Briggs.

Although he has been dropping hints about resuming his boxing career since last summer, the guessing here is that Foreman intentionally delayed a formal announcement until Lennox Lewis took himself off the stage last week. Foreman beating any heavyweight would have immediately provoked questions about Lewis, an opponent for whom he would have been stylistically unsuited and whom he never would have fought.

Here's the part we don't believe: Foreman says he only wants to fight once but, if he is successful, that seems unlikely. While Foreman never wanted to fight Lewis, he *always* wanted to fight Mike Tyson, and this time Don King isn't around as an impediment to that match-up.

Although another fiftysomething former champion, Larry Holmes, threw down the gauntlet to Foreman, Big George says he wants no part of "other geezers." While he hasn't chosen an opponent yet, if we are to believe him it will be someone who hadn't even been born at the time of his Rumble in the Jungle against Ali.

Foreman says he wants to fight "somebody under 30 — a serious fight against one of these young guys."

Earlier this week when word began to trickle out that his sibling was contemplating a comeback, Houston promoter Roy Foreman was asked if he didn't fear for his brother's safety.

"Hey, boxing is a tough business," replied the younger Foreman. "I was afraid for him when he was 20."
February 12, 2004

Tyson has more than a hint of pathos

WASHINGTON

His fight against the Clones Colossus was four days away, but the Prozac appeared to be kicking in already. After a public work-out at Howard University on Tuesday, Mike Tyson spent the better part of half an hour entertaining questions, one of which was phrased in language that might have been better suited to a rap lyric.

"Don't curse like that," Tyson sternly warned his interlocutor. "There are children here."

On the same night that Tyson will square off with Kevin McBride at the MCI Center in Washington, an even more intriguing boxing match will be taking place 200 miles to the north, where Madison Square Garden is presenting a fight between Puerto Rican Miguel Angel Cotto and Muhammad Abdullaev, the Uzbekistani who last defeated Cotto — in the opening round of the 2000 Sydney Games.

Cotto, the World Boxing Organisation light welterweight champion, is undefeated as a pro, and while Abdullaev has lost once, the defeat should probably be marked with an asterisk. I was there at the Mohegan Sun two years ago when Abdullaev, comfortably ahead on points, was decked by Ghanaian Emmanuel Clottey in the 10th round. Abdullaev did not appear to be hurt, and, on instructions from his corner, attempted to gather a bit of rest by remaining on one knee while referee Mike Ortega counted.

Alas, poor Muhammad's English was no better then than it is now, and he stayed down on his knee right through the count of 10.

Most boxing connoisseurs, and to tell the truth, most boxing scribes, would rather be in New York Saturday night, but when the circus is in town, you go to the circus. Sports editors understand that Tyson, despite not having defeated an opponent of note in nearly a decade, remains the most compelling figure in the sport. Cotto-Abdullaev could turn out to be the fight of the year, but you wouldn't take a chance on giving Tyson the skip on the odd chance he might decide to take a chomp out of one of McBride's ears, even though Mike has promised that won't happen.

"I'm not going to bite anybody or break anybody's arm," vowed Tyson at Howard on Tuesday, to which Jeff Fenech, the Australian who is training him for his encounter with the Irishman, added: "Mike Tyson will be fully in control of his emotions."

If I thought I could rely on that I'd pack up and head back to New York right now.

When I checked into my Washington hotel on Tuesday, there was a care package awaiting. The note, which bore the joint logos of Top Rank and Madison Square Garden, was unsigned, but I strongly suspect the handiwork of publicist Fred Sternburg: "You should be in New York . . . We know that this is not your choice and we empathise with your plight," read the message accompanying the contents, which included a bottle of Puerto Rican rum ("to help numb the pain caused by missing the real June 11th fight"), mouthwash ("to remove the inevitable bad taste"), a barf bag, and sterile antiseptic pads ("good for most bites and cuts").

"He truly is an attraction, no matter whether you like him or dislike him," said Don King of Tyson.

King, who promoted Tyson through most of his big money fights, only to wind up on the receiving end of a $100 million lawsuit, has no vested interest in either of Saturday night's shows. The promoter does, however, control three of the world's recognised heavyweight champions, and has a leg up on the fourth, thanks to a World Boxing Council ruling making the winner of an August bout between two King fighters (Hasim Rahan and Monte Barrett) the mandatory challenger for Vitali Klitschko.

Having reached an out-of-court settlement with Tyson, King would love nothing more than to get Tyson, even at his advanced age, back into the title picture.

"It came off the rails for Mike when Mike bit the ear and he had that time off," King mused a few days ago. "Idle time is the devil's workshop. He had a lot of time on his hands and he didn't employ it the right way. But he's paid the penalty for it, and if he's willing to see the error of his ways, I might take him back and help him. He's still an attraction."

Two years ago Tyson filed for bankruptcy protection, having squandered more than $300 million he had earned in the ring.

"I hope he's fighting for the money," said Jose Torres of Tyson. "I don't think he has much chance of becoming champion again, and he's deluding himself if that's his goal. But you know something? I'd be happily surprised if Mike wins the heavyweight championship again."

Torres, the one-time world light-heavyweight champion, was managed and trained by Tyson's boyhood mentor Cus D'Amato, and during Iron Mike's formative boxing years was among his closest confidants. The two haven't spoken in years.

Torres confided the other day that he wasn't altogether confident Tyson could beat McBride.

"I'm not sure he can beat *anybody* now," said Torres.

Tyson once suggested that without boxing he would "just fade into Bolivian." The aura of invincibility that was once his stock in trade has by now been thoroughly dissipated.

"Mike is a student of boxing history, and he's surely aware how badly his legacy has been diminished," said Torres.

Several years ago Tyson took umbrage when boxing scribe Wally Mathews described him as "a rapist and a recluse."

"I am not a recluse," pouted Tyson.

In the gym at Howard University a few days ago he sounded even more pathetic than that.

"It's a lot easier," said Tyson, "to be the heavyweight champion than it is to be a good person."

June 09, 2005

Unassuming Pavlik being hailed as a breath of fresh air

When Kelly Pavlik checked out of his Atlantic City hotel on the morning of September 30th, he was carrying the WBC and WBO middleweight championship belts he had won by knocking out Jermain Taylor the night before.

What he was not carrying was his purse.

After the title fight, the New Jersey Board of Athletic Control had presented the Pavlik family with two cheques. One, for $666,750, represented Kelly's share of his million-dollar purse, less managers' and trainers' fees. The other, for $105,000, was made out to Mike Pavlik, who co-manages his son with Cameron Dunkin.

When the new champion and his dad returned to their room after a night of celebration, Pavlik *pere* had placed the two cheques on the dresser, right beside the coffee pot. The family car was well along the road back to Ohio the next morning when Mike suddenly sat bolt upright.

"I think," he gasped, "I just left the maid a really big tip."

Like three-quarters of a million dollars.

Kelly says he was never as concerned about the misplaced money as his father was, since he knew that cheques that large might be difficult for someone else to cash.

The worst thing that could have happened would not have been if they'd fallen into the hands of an Atlantic City chambermaid, but an Atlantic City elected official. One-third of the membership of the City Council at the New Jersey seaside resort is at this moment either in jail or under indictment, and four of the last eight mayors have been convicted of or pleaded guilty to corruption charges.

And that figure doesn't include the present mayor, Bill Levy, who disappeared a few nights before the Pavlik-Taylor fight in the midst of yet another investigation.

(Turns out Levy, who resurfaced on Tuesday, had checked himself into a substance-abuse clinic; the investigation into whether his worship defrauded the government by falsifying his military records remains ongoing.)

As the Pavliks barrelled down the highway, the panic-stricken Mike Pavlik managed to reach Top Rank publicist Lee Samuels on his mobile phone. Samuels in turn contacted promoter Bob Arum, who immediately stopped payment on the cheques and agreed to issue replacements.

The money arrived in Youngstown a few days later. Kelly Pavlik celebrated his windfall by going on a profligate spending spree: he went out and bought four new tyres for his (old) car, suggesting that the youngster from Youngstown may turn out to be cast in the mould one of his more illustrious but notoriously frugal predecessors, Marvelous Marvin Hagler.

At a New York press conference three days before the Taylor-Pavlik fight Arum (presumably with an eye toward Emanuel Steward, who was present as Taylor's trainer) appeared to commit heresy by comparing Pavlik to Steward's most revered client.

"With all due respect to Tommy Hearns, Kelly Pavlik is the best puncher I've ever seen in the middleweight division," said Arum that day at BB King's nightclub. "And unlike Tommy, he has a chin to go with it." At the same gathering, Pavlik said that "the people who are picking Jermain Taylor because Kelly Pavlik is too slow are going to be surprised. I think my boxing ability isn't recognised by a lot of people."

As it turned out, neither assessment was inaccurate. Battered to the floor in the second round, Pavlik survived a near-knockout and bounced back to take Taylor out in the seventh.

Ironically, Taylor's first career loss came in the first fight in nearly two years that he didn't prepare for by boxing with Andy Lee.

With Taylor defending against a trio of consecutive left-handers (Winky Wright, Kassim Ouma, Corey Spinks), the Limerick middleweight became his stablemate's principal sparring partner. Before the Pavlik fight, Taylor publicist Norman Horton supposed that the steady run of left-handers might have been unprecedented among middleweight champions, but it wasn't. In 1979-80 Vito Antuofermo had back-to-back-to-back fights against southpaws Hagler and Alan Minter (twice). Another former middleweight champ, Roy Jones Jr, once faced seven left-handed opponents in eight fights, but that was as a light-heavyweight.

The unassuming Pavlik comes from a blue-collar background and is already being hailed as a breath of fresh air to the sport.

Meanwhile, Arum is figuring out how to best cash in on his new champion's sudden popularity, and one beneficiary could be Derryman John Duddy.

Pavlik's contract with Taylor included a rematch clause, but (at the insistence of the then-champion, who had hoped to go after Joe Calzaghe once he disposed of

Working Class Hero: down-to-earth middleweight Kelly Pavlik (pictured before an abandoned steel mill in his native Ohio) celebrated his financial windfall by buying four new tyres for his old car.

Pavlik), it specifies that the return bout would be contested at 166 lb, meaning that if it happens at all (Taylor does not at the moment seem eager), Pavlik-Taylor II would be a non-title fight.

The short list of title challengers already appears to have been pared down to two — Duddy and *Contender* (season I) winner Sergio Mora. Arum will be monitoring Duddy's performance against Noe Tulio Gonzalez Alcoba at the National Stadium on Saturday week.

A Pavlik-Mora fight would likely be staged somewhere in Ohio, a reward to the new champion's fans, thousands of whom travelled to Atlantic City for the Taylor fight.

Pavlik-Duddy, on the other hand, would take place in the mecca of boxing — Madison Square Garden — sometime this winter, and the viability of that bout may rest less in Duddy's hands than in those of his cut-man, George Mitchell. The Derryman not only needs to win impressively on October 20th, but must reverse a recent trend by emerging from his Dublin fight without significant residual damage.

October 11, 2007

Hitman follows in great British tradition

That neither Ricky Hatton nor the world's favourite sport has exactly taken America by storm was suggested by a press release distributed two days ago by the promoters of Saturday night's megafight at the MGM Grand Garden.

Under the heading of "Ricky (the Hitman) Hatton, beloved in England, wants US fans to know more of his charismatic personality," the "Did You Know?" section included this titbit: "Ricky is friends with Paul Dalglish, who plays American football for the Houston Texans," news which would have been surprising to that NFL team.

Kenny Dalglish's son, of course, plays *English* football, or soccer, for the Houston Dynamo, a team which just two weeks earlier had won the MLS Cup, but the misinformation was duly reprinted in numerous newspapers and boxing websites around the country yesterday morning.

American sports fans and American sportswriters may be naïve about soccer, but when it comes to self-deception, the eternally optimistic English boxing fan is unrivalled in all of sport.

When tickets for Hatton's fight against Floyd Mayweather Jr went on sale last September, the MGM Grand Garden Arena sold out in half an hour. Of the 17,000 ducats snapped up that day, perhaps 3,000 of them were purchased by British tour operators, but locals estimate that as many as 10,000 of Hatton's countrymen are in Nevada this weekend to support the undefeated Mancunian.

As of yesterday morning, Las Vegas ticket brokers were offering single seats on the floor at $5,000 and up, and four adjacent seats could still be had for a mere $38,000.

It seems unlikely enough that Hatton's army of blue-collar supporters will subscribe at those prices, but a number of Las Vegas casinos will have the fight available on closed-circuit television at $50 a pop, which, given the $54.95 price tag for watching the pay-per-view telecast in one's living room, looks almost like a bargain.

In the meantime, the casinos will spend the next three days cheerfully separating the visitors from across the pond from their money at the gaming tables.

Depending on the always-unpredictable pay-per-view sale in Britain and elsewhere in Europe, Pretty Boy Floyd could wind up with an estimated $20 million for this weekend's exercise. Hatton's take could be as much as $15 million.

Mayweather remains slightly better than a 1 to 2 favourite at the sports books up and down the strip, and the odds would be even shorter but for the recent influx of British money through the windows.

Given the fervour of the Brits, it would be surprising if attendance at tomorrow's weigh-in at the Grand Garden doesn't top the record 7,000 who watched Mayweather and De La Hoya step on the scales in May.

We've seen all of this before, of course. When future Hall of Famer Marvellous Marvin Hagler challenged the very ordinary Alan Minter for the middleweight title back in 1980, Minter was actually the betting favourite at the London bookie shops.

Seven years later the Brits were convinced that Barney Eastwood-managed Herol (Bomber) Graham would inherit the mantle of middleweight greatness once Hagler passed on the torch. Graham was 38-0 when Hagler retired from the ring. The Bomber wound up getting four cracks at world titles, and lost them all.

Saturday night's venue has been the scene of some of these British disappointments. Half a dozen years ago the English had actually managed to persuade themselves that Prince Naseem Hamed, then 35-0, was the second coming of Sugar Ray Robinson — until he was unmasked by Marco Antonio Barrera at the MGM Grand.

An army of supporters at least the size of Hatton's accompanied Frank Bruno to America for his 1996 fight with Mike Tyson at the MGM Grand. Although Tyson had knocked Bruno out in five seven years earlier, this time Bruno was the champion, Tyson had fought just twice since being released from prison, and thousands of beefy Englishmen showed up in Vegas persuaded that their man couldn't lose.

Bruno nearly hyperventilated in his corner before the fight even started. Just before the opening bell he frantically blessed himself so many times that Frank Warren was moved to note that he looked like "the Pope on speed." This time Tyson knocked him out in three.

(The lone exception to a trend which dates back to the dawn of time would seem to be Lennox Lewis, but it should be remembered that the Brits didn't exactly embrace Lewis as one of their own. Though born in London, he was a Canadian citizen of Jamaican stock who lived in the US. When he won, he was English. When he lost, or looked bad, he was a Canadian.)

If Hatton is burdened by unrealistic expectations it is because his fans have never seen him lose. (Mayweather sneered at the Hitman's 43-0 record the other day, noting that "if he'd fought 43 Floyd Mayweathers, he'd be 0-43.) The bout will be Hatton's fourth US outing in a row (and fifth overall, including a four-rounder on a Madison Square Garden undercard 10 years ago). Last year he barely beat Luis Colazzo in Boston, with a first-round flash knockdown furnishing the margin of victory, and then went the distance with the largely untested Juan Urango. This June he knocked out Jose Luis Castillo, but Castillo was but a shell of the fighter who'd given Mayweather two hard fights years earlier.

That the bout is being contested at 147lb probably doesn't bode well for Hatton, who struggled against Colazzo in his only previous fight at that weight. (Mayweather, on the other hand, ventured up to 154 for May's fight against De La Hoya; even as a light middleweight he looked quicker than Hatton did as a welter-weight.)

When somebody mentioned Hatton's "electrifying" style the other day, Pretty Boy scoffed: "If you call hitting and holding and wrestling exciting, then I guess he's an exciting fighter."

Hatton has traditionally been able to wear down his opponents with relentless pressure, but the expectation here is that he won't even be able to catch up with Pretty Boy, who won't stay in one place long enough to engage him on the inside.

Does Hatton have a chance, then? Well, yes. Mayweather has a well-documented history of chronic hand problems, and as late as last week rumours had surfaced that the American had an injured paw and might seek a postponement.

If Hatton can hang in long enough to do some damage to Mayweather's fists with his face, he might be able to make a fight of it.

December 6, 2007

Pretty Boy is sitting pretty on a pretty penny

Charles Arthur (Pretty Boy) Floyd, a Depression-era Oklahoma bank robber and murderer, was romanticised as a sort of Robin Hood of the Great Plains by, among others, Woody Guthrie. (Guthrie's composition *Pretty Boy Floyd* included a line — *Some will rob you with a six-gun/ and some with a fountain pen* — that could have been a paean to a boxing promoter.)

In the 73 years since Pretty Boy's demise, every American whose misfortune it was to have been christened Floyd has at some point in his life answered to the name "Pretty Boy," but Floyd Mayweather jnr makes the unique claim that his nom de ring has nothing to do with Pretty Boy Floyd the outlaw.

"My amateur team-mates gave me that name," insists Pretty Boy Floyd the boxer. "I got the nickname because when my fights finished, I never came out cut or bruised."

At 30 — the age of the original Pretty Boy when he was gunned down in a 1934 FBI ambush — Mayweather has won world titles in five weight classes and is widely considered the world's most accomplished pound-for-pound boxer.

In the process of defeating 38 of 38 professional opponents, he has earned upwards of $100 million (€68 million) in the ring — a figure that could swell by another $20 million when the receipts from tonight's blockbuster fight against Ricky Hatton are tallied. And he isn't shy about letting you know it.

As viewers of HBO's 24/7 promotional series learned last spring, Mayweather routinely walks around with $30,000 in flash-cash in his pockets. "I got money longer than train smoke," boasts Mayweather. "I been riding Bentleys since the 90s."

He has suggested his nickname be replaced by "Money May," and when he founded his rap-music label, he called his firm "Philthy Rich Records".

Although Philthy Rich has yet to produce a commercially successful album, Pretty Boy's connections in the world of gangsta rap run deep: when he fought Oscar De La Hoya last May he was escorted into the ring by the entertainer 50 Cent, who serenaded the crowd with his rendition of Straight to the Bank.

That he is universally admired as a boxer has not translated into personal popularity. When he preceded his training camp for the Hatton fight with a stint on the television programme Dancing with the Stars he was summarily voted off by the viewers.

Pretty Boy: Floyd Mayweather turns on the charm.

And while just 3,000 of Hatton's British compatriots will be among the 17,000 at the MGM Grand Garden Arena tonight, it is a safe bet that at least half the audience would consider a Hatton upset a triumph of justice.

In the ring, Mayweather has not tasted defeat since his controversial loss to the Bulgarian Serafim Todorov in the featherweight semi-final of the 1996 Atlanta Games. He turned pro that October, and two years later won his first world championship, at 130lb, by stopping the Mexican champion Genaro Hernandez.

He has subsequently won titles at lightweight (from Jose Luis Castillo in 2002), light welterweight (knocking out Arturo Gatti in 2005), and welterweight (Zab Judah,

2006), and this May outpointed De La Hoya for the WBC light middleweight title, a belt he relinquished in order to maintain the 147lb championship he will defend against Hatton tonight.

Along the way, Mayweather has kept his name in the news outside the ring as well. He pleaded no contest to assault charges after putting his boot to a bouncer in a 2004 Michigan bar-room fight, and later that year was convicted of misdemeanour battery for punching two women at a Las Vegas nightclub. He was also arrested, but later acquitted, on domestic violence charges brought by a former girlfriend.

And the odd part of it is that Pretty Boy may be the most normal member of his family. These Mayweathers are a case study in dysfunction. Pretty Boy's father, Floyd snr, was a useful welterweight of the 1970s who lasted into the 10th round of a 1978 fight against Sugar Ray Leonard.

Things began to fall apart for Floyd once he began to train on cocaine, and the demise of his ring career was further hastened when he was shot by a drug dealer named Tony Sinclair, the brother of Pretty Boy's mother. (The bullet struck him in the leg. Uncle Tony's aim may have been thrown off when his target used the infant Floyd jnr as a shield.)

In 1994, Floyd snr received a five-year sentence for cocaine trafficking. Two years later, Mayweather jnr wrote a letter to Bill Clinton, unsuccessfully imploring the president to let his father out long enough to watch him box in the Olympics.

It is probably significant that for all his transgressions, Floyd snr was awarded custody of the boy who became Pretty Boy. Junior's mother, a crack addict named Deborah Sinclair, was deemed an even less fit parent.

Although Floyd snr trained his son for a time (and has continued to train many top-flight boxers, including, for a time, De La Hoya), the two no longer speak. Roger Mayweather, who began to work with Pretty Boy when his elder brother was in jail, has trained him for several years.

Roger, who billed himself as "the Black Mamba," was once the WBC junior welterweight champion. In 2006, Roger received a one-year suspension from the Nevada State Athletic Commission for his part in a brawl that erupted after Floyd jnr's win over Judah — though the suspension was somewhat moot since Uncle Roger was soon doing six months in the pokey for beating up the grandmother of his infant son.

"I fought from the bottom to the top," Mayweather jnr reminded a gathering of reporters in Las Vegas last week. "Ricky Hatton never saw his father being shot. He never saw his mom on drugs or his father in prison."

At press conferences and in his adversary's presence, Mayweather has been respectful toward Hatton, but in a remarkably profane, self-involved, four-minute rant recorded at the Philthy Rich studios he dismissed tonight's adversary as "a faggot motherfucker from England".

The snippet is at *http://www.youtube.com/watch?v=Fi3LrdjXXGM*. If you're going to play it on your home computer, get the kids out of the room first.
December 8, 2007

Nothing like Belfast on fight nights

When Howard Eastman walked into the King's Hall the other night, he must have felt as if he were in the *Plaza De Toros* and he was the bull. With a sell-out crowd of 6,100 prepared to passionately embrace one of their own, Brian Peters managed to effectively replicate the McGuigan-era atmosphere for his first boxing card in the North. Saturday night's passion was reflected in an ear-splitting roar that seemed to sustain itself throughout the night, and you had to wonder whether Duddy might be even more daunted by the burden of overwhelming expectation than the veteran Eastman, by the prospect of being fed to the lions for the amusement of the howling crowd.

John Duddy: fighting fit in fight-mad Belfast.

I mean, there are fight towns and then there is Belfast. I spent barely 24 hours there last weekend, and from the taxi driver who picked me up at the airport to the barman who brought the coffee the next morning and everyone I encountered in between, every conversation seemed to revolve around boxing.

Just a few weeks earlier, Juan LaPorte had dropped by my house in New York. To the best of my recollection, the subject of John Duddy never came up that evening, but the old featherweight champion of the early 1980s did recall that in a 68-bout pro career he'd performed in hostile environments all over the world — LaPorte fought Kostya Tszyu in Australia, Wilfredo Gomez in San Juan, and Salvador Sanchez in El Paso, a stone's throw from the Mexican border — but in terms of sheer intimidation, nothing on earth could have prepared him for the crowd at the King's Hall the night he fought Barry McGuigan in Belfast.

It had been more than a dozen years since I'd experienced a fight card at the King's Hall. The most enduring memory of that evening's Barney Eastwood-Don King joint promotion came just before the main event between Chris Eubank and Ray Close.

With the entourages still milling around in the ring just prior to the introductions, a member of Close's posse wearing a leprechaun costume sneaked up behind Eubank and, to the delight of the crowd, pelted him with a fistful of what was supposed to be some sort of magic pixie dust.

What no one had taken into account was that, just before leaving his dressing room, Eubank had liberally slathered himself with a coat of petroleum jelly, so that once he removed his robe his finely-chiseled physique revealed a well-muscled sheen that resembled polished ebony.

After the sneak attack by the leprechaun, the fight had to be delayed for several minutes while the champion's cornermen frantically scrubbed away in an attempt to remove the thousands of bits of glitter that had stuck to his greased body.

In contrast to the controversy that would precede Mayweather-Hatton in Las Vegas several hours later, there were no pre-fight anthem moments at the King's Hall on Saturday night. In obeisance to the season, the main event was instead preceded by the Shane McGowan/Kirsty MacColl rendition of *A Fairytale of New York.*

It had been anticipated Eastman would provide Duddy with his sternest test to date, and he did, unpacking the contents of a kit bag of veteran tricks accumulated over the years in 48 professional outings.

As the fight reached its midpoint it appeared that Eastman had a nose in front. Indeed, I was told later that after six rounds several Derrymen seated in the balcony left in disgust, convinced that their man was inexorably beaten.

But Don Turner has been around even longer than Eastman. (Forty years ago in Harlem, Turner was already a renaissance man who ran with Sugar Ray Robinson, Miles Davis, John Coltrane, and the Black Panther leader H Rap Brown — simultaneously.) The old trainer barely seemed exercised as he reminded Duddy of what he needed to do, and once the Irishman began to use his jab and box, the puzzle quickly fell into place.

Duddy's 96-94 win on the scorecard of referee Seán Russell seemed just, and coincided precisely with our own. The delighted audience slowly filed out of the building, but on this magical evening they were only warming up. The best we could tell, it appeared that every man, woman and child among them had figured out some way to watch the telecast from Vegas.

I spent a few moments in the dressingroom with Duddy and Turner, and then raced back to the hotel to file my copy. Peters had arranged a viewing of the Mayweather-Hatton fight in the bar of another hostelry up the road, and in the wee hours of the morning we settled in with a clientele of fellow scribes, boxing officials, referees, undercard fighters, and fans to watch the ritual slaughter at the MGM Grand.

The loyalties of the company in which I watched the fight in Belfast were even more pro-Ricky than at the Vegas venue itself — and it wasn't just Englishmen making all that noise at the MGM. (Mayweather might just be the best practicing boxer extant right now, but he's pretty easy to dislike.

Throw in his Uncle Roger in the corner and it's a safe bet that not a few American sportswriters were secretly harboring hopes for a fluke upset, too.) Far too much was made of the predictable hissing and booing that accompanied Tyrese Gibson's tone-deaf rendition of *The Star-Spangled Banner*. (If I'd been there, I might have booed it myself.)

A day later I heard one British television commentator suggest that the disrespectful episode might have cost Ricky the fight by predisposing referee Joe Cortez against the Englishman; the truth of the matter is that the outcome would have been the same even if Ray Hatton had been the referee.

A few days before the fight I had somewhat facetiously noted that Hatton's best hope might lie in trying to damage Mayweather's fists with his face, but Ricky apparently took the advice to heart.

Apart from the hotel where we'd watched the fight, Eglantine Avenue is a residential neighbourhood. As I walked back to my own quarters at six in the morning I was startled to hear a familiar voice booming from an open window. I looked up and saw a large gathering in a third-storey apartment. The inhabitants had thrown open the windows and turned up the volume so their neighbours could share in the transmission from Las Vegas. So here I was standing on a deserted street where I'd never been before, listening to Larry Merchant interview Floyd Mayweather. It would have been a positively surreal moment anywhere else in the world. In Belfast, it seemed almost normal.
December 13, 2007

WHAT IT WAS, WAS FOOTBALL (OURS AND THEIRS)

On Oakland Raider fan: they dress in basic black, augmented by studded dog-collars, chains, Darth Vader face shields, swastikas, switchblades, and body odour. They are the most vocal, most animated, and, some would say, most dangerous collection of football fans outside Britain.

'Vicious' press campaign led Stapleton to quit

FOXBORO

His team was one of only two which did not reach the playoffs in Major League Soccer's inaugural season. He endured a season-long battle with the club's star player and a running feud with some of its more vocal supporters. In the end, however, it was what he perceived as a "vicious" media campaign and the effect it was having on his family that led Frank Stapleton to tender his resignation as coach of the New England Revolution last week.

"I just don't need any more pressure put on my family," said Stapleton. "I'm trained to deal with this stuff, but just because you're married to a footballer doesn't mean she (wife Chris) can cope with it. Your kids and your family are not immune. I tried to keep them away from it as much as possible, but ..."

In a 17-year professional career at Arsenal, Manchester United, and Ajax, Stapleton thought he had endured the best the English tabloid press could dish out,

Frank Stapleton in his Manch-ester United playing days.

but, he said this week, on a personal level, this was even worse.

"I don't expect not to be criticised, but this became an ongoing situation. It was as if there was a rivalry between the Boston papers to see who could be the most vicious."

Indeed, the soccer correspondents from both Boston dailies, the *Herald* and the *Globe,* had called for his head well before the season ended, and he has waged an unseemly, summer-long public squabble with popular Revolution defender Alexi Lalas.

"I place a lot of the blame for this on myself," said Revolution owner Jonathan Kraft, who desperately attempted to talk Stapleton out of his decision. "We put Frank in an incredibly difficult situation by hiring him just three days before the combines. By the time he came on board every other coach in the league had a say in determining his allocated players, but Frank had to play the hand he was dealt. We actually handcuffed him."

Only when his team, opened its pre-season training camp in Florida last March did Stapleton discover that Italian striker Guiseppe Galderisi, supposedly his most experienced player, had not seen action since the previous September and was far from match-fit. After several unproductive games, Galderisi was placed on waivers and sent packing in early May, a move which was immediately met with a storm of protest from Lalas, Galderisi's friend and former teammate from Padova in Italy's

Serie A. Even as Lalas sulked, Galderisi was eventually claimed by the Tampa Bay Lighting, and played productively as that team finished with MLS' best regular season record.

In the meantime, the Revolution were utterly bereft of a proven goal scorer over the first half of the season, a situation which was so desperate that, at one time, there was serious talk of the 40 year old Stapleton activating himself.

In late July the gifted American international Joe-Max Moore was signed from Nuremburg of the German *Bundesliga*, and scored 11 goals over the final 14 games.

Stapleton had also become increasingly frustrated by the level of commitment Lalas was displaying in club matches. (Those who witnessed Lalas' gritty *mano-a-mano* Foxboro duel with Niall Quinn in June's US Cup match, three days after a display of sublime indifference in a Revolution game on the same pitch, glimpsed the situation in microcosm.)

In addition to his frequent absences when called to national team duty, Lalas successfully lobbied his way onto the US Olympic team as one of the over-23 additions — against the wishes of Stapleton.

"I think (Lalas) had expected to have a say in how the team would be run, and once he saw early on he wasn't going to be able to influence things the way he wanted, he couldn't wait to get out of town," said Stapleton. "He couldn't wait to get away to the national team, and he couldn't wait to get off to the Olympics. His attitude in training was diabolical, and he didn't work on any aspect of his game."

Matters came to a head in mid August, when Stapleton sat Lalas down for a televised game against the New York MetroStars at Giants Stadium. A television audience watched America's most visible soccer player sulk on the bench for 90 minutes as his team lost 4-1.

While Lalas was subsequently returned to the lineup (after some gentle nudging from the front office, Stapleton later revealed), apologised for his behaviour ("I've been acting like a jerk," he admitted), and did perform with renewed vigour thereafter, two days after the season ended he had lunch with the *Herald* and *Globe* soccer writers and informed them that if Stapleton returned to the Revolution next year, he, Lalas, would not.

The Revolution proceeded to stumble to the wire, losing their last three games outright to finish with a 15-17 record. In the end, the club could have reached the playoffs by winning its last game against the Columbus Crew. They lost 1-0, on a goal, ironically enough, conceded when a cross slipped underneath Lalas' foot.

A crowd of over 38,000 turned out for the finale. Despite its shortcomings on the field, the Revolution finished third in MLS attendance.

Inevitably, Stapleton's resignation has been interpreted elsewhere as a victory for Lalas, although the player himself declined to gloat afterwards. In Stapleton's own view, it had more to do with his young sons being taunted at school over what they were reading in the papers.

"If I have a regret, it's that we didn't give the fans what they wanted and deserved," said Stapleton as he took his leave. "There were times when they could have come down on us, but they stuck behind us. I've played all over the world, and without a doubt the (Foxboro) crowd was the best I've ever been involved with."

Asked where the search for a successor might lead, Kraft said, "I'd like to find a guy with all the qualities of Frank Stapleton."

October 03, 1996

Mexico passes NFL test with ease

MEXICO CITY

At the *Zocalo*, the cobbled city-centre marketplace that ranks second only to Moscow's Red Square in sprawling urban gathering places, a group of tribal dancers were about to perform their ancient Aztec rituals for the benefit of the *Turistas*. As their leader stripped down to his bare chest and prepared to don his peacock-feathered head-dress, he removed his last 20th century garment — a maroon sweat-shirt emblazoned with the logo of the Washington Redskins.

With Commissioner Paul Tagliabue cast in the role of a latter-day Hernando Cortez, the National Football League continued its relentless conquest of the world's television markets last Monday night with a pre-season game at *Estadio Azteca*, the site of the 1986 World Cup. The participants were identified in the game programme as the *Vaqueros* of Dallas and *Los Patriotas de Nueva Inglaterra*.

Since inaugurating its "American Bowl" series with a Bears-Cowboys game at Wembley a dozen years ago, the NFL has staged 33 of these contests in far-flung locales from Tokyo to Dublin, none of them in venues more generally inhospitable than the Mexican capital, where the primary pursuits of the natives tend toward soccer, bullfighting, and robbing *Gringo* visitors at gunpoint.

Players from both teams, as well as the members of the NFL travelling party and media, were advised not to leave their hotel without armed guards. As a safeguard against the malady commonly known as "Montezuma's Revenge," each player was warned about eating any dodgy tacos and issued two litres of bottled French water upon arrival, with instructions to drink nothing else. Moreover, there were hundreds of pistol and shotgun-packing *Federale* security forces guarding the field at *Azteca*.

It was, in short, like playing an exhibition game in Beirut, but make no mistake about it, the NFL will be back. If you're looking for reasons, there were 106,424 pretty good ones in attendance on Monday night.

The NFL's motivation in this ongoing global exercise is threefold. First, most obviously, is the nurturing of fertile television markets. (The league already has contracts with two Mexican networks.) Second is the enhancement of marketing and merchandising opportunities — and despite the abject poverty in which most of Mexico City's 22 million populace lives, it was startling to see how many natives one found trotted out in the regalia of one NFL team or another.

The third, more subtle goal involves the exploration of eventual expansion sites for the inevitable day the league decides to extend its composition beyond the borders of the United States. If Dublin flunked this test (the 30,000-odd announced at Croke Park for the Steelers-Bears exhibition last July was the second-smallest crowd to watch any of these American Bowls), Mexico City appears to have passed it with flying colours.

Tagliabue himself has repeatedly pointed to the Mexican capital as a "priority market." Patriots owner Robert Kraft said this week that he would "enthusiastically support" Mexico City as a future NFL site, and Dallas owner Jerry Jones confidently predicted a Mexico City NFL franchise "within your lifetime."

Texas was once part of Mexico, and while the Cowboys' status as "America's Team" may have diminished somewhat over the past half-dozen years, their claim to being *Mexico's* team remained unchallenged. South of the border, Dallas gear outsells that of all the other 29 teams combined.

Given their penchant for tunnel vision, NFL coaches generally detest participating in these games, simply because it disrupts routine, but New England's Pete Carroll managed to find a silver lining.

The game represented, claimed Carroll, a "perfect opportunity" to prepare his Patriots for their September 7th season opener in Denver, where the New England team will play a Monday Night game against before a hostile crowd at a 5,280-foot altitude.

The game, in short, was supposed to serve as a dress rehearsal, with Troy Aikman and Emmitt Smith serving as stand-ins for John Elway and Terrell Davis, the *Azteca* for Mile High Stadium, and the Mexican *aficionados* playing the part of Denver's boisterous crowd.

By half-time the Patriots had scored three touchdowns, had three more called back by holding penalties, and missed two more opportunities when quarterback Drew Bledsoe overthrew wide-open receivers ("I'm going to blame it on the altitude," joked Bledsoe), and any notion that the Cowboys were Mexico's Team had been thoroughly dispelled, as each Dallas miscue (and there were plenty of them) was greeted by tens of thousands of shrill whistles.

And actually, the Cowboys got off easy. A day before the Cowboys lost to the Patriots, the favoured Puebla Executives lost a 3-2 soccer game to Atlas in the Mexican First Division. As the losers filed out of Cuauhtemoc Stadium, displeased Puebla supporters were waiting for them with sticks and chains, and stoned the team bus as it departed the car park.

Indeed. No one threw rocks at the losers on Monday night, but while the game was in progress somebody broke into the Cowboys' locker room to steal wallets and jewellery belonging to 18 Dallas players.

August 21, 1998

Shootout bites the dust in US game

FOXBORO

Unless you happen to be a particularly devoted *aficianado* of South American soccer, Marco Etcheverry's name might be unfamiliar to you. The 29-year-old Bolivian midfielder's exposure on the world stage has been fleeting indeed.

If memory serves, between a nagging injury and the birth of his first son that June, Etcheverry did not make the trip to Dublin for Bolivia's friendly at Lansdowne Road which preceded the 1994 World Cup, and when the tournament proper began in this country, his appearance was so brief, and his departure so swift, that if you so much as blinked you probably missed it.

Etcheverry, still nursing a groin strain, wasn't supposed to play at all when Bolivia faced Germany in Chicago in the first game of USA '94, but with his side trailing 1-0 he was brought on in the second half, and stayed on the pitch for less than three minutes. With the referee staring over his right shoulder, he delivered a swift boot to the shin of Lothar Matthaeus. Out came the red card, with it a two-game suspension, and Etcheverry's World Cup was over.

Nicknamed *"El Diablo,"* the swarthy, dark-maned Etcheverry has served for the

Marco Etcheverry: "Do you have a match, my friend?"

past four years as the captain, playmaker, and linchpin for DC United, which played its fourth consecutive MLS Cup last Sunday at Foxboro Stadium. The 2-0 win over the Los Angeles Galaxy established DC United as the most dominant club team in the history of American soccer.

("Well," noted a wag, "that certainly makes them a tall bunch of midgets, doesn't it?")

DC United's dominance over that brief span is all the more remarkable because when Major League Soccer divided up its modest spoils at its inception four seasons back, parity was the goal. The original eight teams were allegedly created equally, and it was only by a combination of good fortune and perceptive personnel moves that one emerged head and shoulders above the others.

Having accidentally created a dominant team, MLS spent the next three years attempting to whittle United down to everybody else's size, forcing upon it several salary-cap inspired trades that robbed the team of its top scorer (El Salvador's Raul Diaz Arce), as well as several of its better American players. (John Harkes was traded to New England, Roy Wegerle to Tampa Bay and Tony Sanneh was sold to the Germans.)

The club even changed coaches last year, when Bruce Arena left to take over the helm of the US national team, and was replaced by Dutchman Thomas Rongen. Still, DC remains at the top of the heap, and that the principal constant has been Etcheverry is hardly a coincidence. The Bolivian came from Chile's Colo Colo to start United's first game in 1996 and, apart from a brief loan to Barcelona over the winter of 1997-98, has been there since. In 1998 he was named the league's Most Valuable Player, and at a Saturday night gala preceding Sunday's championship game was named to the league's "best XI" for the fourth consecutive year.

A world-class distributor of the ball, Etcheverry's other stock in trade will go by the boards next year. Over the years he has scored a record 16 shootout goals, but, largely at the urging of new MLS commissioner Don Garber, the league's competition committee last week voted to do away with that ghastly tie-breaking procedure.

About time, Alan Kelly agrees. Kelly, who collected 47 caps playing for Ireland and then sired another generation of Irish internationals in Gary and Alan, serves as the goal-keeping coach for DC United. Even as the champagne flowed freely in the DC dressing-room on Sunday afternoon, Kelly conceded that he had felt downright silly every time he attempted to explain the shootout to somebody back home.

When MLS squeezed out commissioner Doug Logan last summer and brought in Garber, whose background had been in trying to sell American Football to the Europeans, the US soccer community had reacted with understandable trepidation. Garber, by his admission, knew even less about the sport than did his predecessor.

However, watching the fits and starts of MLS from his European base had provided Garber with a unique perspective. And he proved to be a good listener.

For four years MLS had played a soccer-like game that occasionally reminded people of the real thing. By bastardising the rules in an effort to make them more palatable to the ordinary American fan, MLS had not only consistently alienated the hard-core soccer audience in the US, but held itself up to ridicule around the rest of the world. Garber, recognising that perception, wasted little time in his brief term in office in attempting to remedy both situations.

Convincing the MLS owners was not easy. We're talking about a group of men, after all, who came to the sport still convinced that the greatest threat to world peace was the 0-0 draw.

"As part of the most popular sport in the world, Major League Soccer has decided to bring our rules of competition in line with those of most internationally-respected leagues," said the new commissioner as he formally unveiled the sweeping changes earlier in the week. "Millions and millions of fans in America follow soccer the way it is played across our globe. Our audience has spoken, and we have listened."

Even in agreeing to scuttle the shootout, the MLS moguls still did not quite get it. By insisting on two, five-minute golden goal overtime periods for regular-season games, the owners revealed that they still don't understand that a draw is not only an acceptable soccer result, but sometimes quite a desirable one. The philosophy in America still echoes that of the old college football coach, Duffy Daugherty, who coined the phrase: "A tie is like kissing your sister".

The new commissioner also convinced the owners to have the game clock run forward rather than backward, a paean to American convention MLS had utilized over its first four seasons.

When we interviewed him just before the '94 World Cup, incidentally, Marco Etcheverry didn't speak a word of English. When we ran into him in the boozy United dressing-room following Sunday's win, he had a fat cigar clenched between his teeth and asked, in perfect English: "Do you have a match, my friend?"
November 25, 1999

Former diplomat shows his real tact

Late one glorious Saturday morning in the summer of 1994, I arrived at the European Club in search of a game of golf. Although the timesheet was quite full, Miss Ruddy assured me that if I didn't mind waiting 45 minutes or so I could probably play with the Canadian Ambassador.

Which is how I came to meet Mike Wadsworth.

Major Wadsworth arrived in due course, accompanied by a fellow who had been one of his college football team-mates at Notre Dame some 30 years previously. Having been thus provided with something of a common ground, we spent a pleasant afternoon on the links at Brittas Bay, not to mention a profitable one: with the passage of time, I cannot recall whether His Excellency played off 16 and I relieved him of 15 quid or vice versa, but those numbers remain (almost) indelibly etched in my mind.

It was several months later that I read, somewhat to my surprise and amusement, a wire-service story reporting that Dick Rosenthal, the long-time athletic director (AD) at Notre Dame, had decided to retire. The story went on to say that Rosenthal had agreed to remain in the job until the following spring, when his successor, Major Michael Wadsworth, completed his term as Canada's Ambassador to Ireland.

Now, as difficult as this might be for the uninitiated to imagine, in certain quarters this transformation — from serving as one's emissary to the Irish to overseeing the conduct of the Fun and Games Department of the *Fighting Irish* — was viewed as a step up in the world. And there seemed little doubt that the image of the Golden Dome and Touchdown Jesus was at that time in need of a fresh makeover.

A year earlier I had been in South Bend for 10 days or so, straddling the period between Notre Dame's win over Florida State in the 1993 version of the "Game of the Century" and the shocking, last-second loss to Boston College the following Saturday. The football coach at the time, the legendary Lou Holtz, was attempting to hold things together in the face of a brewing mini-scandal. At least one player had tested positive for steroids, and the word on the street was that he might not be the only one.

The Fighting Irish were practising indoors that week. Those of us who comprised the "out-of-town press" were not allowed to view these preparations, presumably on the grounds that one of us might transmit a bit of espionage to Bobby Bowden, the Florida State coach. We were asked instead to remain in a holding area off in another corner of the gym as we awaited our audience with the great Holtz.

Not 10 feet from the designated spot where we had been instructed to wait stood a large table, which, once the practise session concluded, rapidly began to fill with glass vials containing urine specimens, collected from an ostensibly random sampling of Notre Dame players as they filed off the floor. There was little doubt that this exercise was being conducted for the benefit of the visiting media. Drug testing had become a spectator sport.

It was into this wholesome atmosphere that Mike Wadsworth stepped, replete with his concept of reform and an ambitious five-year plan designed to restore Notre Dame's athletic reputation to its traditional position of grandeur.

It proved a more difficult task than even he had imagined. It is generally accepted that Holtz's decision to resign came after some gentle nudging from the new AD. (An age discrimination suit filed by sacked assistant Joe Moore also blossomed into an unwelcome front-page story after Wadsworth had assumed the reins.) Nor did it do much for Wadsworth's cause when the Irish went 5-7 last fall, a record that represented Notre Dame's worst football season in decades.

Although Wadsworth was able to put his stamp on certain matters — suffice it to say that Notre Dame would never have played a regular season game at Croke Park under one of his predecessors — he found himself increasingly at loggerheads with the college administration. Just last year, when he attempted to hire Rick

Majerus to succeed John McLeon as basketball coach, he was rebuffed by the Rev Edward A. Malloy, the university's president.

In the end, though, it was neither a losing football team nor a disagreement over hiring practises which proved Wadsworth's undoing. Rather, it was Kimberly Dunbar.

Lest the reader jump to untoward conclusions, Ms Dunbar was most assuredly no Monica Lewinsky. Indeed, the evidence at hand suggests that she was nothing more than an overzealous if somewhat deranged Notre Dame supporter. Described as a worshipful "booster" in both court documents and the subsequent NCAA investigation, she had, it developed, embezzled funds in the amount of $1.2 million from her employer, and spent most of it lavishing gifts on a dozen Notre Dame players over a five-year period more or less coinciding with Mike Wadsworth's watch.

In the eyes of Father Malloy and the university administration, the unforgivable aspect of this transgression was not the criminal act itself – that Ms Dunbar had stolen $1,200,000 from her employer — but rather that she had distributed the funds in a manner which compromised the athletic eligibility and amateur integrity of Notre Dame players. When the NCAA, for the first time in Notre Dame history, slapped the football program with probation (with the concomitant loss of two scholarships), Wadsworth's fate was sealed.

This week Father Malloy announced that, "by mutual agreement," Wadsworth had agreed to end his tenure with the expiration of the five-year contract he had signed when he left Ireland, but Wadsworth made it clear that he would have preferred to stay for at least another year.

"But there is a broad perception that there's a problem, and perception is very important," sighed Wadsworth. "The best way of dealing with this is to turn the page and start afresh."

The Major could, one surmises, always return to the Canadian Foreign Service, but after his five-year brush with the Big Time, life as a mere ambassador will seem like very small potatoes indeed.

February 10, 2000

Mickey Mouse world of the MVP

TAMPA

A whole generation of Americans has by now grown up believing it to be a Super Bowl tradition as old as the F14 flyover: the moment the final gun sounds to end the game, an interviewer catches up with the game's Most Valuable Player as he is being borne off the field on the shoulders of his team-mates and breathlessly asks: "Hey, Joe Blow! You've just won the Super Bowl! What are you going to do next?"

To which Joe Blow, who has been handsomely compensated by prior arrangement, gleefully replies: *"I'm going to Disney World!"*

A day later this exchange will have been packaged, along with footage of Joe Blow and his family happily cavorting with Mickey and Goofy, in a commercial spot presumably designed to help those American families still undecided in their plans for February's school holidays to make up their minds.

Contrary to popular supposition, the arrangement with the Disney people does not predate the invention of the face-mask. It was, in fact, conceived just 15 years ago. Phil Simms, the New York Giants' quarterback, was the first to utter the phrase, which has been repeated by every Super Bowl MVP since.

Joe Montana and Jerry Rice. Troy Aikman and Emmitt Smith, they've all done it. Last year it was the Rams' Kurt Warner (Cinderella himself?). But as Super Bowl XXXV drew nigh, the Disney people realised that they had a potential nightmare on their hands: what if the Baltimore Ravens won and Ray Lewis was the MVP?

It would hardly do, after all, to pay a man who less than a year earlier stood accused of two murders to stand up and shout *"I'm going to Disney World!"* And if he did show up at the Magic Kingdom, which family would Lewis bring to the parade? The three children he has by one woman (not his wife) in Florida, or the one child by the other woman (not his wife) in Maryland?

If he was wavering before Super Bowl week, Disney CEO Michael Eisner quickly made up his mind once the Ravens got to Tampa. Grilled by a battalion of reporters and television types, an unrepentant, arrogant, and defiant Lewis wasted little time in embracing the villain's role. Asked if he had spoken to the families of the two men slain in an Atlanta nightclub last year, Lewis replied "Nah. Why should I?"

Although the murder charges had been dropped in a plea-bargaining arrangement (Lewis pleaded guilty to obstruction of justice and testified against two co-defendants), the NFL had fined Lewis a record $250,000.

Getting paid to go on Mister Toad's Wild Ride might have been the perfect way to end his bizarre year, but in the days before the game Disney quietly backed off its usual arrangement and declined to contract themselves to using the Super Bowl MVP in the traditional promotion.

The Ravens naturally won, defeating the New York Giants in a sloppy game that may have been the worst-played Super Bowl in the history of the event. For the first time, fans were allowed to participate in the MVP voting via an Internet poll, but their vote would count just 20 per cent of the total. The remaining 80 per cent of the electorate remained in the hands of a 15-man (or actually, 14 men and one woman) media panel.

Lewis, of course, won the award, even though it was by no means clear that he was even the Most Valuable *Lewis* in Super Bowl XXXV. Ravens' running back Jamal Lewis ran for over 100 yards and a touchdown. Baltimore return specialist

Ray Lewis of the Baltimore Ravens: caused something of a dilemma for both Michael Eisner of Disney, and the NFL with regard to their bandana policy.

Jermaine Lewis raced 84 yards to score on a third-period kick-off return, and accumulated 145 yards in returns on the evening.

Ray Lewis had what was for him a comparatively pedestrian game, but he was unquestionably the heart and soul of a defence as dominating as any ever to appear in the biggest game of the year.

He might not have been a landslide choice, but put it this way: it wasn't the most outrageous vote to take place in Florida this winter.

If the Disney people showed great judgment, their counterparts from Ford weren't so fortunate — or so prescient. Having committed to presenting one of their cars to the Most Valuable Player, the company suffered a dual indignity, inasmuch as reporters with long memories could point out that Lewis departed the last two Super Bowls in Ford products. A Lincoln Navigator limousine served as the getaway car for Lewis and his posse following last year's Buckhead murders, and this year he got the keys to a new silver Ford Explorer.

Disney, in the meantime, had quietly made their arrangements backstage, and when the game was over they had a crew ready to film Baltimore quarterback Trent Dilfer shouting *"I'm going to Disney World!"*

He might not have won the MVP election, but Dilfer was hardly undeserving of the commercial spot. His was a wonderful rags-to-riches story in any case. A year earlier (while Ray Lewis was in jail, as a matter of fact), he had been released by his career-long team, the Tampa Bay Buccaneers. (His departure was enthusiastically supported by the more rabid Bucs' fans, some of who used to regularly boo Dilfer's wife when she ventured out in public.)

Signed by the Ravens, he had spent the first half of the season in a backup role, and got the quarterback's job in late October largely by default after starter Tony Banks sputtered. After losing to Pittsburgh 9-6 in his first outing, Dilfer led the Ravens to 11 straight wins, including last Sunday night's.

So there they were in Orlando on Monday: the more wholesome Dilfer, along with his wife and three children, riding down Main Street in a ticker-tape parade.

When the issue of his non-invitation was brought up after the game, Ray Lewis had but one cryptic comment:

"I ain't goin' to no Disney," he muttered.

February 01, 2001

Some heads are political footballs

When the National Football League moguls convened in Palm Desert, California for their annual spring owners' meeting this week, several pressing items headed up the agenda. With the league set to expand to 32 teams in 2002, a new divisional realignment is in the cards, and the future of instant replay in reversing or upholding officials' on-field calls was a matter still obviously in need of some tweaking.

While the owners, finding themselves unable to arrive at a consensus, tabled both of those topics for future discussion, they did find themselves in apparently unanimous agreement on one momentous issue.

Bandanas

For the past decade, harkening back to the NFL debut of Deion Sanders, certain players have increasingly taken to protecting their carefully coiffured hairstyles by wearing colourful kerchiefs underneath their helmets.

The devotees of this fashion seem to fairly revel in the fact that it conjures up an image of the dastardly 18th-century pirate, although, to tell the truth, a 300lb lineman with a kerchief on his head is apt to come off looking less like Captain Blood than Aunt Jemima.

The owners, along with NFL commissioner Paul Tagliabue, knew they had to tread somewhat gingerly when it came to an issue with patently racial overtones. By and large the demarcation line is clear: Black guys wear bandanas. White guys don't.

So rather than come down with a heavy-handed decree from the commissioner's office, or have the owners submit it to a vote among themselves, the NFL owners assayed a deft end-run: In what was, depending on one's perspective, either a tactful bit of diplomacy or an act of incredible cowardice, they handed *L'Affaire* Bandana off to a subcommittee, packaged it in the midst of several other "sportsmanship" issues, and then marched Dennis Green out to make the announcement to the press.

Cute.

Green is the head coach of the Minnesota Vikings. He also happens to be black. He serves on the NFL's competition committee, and even more conveniently, he has for the past 10 years enforced a Vikings' team rule forbidding bandana wear on Sunday afternoons.

"It has nothing to do with anything other than the football uniform," explained Green. "You don't see baseball players wearing them — and just because the commissioner says the Vikings don't wear them doesn't mean it's me against the black guys. The uniform consists of what a player wears — and that's from the shoes to the top of the head."

The league's contention is that wearing individual accoutrements violates the league's uniform policy. "We have exacting uniform standards for everything except what people put on their heads," said Tagliabue in defence of the proposed regulation.

Indeed, the NFL employs its own brand of Fashion Police. At each and every game, a representative of the league office — usually a former player — is on duty

An illustration depicting the last stand of General Custer at the Battle of Little Big Horn, June 25, 1876. The Garryowen air was in Custer's time, and remains to this day, the regimental anthem of the Seventh US Cavalry,

in the press box. This fellow's sole function is to issue citations for uniform viola-tions. Players can be (and are, regularly) fined for everything from having their shirt-tails out to baggy stockings to displaying excessive tape on their shoes.

There are even guidelines regulating the length and colour of allowable acces-sories such as towels and gloves. Since bandanas have been around for more than a decade, you might ask, why are the owners only now getting around to addressing the subject?

Two words: Ray Lewis.

The NFL's carefully-cultivated image took several big hits last season, but none larger than that engendered by the spectacular season of the Baltimore linebacker, who began 2000 in an Atlanta jail cell, accused of a double murder, and finished it as Super Bowl XXV's Most Valuable Player.

That Lewis' swaggering, defiant, and decidedly unrepentant stance was accom-panied by a bandana atop his head may have doomed the fashion forever.

It was announced, in any case, that Green's subcommittee had voted 8-0 to Ban the Bandana, making ratification by the owners a likely formality.

That this recommendation came as part of an overall endorsement tightening existing rules against taunting, trash-talking, chest-bumping, and extraneous showboating makes it clear enough that the owners have grown both wary and weary of the thuggish image which has come to be equated with the bandana brigade.

You may rest assured, however, that the bandana devotees aren't going to see it that way. They are going to claim that the league is trying to stifle expressions of individualism, and, moreover, they're going to claim that the proposed new rule is racially inspired. And they could be right on both counts.
March 29, 2001

From Turin, via Garryowen, to Foxboro

The Winter Wonderland atmosphere only made it more surreal. The blizzard which had begun two hours before kick-off had dumped six inches of snow on Foxboro Stadium last Saturday night, and now, in the ninth minute of overtime, several New England Patriots availed of their final time-out, feverishly kicking the snow away to clear a spot where the ball would be placed for a game-winning field goal attempt.

From across the line of scrimmage, several Oakland Raiders were simultaneously doing their level best to kick the snow right back from whence it had come.

Despite the treacherous footing — imagine an ice-skating rink with half a foot of snow on the surface — the Patriots kicker had miraculously booted a 45-yard field goal with 27 seconds left in regulation to bring his team, which had trailed 13-3 with eight minutes to play, level at 13-all, and now he capped the dramatic comeback by drilling the kick home.

As the placekicker was borne off through the driving snow on the shoulders of his team-mates, the stadium rocked with delirious glee. Over 60,000 had remained rooted (and possibly frozen) to their seats, and now they positively exploded in delight at the realisation that the Patriots, who opened the season a consensus pick for the AFC East cellar, were one game away from the Super Bowl.

New England was still basking in the afterglow two days later when I chanced, on my car radio, to hear the Irish-American folksinger Tim O'Brien perform a song called "Mick Ryan's Lament." O'Brien, a Virginia-born musician now living in Nashville, explored his Irish roots in a recent album entitled *Two Journeys*, on which he was accompanied by, among others, Kevin Burke, Paddy Keenan, Tríona Ní Dhomhnaill, and Maura O'Connell.

The song in question, sort of a "Willie McBride comes-to-America," is ostensibly the first-person account of a young fellow who flees Ireland in 1848, presumably one step ahead of the authorities. Voicing his disdain for his cousins who escaped the Famine by taking the King's Shilling, he and his brother arrive in "Amerikay," where they enlist in the Union army to fight in the name of freedom at the battle of Vicksburg.

Mick survives this encounter (his brother, Paddy, does not), but remains in the army one war too long, and perishes, ironically, at Custer's Last Stand in June of 1876. Only belatedly does he recognise that in going off to subdue the Sioux he has in the end "turned into something I hated," and given his life in the service of a cause not terribly unlike the one he left Ireland to escape.

The catchy refrain, as enunciated by the now-deceased Private Ryan, goes:

The band, they played the Garryowen
Brass was shining, flags a-flowin'
I swear if I had only known
I'd have wished that I'd died back at Vicksburg.

A noble sentiment, to be sure, but historically an inaccurate one.

In his liner notes to the album, O'Brien says of the Robert Lee Dunlap-composed "Mick Ryan's Lament" that "the tune 'Garryowen' was George Armstrong Custer's marching theme, and was likely heard by Sitting Bull and his tribe at the Little Bighorn".

While the Garryowen air was in Custer's time and remains to this day the regimental anthem of the Seventh US Cavalry, quite certainly neither the Hunkpapa Sioux chief Sitting Bull nor Custer heard it played on the day of the battle — and, moreover, if they had, the New England Patriots would have lost, or at least would have had to figure out a different way to win, last Saturday night.

Born in Turin in 1834, Felix Villiet Vinatieri trained as a classical musician at the conservatory in Naples before emigrating to America in 1859. He served with the Union army during the Civil War and was discharged in 1870 at Fort Sully in the Dakota Territory, where he chose to settle.

Marrying a local girl, he earned his living teaching music while pursuing his greater dream as a composer.

When the Seventh Cavalry, under the command of Custer, arrived in the Dakotas three years later, the town of Yankton staged a ball. Custer was sufficiently impressed by the sophistication of the music performed that he summoned the band's leader.

Custer explained to Vinatieri that his present military bandleader had requested to be relieved, and offered him the position of chief musician. Vinatieri agreed, and, after travelling to Minnesota to be officially sworn in, was appointed bandleader of the Seventh Cavalry.

Although Vinatieri and his musicians accompanied Custer on many of his forays through the west, the 1876 Little Bighorn excursion was not one of them. While it seems unlikely that Custer fully comprehended the danger lying in wait for him (if he had, he most assuredly would never have marched off that morning), he understood enough about the circumstances to realise that announcing the operation with a marching brass band probably wasn't a great idea.

At Custer's direction, Vinatieri and his 16 musicians, most of them Germans, remained behind with the regimental supply steamboat, moored on the Powder River, under orders not to engage in the battle; thus it was that none of the musicians was among the 276 men and officers killed that day.

(Since the Sioux were of the belief that separating a decedent from his privates would deny him entrance into heaven, all the bodies save Custer's were scalped and mutilated, a circumstance somehow overlooked in Mick Ryan's somewhat sanitised message-from-the-grave.)

Eventually captured, Sitting Bull went on to tour Europe as part of Buffalo Bill Cody's Wild West Show. Felix Vinatieri was honourably discharged later that year and returned to his adopted hometown to resume his life as a civilian musician and, perhaps even more significantly, from a football standpoint, to father several children.

A composer of some renown, Felix wrote marches, polkas, waltzes, overtures and two of America's earliest light operas before dying, of natural causes, in Yankton, South Dakota in 1891 — a year after Sitting Bull, and 81 years before his great, great-grandson Adam Vinatieri, the place-kicking hero of last Saturday night's win against the Raiders, was born in the same city.

Jan 24, 2002

Raiders rev up and head for town

SAN DIEGO

That loud belch you just heard meant another Raiders fan has arrived in San Diego. Both the Oakland Raiders and Sunday's Super Bowl opponents, the Tampa Bay Buccaneers, employ the skull-and-crossbones as a symbol, but only one of them actually means it.

Their supporters call themselves "Raider Nation." On game days they are given to painting their faces in the black-and-silver colours of the Raiders.

They dress in basic black, augmented by studded dog-collars, chains, Darth Vader face shields, swastikas, switchblades, and body odour. They are the most vocal, most animated, and, some would say, most dangerous collection of football fans outside Britain.

When the New England Patriots played in Oakland late last year, a group of Boston businessmen and their wives had leased a luxury suite at Network Associates Coliseum for the Sunday Night game.

During the fourth quarter a nervous security guard visited the suite and, eyeing the boisterous crowd in the stands, warned the occupants: "Lock the door. And don't come out for at least an hour after the game."

The Raiders themselves arrived in San Diego for Super Bowl XXXVII on Monday night. Their fans have been trickling in all week, and the rest of them will be along as soon as they make bail.

San Diego is only 498 miles by freeway from Oakland, well within the driving range of a chopped Hog or a 1975 Chevrolet pick-up, which appear to be the vehicles of choice for people who wear dog-collars on Sunday.

By game time on Sunday, the car-park at QualComm Stadium will look like a casting call for a remake of The Road Warrior. The cheapest tickets for Super Bowl XXXVII carry a face value of $400. Club seats are $100 more, but you won't find any in either denomination for sale at the box office. According to the NFL's arcane distribution formula, 11,800 tickets are earmarked for the fans of each competing team, but a glance at the classified ads in the San Diego newspapers suggests that those have already been spoken for.

The asking price for Super Bowl tickets is roughly four times face value, and with Sunday's game scheduled to be played in one of the smaller venues, 67,500-seat QualComm, the scalpers who masquerade as licensed ticket brokers in California still hope to make a killing.

But the tour operators whose usual practice is to snap up tickets in anticipation of packaging them with hotel rooms and round-trip airfare weren't counting on the Raiders reaching the Super Bowl for the first time in 19 years.

For the most part Raider fans rarely fly, they drive, and a fellow whose day job involves operating a methedrine lab isn't likely to sleep much anyway. When a Raider fan does nod off it's usually in the back of his truck — and that's a few days after the game, when the beer finally overtakes the speed.

It would be misleading, however, to suggest that Raider fans don't ever get on airplanes. Take the case of Charles Dawson Jones, who in 1990, despite no visible means of support, attended every Raiders game, home and away. Only after the security cameras were examined did it come to light that Jones had financed his devotion to the skull-and-crossbones by robbing 24 Sacramento-area banks.

The proximity of San Diego, not just to Oakland but to the Raiders' former home in Los Angeles, can only enhance the fears of the NFL hierarchy.

When the Raiders travel downstate to play the Chargers in their annual divisional game, QualComm is transformed into the southern California branch of the infamous "Black Hole," as its denizens describe the Oakland stadium.

The toothless swarms from northern California are augmented by the team's old fans from Los Angeles, otherwise known as the Crips and the Bloods. This trend is a hold-over from Raider-owner Al Davis's eight-year tenancy in the LA Coliseum, during which gang violence became a staple of Raider games.

In what has taken on the trappings of a cyclical pattern, Raider fans have in recent years showed up in San Diego in such profusion that Charger fans became thoroughly intimidated, and not without good reason. Two years ago, an Oakland fan demonstrated his allegiance by stabbing a San Diego fan. (That perpetrator is now serving a five-year sentence, but has undoubtedly petitioned for a furlough so he can attend Sunday's Super Bowl.)

The year before that, a group of Raider fans began beating up Charger fans in the stands with such enthusiasm that the teams stopped the game so the players could watch.

Given this tradition and the likelihood that history will repeat itself, Charger fans have taken *en masse* to selling their tickets for the annual Oakland game to Raider fans, pocketing the money and watching the games from the safety of their living rooms while leaving their remaining compatriots at the mercy of the Harley-Davidson set.

Super Bowl XXXVII, in fact, may mark the first time in the history of the event in which Satan has an active rooting interest. I mean, you could approach a man on the street in any one of a 100 cities and ask the question: "What is Lucifer's favourite football team?" and a 100 out of a 100 would reply "The Raiders".

Ever the NFL maverick, Al Davis has always traditionally stocked his rosters with the bottom feeders of the NFL scrapheap. The present incarnation of the Raiders is somewhat unusual, in that as far as we can tell it doesn't include a single convicted rapist, but the team's fans more than make up for that oversight.

Two dozen of the Raiders' more enthusiastic supporters were detained by police after celebrating the team's 41-24 win in last Sunday night's AFC championship game by trashing several blocks of downtown Oakland, torching an car repair shop, and overturning several cars.

You couldn't help but wonder what they might have done if the Raiders had lost that game. The answer could be forthcoming in San Diego this weekend.
January 23, 2003

A clean breast of it

HOUSTON

In certain parts of the world when a stranger suddenly moves to disrobe in the midst of a crowd he (or she) can expect a bullet between the eyes, on the entirely reasonable presumption that he (or she) might be a suicide bomber.

We're not suggesting here that somebody should have shot Janet Jackson for flashing a breast during last Sunday's Super Bowl half-time show in Houston, but in the case of Mark Roberts, it might not have been a bad idea.

With her brief flash of semi-nudity Ms Jackson not only upstaged the New England Patriots' 32-29 come-from-behind win in Super Bowl XXXVIII, but accomplished the unthinkable by becoming the most talked-about member of her own family.

She has in the process managed to divert the attention of George W Bush ("It's important for families to be able to expect a high standard when it comes to programming") from his misguided exercise in Iraq, and to attract the disapprobation of everyone from National Football League Commissioner Paul Tagliabue to Michael Powell, the chairman of the Federal Communications Commission, whose father Colin happens to be the Secretary of State.

The Houston constabulary received dozens of calls from Bible-thumping locals who wanted Jackson and her co-conspirator Justin Timberlake arrested for their impromptu striptease, in which Timberlake, after repeatedly mouthing the refrain "*Got to have you naked by the end of this song*" proceeded to deliver, ripping down the right half of Jackson's bustier to expose her right breast, which was adorned with some sort of sunburst tassle dangling from her pierced nipple.

We are taking all of this on faith, of course. Not more than a handful of the 71,125 in attendance at Reliant Stadium Sunday evening had the vaguest inkling that this had taken place, although the millions watching on television, including the president, evidently had a better view.

The television audience was only vaguely aware, on the other hand, that Roberts, the 39-year-old Liverpudlian who pulled a similar stunt at Croke Park last summer, delayed the beginning of the second half by several minutes, but everyone in the stadium saw way too much of him.

Roberts sneaked on to the field by disguising himself in a tear-away costume crafted to resemble one of the game officials' outfits.

The moment he shed it, the television cameras cut away, but here's the problem: what if Roberts had had Semtex — or a gun — under his coat instead of a G-string? As the Carolina Panthers lined up for the second-half kick-off, it became apparent

The infamous "wardrobe malfunction." Janet 's breast with tassle. Bloke on right, Justin Timberlake.

that they were in danger of being flagged for having too many men on the field. The 12th proved to be Roberts, who shed his zebra-striped coat and began dancing around, wearing just a football-shaped codpiece.

It was only after Carolina placekicker John Kasay pointed him out that any of the hundreds of yellow-jacketed security guards on duty even began to move in Roberts' direction. Once the NFL's hired muscle gave chase, a couple of Houston policemen half-heartedly jogged out behind them.

Even then, it wasn't one of the gendarmes who brought him to earth, it was Patriots' linebacker Matt Chatham, who levelled him when he reached the New England end of the field.

The English interloper was handcuffed, hog-tied, and bundled off to the local jail. He has been charged with criminal trespass and public intoxication.

Upon being booked, Roberts gave his occupation as "international streaker." But couldn't he as easily have been an international terrorist?

Security for this Super Bowl was supposed to be the tightest in history. Every patron entering the stadium Sunday night had his hand-baggage searched, twice, and had to pass through two separate metal detectors. There were concrete barriers, security fences, and a no-fly zone in the vicinity of Reliant, none of which deterred Roberts from gaining access to the field.

According to Houston police, he had simply bought a front-row ticket and hopped over the fence.

(Given the exorbitant price of tickets — Roberts' had a face value of $500, but would have fetched at least $3,500 on the street — you might wonder how he came to be seated in such a choice location. One clue is that he had the imprimatur of an Internet gambling casino stenciled across his chest and back.)

One would think that such an embarrassing breach of security would have NFL officials falling all over themselves to explain it away, but there was barely a peep out of the league about the streaker.

The NFL people have been too busy apologising about Janet Jackson's breasts.

Within 15 minutes of l'affaire Jackson, a communiqué from CBS apologising for the incident was being circulated throughout the press box, and, terming the Timberlake-Jackson *pas de deux* "totally inconsistent with assurances our office was given about the content of the show," NFL vice-president Joe Browne said: "It is unlikely that MTV will produce another Super Bowl half-time (show)."

Unsurprisingly, switchboards at CBS affiliates across the country lit up, fielding phone calls from indignant viewers. Powell, whose board oversees radio and television stations throughout the land, termed it a "classless, crass and deplorable stunt".

New England quarterback Tom Brady threw three touchdown passes and was named Super Bowl XXXVIII's Most Valuable Player, but, he joked the next morning: "I thought the tackle on the streaker was the best part" of the game.

A few days before he left for Houston Brady had travelled to Washington as Bush's guest for the State of the Union Address, but he did not appear to share the president's horror over Janet Jackson's overexposure.

"I didn't see the half-time show, but I heard about it," said Brady. "I wish I *had* seen it."

February 05, 2004

Hi, would you like to play in the Super Bowl?

JACKSONVILLE

On the evening of January 22nd, Eagles tight end Chad Lewis gathered the second of his two touchdown catches in the NFC Championship game, but landed somewhat awkwardly as he came to earth in the end zone.

The score had put the Eagles on top, 27-10, and more or less ensured that the Philadelphia team would be making its first trip to the Super Bowl in nearly a quarter century, but Lewis' jubilation was short-lived.

When fellow tight end LJ Smith rushed over to congratulate his team-mate, the first words out of Lewis' mouth weren't, "We're going to Jacksonville," but "I think I just broke my foot."

His diagnosis was confirmed by X-rays. Lewis had suffered a Lisfranc fracture, and underwent surgery the following morning.

At 4 p.m. on Monday, January 23rd, the telephone rang in the field office of a construction project in southern New Jersey. Jeff Thomason, the assistant project manager for the Toll Brothers Construction Company, was summoned to the phone and was surprised to learn that the voice on the other end belonged to Eagles coach Andy Reid. He wanted to know if Jeff could come out and play.

Thomason had been happily retired from professional football for two years, and was making a decent living in the construction business. He had spent 10 years in the NFL, all as a reserve, in the employ of the Green Bay Packers and later the Eagles. Now the coach who had cut him two years earlier wanted to know if he could spare the time to come play in the Super Bowl.

Thomason hastily arranged for two weeks' vacation time, and the next morning reported to the Eagles' complex in South Philly. After a brief audition he was signed on the spot. "I was able to still catch the ball and do okay," said Thomason.

Reid explained that while other tight ends of a more recent vintage were available on the market, he had several good and compelling reasons for turning to the tried-and-true.

"One was that Jeff already knew our system," explained the Philadelphia coach. "We wouldn't have to spend time giving him a crash course in the plays. Another was that we knew he had kept himself in tremendous shape. He's been training for and participating in triathlons since he left football."

"It's kind of like riding a bike," said Philadelphia offensive coordinator Brad Childress after putting Thomason through two days of drills. "Jeff came in, did all the motions and knows right where to be. He hasn't forgotten anything. Some of the nuances are different, but I think he'll be able to fill that role."

The Cinderella story was so compelling that when the Eagles were trotted out on the field at AllTell Stadium for Tuesday's Media Day sessions, Thomason was provided with his own podium, an honour more commonly reserved for more prominent players like Pro Bowlers Donovan McNabb, Terrell Owens and Jevon Kearse.

Media Day is one of those curious Super Bowl traditions. Five days in advance of the game, players from both teams arrive at Sunday's venue in game regalia, and several thousand print, radio and television journalists are turned loose for an hour's feeding frenzy.

Thomason had been through a couple of these before. In his Green Bay days he'd been a participant in two Super Bowls, but, he said, Wednesday's experience was "incredible. My last two media days, when I was with the Packers, I was over in the corner trying to *get* someone to talk to me. This is definitely a thrill."

And an even bigger thrill, it appears, for his fellow hard-hats back at Toll Brothers, who will have a vicarious rooting interest when Super Bowl XXXIX kicks off Sunday evening.

Not that Jeff was wielding a sledgehammer on the building site. He spent as much time crunching numbers behind a desk as he did actually surveying the progress of the job. "But how many guys sitting at their desks get a phone call to come play in the Super Bowl?" he asked, as if he still couldn't believe it.

During the two years he spent away from football, Thomason said he hadn't missed the daily grind or the bumps and bruises, "but I missed the guys. I think the camaraderie and the life is what most retired players go through. It's a great life. You work your tail off in the season, and in the off-season you have a lot of free time."

At the same time, said Thomason, his recent return has given him a new appreciation of his former life. "Definitely. I've been out there working 10 and 12-hour days with weekends off. I can't put into words how lucky I am to be playing football again. I'm thrilled to be here, but it's all kind of surreal to me."

Thomason won't just be window-dressing in Sunday's Super Bowl. Reid said this week that he reckons the construction worker will be on the field for 15 to 20 plays — "about what our second tight end normally does." That his first game in 25 months will be against the defending world champions doesn't make his re-entry any easier.

The biggest test, of course, will come on Sunday, the first time a New England defender pops him in anger.

"That first hit will be interesting," mused Thomason. "I know it'll be a real eye-opener for me. I'm just thankful we've had the two weeks to prepare for the Super Bowl. If it had been one week it would have been tough, but this gives me time to catch up."

Though he clearly is enjoying the experience, Thomason hasn't been tempted to make a full-time comeback.

"No, this is my final one. It will be my swan song. After the Super Bowl I'll go back to work at Toll Brothers. I'll go back to my desk and sit there and wonder what happened to me over the last two weeks.

"Besides," he added. "I can't take any more time off. I've just used up all my vacation time for the next year."

February 03, 2005

HAVE ANOTHER PRETZEL, MR PRESIDENT?

President Bush and his advisors in session on September 13, 2001, two days after terrorist attacks on the Pentagon and the World Trade Centre.

Secret of the eagle that Clinton landed

In the course of the visit to Dublin of America's First Family on Tuesday, Hillary Clinton prefaced her remarks at the US Ambassador's residence by voicing her husband's principal regret about the brevity of the trip: "Bill is heartbroken he can't play golf."

Outside the rain was falling on a chilly, windy, wintry day, and at the Oireachtas ladies chuckled politely, assuming the remark to have been made at least half in jest, but my guess is she was telling the truth. William Jefferson Clinton is a certifiable golfing fool, and it wasn't the weather that kept him away. If they'd built a few more hours into his schedule, he'd have been out to Portmarnock in a flash.

One summer evening half a dozen years ago I found myself in Washington, and had dropped by the East Potomac Golf Club for a chat with my friend and swing guru, Julieta Stack. After her last lesson of the evening we had headed out for a bite to eat, but upon arriving at an Indian restaurant on Capitol Hill, we found the sidewalk outside swarming with members of the local constabulary.

Stick-ups in Washington are not uncommon, even in the shadow of the White House, and we at first took this to be the case. As we approached, I asked one of the gendarmes if there was a problem.

"No, sir," he replied, "but if you're going in we're going to have to search you." When I asked why, he replied "because the President is having dinner inside."

After submitting to a pat-down, we entered the restaurant to find Bill, Hillary and Chelsea Clinton seated at one table, along with presidential adviser Mack McLarty and his wife Donna. Most of the other tables were occupied by Secret Service men vainly attempting to appear inconspicuous.

Once we had taken in the scene and placed our order, Julieta reached into her purse, took out one of her business cards identifying her as a certified LPGA teaching pro, and scribbled a note on the back. She then summoned our Punjabi waiter and asked him to deliver it to the man across the room.

The note read: *"Dear Mr President, I've seen that swing on television, and I think I can help."*

Bill Clinton acknowledged the note with a smile and a cheery wave towards our table, and stuck the card in his pocket. Three weeks later, the leader of the Free World showed up, unannounced, at East Potomac. Julieta, much to her regret, was off that day, but the President went out and played a round on the scruffy municipal course anyway.

Bill Clinton, probably the best-golfing president since Kennedy, and certainly the most avid since Eisenhower, achieved an historical milestone of sorts by becoming the first president to actually lower his handicap (from 13 to 12) while in office. This is no mean feat, particularly when you consider that every time he sets out on the links, his every shot is scrutinised not only by his playing partners and the odd reporter, but by a squadron of secret servicemen in motorised golf carts — not to mention the obligatory police sniper and another fellow who follows along bearing the secret codes for unleashing a nuclear attack.

While he has played with many of the top golfers of his era, Clinton confessed to being intimidated by playing with only one — Christy O'Connor, he confessed to Tom Friedman of the *New York Times* in an interview which appeared in *Golf Digest* this autumn. Two summers ago the President played a round with Himself at Ballybunion.

Clinton enjoys the company of golfers. "I get to play with all these pros and other good golfers, and they give me all this good advice," explained the President.

Clinton, who has been trying to arrange a game with the disabled golfer Casey

President Bill Clinton: no witness to his miracle three-iron.

Martin, said he would also like to play with Tiger Woods and David Duval. He was even gracious in recalling the implicit snub when the victorious 1993 US Ryder Cup team declined an invitation to visit the White House.

Several of that year's Ryder Cuppers were irate over a measure passed early in the Clinton administration which had increased their already-healthy tax bite, and one of them, Paul Azinger, had also labelled the President a 'draft dodger' over his anti-war stance during the Vietnam era — a charge which prompted a colleague of mine to ask at the time "Excuse me, but exactly what war did Paul Azinger fight in, anyway?"

When Friedman asked President Clinton to name his favourite courses, by the way, the first word out of his mouth was Ballybunion.

Once, when he was Governor of Arkansas, Clinton recalled, he was feeling sufficiently stressed-out that he cancelled his appointments for the afternoon and sneaked out to a local course.

He encountered a doctor who was also playing hooky from his office, and the two made up a game.

During the course of the round, Clinton smashed a 260-yard drive that missed the fairway and came to rest beneath a tree. Assaying his unenviable position, he tried the only stroke available, played "a three-iron, off my back foot," and miraculously holed the shot from 175 yards.

His jubilation quickly subsided when he realised he was in the precise position of the proverbial priest who went out to play on Sunday morning and made a hole-in-one: Who was he going to tell?

"I'd just hit the best shot of my life and made an eagle, and I couldn't tell a soul about it," he recalled years later. "But at least I had a witness."
December 14, 2000

I'd like to thank all the little people

Kevin Spacey, Michael Caine and Denzel Washington have to sweat it out for another 38 days. For me, the wait is over. The Academy of Motion Picture Arts and Science released its list of nominees for the 72nd annual Academy Awards on Tuesday, and for some unfathomable reason my name was not on the list.

While no one was exactly tipping me actually to win an Oscar for my motion picture debut in Ron Shelton's new boxing film *Play It to the Bone,* the smart money had it that I'd at least be nominated. Not that it's much consolation, but my costars — Woody Harrelson and Antonio Banderas — weren't nominated either.

Harrelson and Banderas play a couple of over-the-hill middleweights who are exhumed to fight each other in Las Vegas. The way the storyline goes, they are summoned to fight on the undercard of a bout between Mike Tyson and a fictitious Russian named Alexei Rustikov after the principal supporting bout falls apart at the last minute, and they speed their way across the desert from Los Angeles.

Apart from the fact that Harrelson, whose head is shaven and body heavily tattooed for the role, looks an awful lot like the real-life boxer Angel Manfredy, and Banderas like Arturo Gatti-as-Zorro, the bare bones of this tale are taken from an episode which actually occurred several years back. Brought in at the last minute, the two palookas surprised everyone by putting on the Fight of the Year.

My role? I play a bearded, portly, jaded newspaperman seated at ringside. Suffice it to say the make-up girl was not overly taxed the afternoon they shot my scenes.

Director Ron Shelton, who also wrote the screenplay, is a former minor league baseball player who relied on that experience to make his breakthrough film *Bull Durham* a dozen years ago. Although he has made several other movies, he is best known for his work in the sports genre, having branched out into the worlds of golf *(Tin Cup)* and playground basketball *(White Men Can't Jump),* in addition to having made *Cobb,* a jaded portrait of the legendary 1920s baseball curmudgeon Ty Cobb.

I first met Shelton a decade ago. By chance we had been seated at ringside together at a fight at Caesars Palace, and it turned out we had formed a mutual admiration society a few months earlier, by virtue of having each contributed a story to a baseball anthology published that year.

I had written about Bill (Spaceman) Lee, the eloquently eccentric pitcher from whom Shelton had occasionally borrowed in Bull Durham, and Ron had written about Steve Dalkowski, a legendary pitcher who reputedly could throw harder than any man who ever lived, but whose near-sightedness at once terrorised minor league hitters and kept him from reaching the big time. I had greatly admired Ron's piece, and he had loved mine.

Although the main event is supposed to feature Tyson (who was paid for his appearance in the film), the fight scenes for *Play It to the Bone* were actually shot at the Mandalay Bay a few days before last May's Oscar De La Hoya-Oba Carr welter-weight title fight.

In the interest of verisimilitude, several of us who make part or all of our living writing about boxing were corralled to form the ringside press section, which was then filled out by those who presumably could pass as boxing scribes. Top Rank matchmaker Bruce Trampler, for instance, who wouldn't be caught dead at a Tyson fight, is seated in the front row, furiously taking notes.

We were about half an hour into the first day's filming when a horrified Shelton

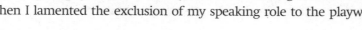

shouted "Cut!" and came scrambling out from behind the cameras to confront De La Hoya's cut-man Chuck Bodak, seated in the press section.

"Chuck, you can't be sitting there!" said the exasperated director.

"Why not?" asked Bodak, a bald-headed fellow with a white beard who is one of the more recognisable cornermen around.

"Because in the scene we shot yesterday you're working in Woody's corner," Shelton reminded him. "This is supposed to be the same fight!"

Kimball was curiously omitted from a studio publicity still of fellow cast members Woody Harrelson and Antonio Banderas.

The script called for Harrelson and Banderas to start belting one another around, each hitting the deck with alarming regularity. We writer-types were supposed to "be ourselves," but Shelton liked my extemporised line — *"Holy shit!,"* as Harrelson thudded to the floor — so much that he incorporated it, and I wound up shouting the phrase a good two dozen times through the numerous takes we shot that afternoon.

By the end of the day, my voice-box was nearly as sore as Woody's backside.

As it turned out, my line stayed in the movie, but since it is delivered with me off-camera, no one will ever match up the voice with its author. This sad fact was relayed to me several months ago after George Foreman's publicist, Bill Caplan (who plays the ringside physician in the film), viewed a screening of the finished product.

When I lamented the exclusion of my speaking role to the playwright Israel

Horovitz, he reminded me by way of consolation: "There are no small parts, only small actors."

That is certainly true enough. Between the ringside fans and the guests at a pre-fight party, the roster of Bone cameo roles read like a Hollywood Who's Who: Kevin Costner, Drew Carey, Wesley Snipes, James Woods, Tony Curtis, Rod Stewart and President Clinton's reputed former mistress, Gennifer Flowers, all had roles even more brief than mine, but it did make for one hell of a cast party.

Most of my footage, alas, wound up on the cutting-room floor, a fact which may have influenced the Academy selectors who failed to nominate me for an Oscar. In fact, by my count your man in Hollywood is only on camera four times, and fleet-ingly at that. (Though it's easier to pick me out than it is to, say, find Steve Collins in that pub in *Michael Collins*.)

While Play It to the Bone didn't garner a single Oscar nomination, there is some consolation in the fact that the year's other, more heavily-hyped boxing film, The *Hurricane*, got only one. And it goes without saying, we had more fun making ours.
Thu, Feb 17, 2000

Pro sport back to work after the outrage

NEW YORK

We were midway across Long Island Sound two days ago when the ferry gunned its engines and abruptly altered course, sending hundreds of jittery passengers out onto the decks to see what the problem was. The Coast Guard marshal assigned to the voyage, a sidearm strapped to his waist, quickly assured everyone the boat hadn't been hijacked, but had taken the precautionary manoeuvre to steer clear of a disabled Greek freighter which was making its way up the Sound toward New York under a Coast Guard escort.

A week after two airplanes demolished the World Trade Center, black puffs of smoke could still be seen in the drifting clouds, and, to the west, a smog-like thermal inversion hung over Manhattan. As we made our way to Orient Point, I got my first glimpse of one of those spectacular, blood-red sunsets New Yorkers had been describing for days.

The New York Jets were not at their Hempstead training camp when I arrived on Long Island. On Tuesday, which would normally have been the players' day off, they had gathered *en masse* at the Salvation Army headquarters on 14th Street in Manhattan and were helping to load trucks with boxes of supplies, ranging from food and water to bibles. Along with coach Herman Edwards and millionaire owner Woody Johnson, the players were wearing red T-shirts that read "Emergency Disaster Services" as they joined in with the other volunteers.

A day earlier, members of the New York Giants had visited the World Trade Center site, and Tuesday, in Washington, the Redskins paid their own visit to the Pentagon. Then, yesterday, it was back to work, as 31 NFL coaches began to draw up their own battle plans for Sunday's NFL games, the first to be played since the September 11th outrage.

Major League baseball, which extended its season by pushing last week's cancelled games into October, resumed play this week. The nation's major colleges, some of whom play to even bigger crowds than those attending professional sporting events, will also resume their slates this weekend.

(For their games in Pittsburgh this week, the New York Mets asked and received permission to wear baseball hats of New York City firefighters and policemen. All Major League uniforms have been augmented with miniature American flags.)

Several of the Jets, who play the Patriots in New England Sunday afternoon, have asked that the team travel to Foxboro by chartered coach rather than airplane. (Edwards, while not unsympathetic to the position, doesn't sound as if he's going to go along with it, but at least one NFL team, the Carolina Panthers, will stay on the ground, travelling by bus to Atlanta.) Reflecting on last week's loss of thousands of lives in New York, Washington and Pennsylvania, it has occurred to many that the death toll could have been increased tenfold had the terrorists decided to take out a stadium jammed with 60,000 spectators.

On Monday, a Tampa area newspaper played to this sentiment with a front-page, full-colour photo of an empty Raymond James Stadium, where the Buccaneers would have been playing the Philadelphia Eagles the previous afternoon.

Ten years earlier, just across the street, Tampa Stadium had staged Super Bowl XXV literally days after the commencement of our own little jihad called Operation Desert Storm. Security precautions seemed extreme at the time (I remember being "wanded" and having my briefcase searched on my way into a practice session), but it appears we're going to have to get used to it this time around.

I don't pretend to be able to fathom the minds of terrorists, particularly those who could cook up something as insidious as the September 11th game plan, but it strikes me that in many cases players may merely be flattering themselves, and that certain fears currently prevalent in the sporting world may be misplaced.

Clearly, had the hijackers who pulled off last week's assault been bent on inflicting the maximum death toll, they wouldn't have struck on Tuesday but Sunday, and they would have attacked sporting venues instead of what they did. It seems evident that the World Trade Center and the Pentagon were chosen largely for their symbolic value and that the attendant loss of life came in what military types like to describe as "collateral damage".

President Bush has promised to wage "war" against the enemy (although it seems clear he has only a vague idea of who that might be), and the nation has been

The moment of impact when hijacked United Airlines Flight 175 from Boston crashed into the south tower of the World Trade Center and exploded at 9:03 am on September 11, 2001.

whipped up to a feverish battle pitch unseen in this country since the second World War. Every other American house flies the Stars and Stripes, every other roadside business has a patriotic message lettered on its billboard.

On the first day of deer hunting season each year, zealous American marksmen kill an amazing number of family dogs, so it shouldn't be surprising that in Arizona this week, a vigilante shot and killed a turbaned Sikh from India on the assumption that he was an Arab. Down the street from where I live, some latter-day patriot set ablaze a petrol tank at a station whose owner proved to be a Lebanese Christian.

In this climate, Don King has rescheduled the Felix Trinidad-Bernard Hopkins middleweight championship fight originally scheduled for September 15th for Madison Square Garden a week from Saturday. Although it seems clear they will still be pulling bodies from the rubble of the World Trade Centre then, the September 29th date became available when a wrestling championship was cancelled.

Security has already been beefed up for the sold-out event. Upwards of 19,000 spectators will be obliged to pass through metal detectors, and weapons will be confiscated. The Garden confirmed they had planned to take elaborate precautions even before the bombings, but now the measures will be in place to protect the fighters' supporters from terrorists, real or imagined, rather than from one another. Such has become the landscape of the American sport, now and for the foreseeable future.

September 20, 2001

Bush and Dolphins choke at home

What is it with these Bush presidents, anyway? You may recall that a decade ago the incumbent's father, George Bush, lost both face and stomach when he first barfed on one of his hosts and then passed out at a state dinner in Japan. Now the son sits down to watch a football game and emerges from the experience looking as if he'd just gone a few three-minute rounds with Mike Tyson.

Although I wasn't in the White House rec room on Sunday evening when the Miami Dolphins nearly killed the Leader of the Free World, I have a pretty good guess as to precisely what the fateful moment might have been.

Here was George W Bush, watching the National Football League play-off game between the Dolphins and the Baltimore Ravens. With just under nine minutes left in the game, Miami appeared on the verge of getting themselves back into the game when quarterback Jay Fiedler dropped back to pass and lofted a spiral in the direction of wide receiver James McKnight, who was streaking for the goal line.

McKnight had opened up a two-stride lead on Ravens defender Duane Starks, and Fiedler's pass couldn't have been better thrown. Somehow it slipped right through McKnight's hands, bounced off his shoulder pad, and careered into the air, dropping straight back down into the arms of Starks, who gathered it in without even breaking stride and headed off in the opposite direction.

Game, set, and match.

The next thing anybody knew, the fans were pouring out of Pro Player Stadium, and the president of the United States was rolling around on the floor turning an apoplectic blue, a pretzel lodged in his throat.

Now, we're only guessing that Bush was rooting for the Dolphins, but it's a pretty fair assumption. Next to his native Texas, Florida is the state nearest and dearest to the President's heart. His younger brother is the governor there, and it was his controversial win in that state which eventually provided his margin of victory in the last election.

So what do the Dolphins — the only home team to lose in last weekend's first play-off round — have in common with the president?

Answer: they both choke at home.

There wasn't much point in trying to cover this one up, since the visual evidence was indelibly etched on the presidential face. The official explanation for the shiner below his left eye — that Bush first (a) choked on the pretzel, (b) then fainted, and (c) landed face-first on the carpet, where (d) his spectacles cut him high on the cheekbone, after which he was (e) revived by the First Dogs licking his face — doubtlessly came after presidential advisers concluded that nobody was going to fall for the old "I walked into a door" story again.

Now, your first reaction to the news was probably the same as mine, which is undoubtedly why the White House almost immediately issued a communiqué from Dr. Richard Tubb insisting that "there was absolutely, positively, no suggestion on physical examination that any alcohol was involved" in the misfortune suffered by the nation's most prominent teetotaler.

To which we would merely ask: name the last time you saw anybody eat a pretzel without a beer in his other hand.

The presidential mishap has, needless to say, sparked comparison to similar adventures by Bush's predecessors: It might be a stretch to tie his father's unfortunate experience with Japanese cuisine to the world of sport, but Bill Clinton's tumble down the stairs at Greg Norman's house, Gerald Ford taking target practice on golfing spectators, and Jimmy Carter's encounter with the "killer rabbit" on an ill-fated canoe trip surely qualify.

And who could forget the night Massachusetts Governor Michael Dukakis, the opponent for Bush *père* in the 1988 presidential election, broke his arm when he took a spill while running a late-night foot race against his New Jersey counterpart Brendan Byrne across the front lawn of the Governor's mansion?

Surely some irony exists in the fact that the actual "doomsday" box containing the codes for unleashing global nuclear attack is known, in Secret Service parlance, as "the football". We can't help wondering: is it really wise that the president should be left alone with this device and his television remote in the same room, at least until the playoffs are over?

In the days since the "fainting spell" America's television talk-show hosts have, needless to say, had a field day with the episode. NBC's Jay Leno pointed out that the Secret Service had spent all this time worrying about Osama Bin Laden when the real enemy lurked in the form of "Mister Salty". On CBS's Late Night, David Letterman noted that Bush was only out cold for four seconds.

"Fortunately," added Letterman, "it was the same four seconds Dick Cheney was conscious."

Listen, it could have been worse. What if his brother had been the governor of, say, North Carolina, where the Panthers went 1-15 this season? Cheney might have been running the country by October.

None of this bodes very well for the White House Super Bowl Party two weeks from Sunday. Last we heard, Mrs Bush has ordered the caterer to revise the menu to include soft-serve ice cream, strained carrots and warm milk.

January 17, 2002

Bitter twist to the true story of a hero's end

So now Pat Tillman's death turns out to have been an own goal. As even those who have never watched a National Football League game must know by now, Tillman was the former Arizona Cardinals safety who spurned a $3.6 million contract renewal to become a US Army Ranger in the wake of the September 11th attacks.

He had already served at least one tour in Iraq and had somehow wound up in Afghanistan when he was killed on April 22nd in what was described as an "ambush" when his patrol allegedly came under fire near the Afghan-Pakistani border. The nature of his life and the supposed circumstances of his death conspired to elevate him to heroic status.

"Pat Tillman," New England Patriots owner Robert Kraft reflected in a conversation with me a few days later while the 2004 draft was in progress. "I've been thinking about him all weekend.

"Think about it," said Kraft. "When you consider all the qualities that make a football team great — courage, toughness, perseverance, hard work, and an almost noble sense of purpose — this guy embodied them all. In the end, he was the ultimate team player. I've been thinking about him all weekend, even in the draft room, because I don't think that we as a league can forget this guy. He was the kind

A police officer holds a memorial card for Pat Tillman, killed by 'friendly' fire while serving in Afghanistan.

PAT TILLMAN

of guy I'd want on my team — in any business."

At the time the voices of dissent were decidedly muted, although a University of Massachusetts student was reprimanded for writing an op-ed story in the campus newspaper in which he described Tillman as "not a hero, but a Rambo," and cartoonist Ted Rall received death threats after the publication of a cartoon which asked whether Tillman should be remembered as a hero, a sap, or an "idiot".

Just a few days ago — ironically enough, on the holiday weekend Americans celebrate as Memorial Day — it came to light that Tillman wasn't killed by terrorist-minded Islamic extremists at all. He was shot by his own team-mates in one of those bungled operations that calls to mind those reports which accompany the first day of deer-hunting season, when you can take it for granted that some trigger-happy sportsman is going to mistake either one of his hunting partners, the farmer's cow, or your family dog for a 14-point buck.

That everyone from George W Bush to NFL commissioner Paul Tagliabue to we in the media — the player's likeness graced the cover of Sports Illustrated the week after his death — rushed to confer immortality after Tillman made the ultimate sacrifice is understandable. As a nation we were eager to believe the army's official version of Tillman's tragic demise, which turns out to have been a fanciful illusion — sort of like Weapons of Mass Destruction.

Consider *Sports Illustrated's* dramatic account: *"The rangers scrambled out of their vehicles as they came under ambush and charged the militants on foot. Suddenly Pat was down, Pat was dying. Two other US soldiers were wounded, and a coalition Afghan fighter was killed in a firefight that lasted 15 or 20 minutes before the jihadists melted away."*

Author Gary Smith may have been guilty of slightly embellishing the known "facts," but his description relied heavily on the army's account.

In the version given by an army spokesman who confirmed Tillman's death in April, the football star had been killed in a "firefight" on a road southwest of the US base at Khost. After coming under fire, Tillman's patrol got out of their vehicles and gave chase, a path which directly led to the ambush.

"Through the firing, Tillman's voice was heard issuing fire commands to take the fight to the enemy on the dominating high ground," another army version claimed. *"Only after his team engaged the well-armed enemy did it appear their fire diminished."*

Only six weeks later — after Tillman had been posthumously awarded the silver star and purple heart, been promoted to corporal, been lauded by Congress and had a plaza at the Cardinals' new stadium named in his honour — did the truth begin to emerge. Tillman wasn't killed by "enemy" fire, because there wasn't any enemy present. He was shot by his fellow soldiers.

Despite what were described as "constricted terrain and impaired light conditions," Tillman's detachment had split into two on this particular recon mission. Apparently somewhere in between the groups, a rogue land mine exploded.

Assuming they had come under fire, both groups began shooting wildly at one another. Pat Tillman, along with two other rangers, was killed by what the army chooses to oxymoronically describe as "friendly fire".

Tillman was hardly the first soldier to have been killed by his men. In the American Civil War, Confederate General Thomas "Stonewall" Jackson was mortally wounded in an artillery barrage from troops under his command, and credible accounts have been advanced that Michael Collins' demise at Béal na mBlath might have come under similar circumstances. It hasn't diminished their heroic status — nor should it Tillman's, however misguided his participation in Bush's adventure may have been.

Interviewed by NBC news at the Cardinals' Phoenix facility in the aftermath of the September 11th attacks, Pat Tillman may have foreshadowed his fate when he reflected: "My great grandfather was at Pearl Harbor, and a lot of my family has gone and fought in wars, and I really haven't done a damn thing as far as laying myself on the line like that."

"He gave up more than anyone I know to serve," said a fellow soldier upon learning of the actual circumstances of the football player's tragic end. "A lot of us sacrifice something, but no one sacrificed as much as he did to join. It doesn't really matter how he was killed. It's sad."
June 03, 2004

Welcome to the arms of Athens . . .

ATHENS

When one reflects on the unhappy events of Munich in 1972, as one must in the midst of the armed camp that is Athens in 2004, one is reminded that the official version of what happened on that fateful morning requires a virtual suspension of disbelief.

For 32 years now the world has blithely accepted the contention — a preposterous one, when you think about it — that German "sharpshooters," firing blindly through helicopter windows across the tarmac in the half-light of dawn, killed nothing but Palestinians, while each and every one of the Israeli hostages was killed by grenades exploded in a final gesture of defiance by the dying terrorists.

Now, one might reasonably argue the point is moot, since the Munich hostages were essentially doomed the moment the first shot was fired, but the official version of events presumed a level of marksmanship that did leave one wondering why these fellows weren't on the German Olympic rifle team instead of in the *Bundeswehr*.

Those questions have haunted me for better than three decades.

Then, a couple of months ago in New York, I happened to be watching an archived film about the Munich massacre, in which a German official was queried on this very point.

"*Charpchooters?*" he replied. "*Zey vere not 'charpchooters'. Zey vere chust . . . men viz guns.*"

The entire security framework here in Athens is based on the hypothesis that not only are the good guys all armed, but that they actually know how to use their weapons.

During the British Open at Troon last month the golf writer-*cum*-novelist Dan Jenkins informed me his daughter Sally would also be covering the Olympics in Athens.

Sally Jenkins, in addition to her role as Lance Armstrong's Boswell, is a featured columnist for the *Washington Post*, and in preparation for her Olympic assignment, said her father, for the past several weeks she'd been attending classes in conversational Greek.

"So far, the best I can gather, she's learned two useful sentences," Dan told me. "One is '*I'd like some more red wine, please.*' The other is '*I'm down here under the rubble*'."

A recent survey indicated 52 per cent of Americans polled thought it likely there would be a terrorist attack during the Athens Games. My more informal calculations would suggest the percentage of American sports editors holding this view is even higher.

Changing planes in Amsterdam en route from Dublin to Athens last Sunday I ran into my friend Steve Springer of the Los Angeles Times, who told me that not only had everyone in his paper's travelling party, but the entire *Chicago Tribune* family, been required to endure seven hours of terrorist-response training.

Upon arrival at his Athens hotel, said Springer, he and his colleagues were all being issued gas masks, which they were supposed to don at the first whiff of trouble.

This struck me as just plain silly. For one thing, I doubt even seven hours of intensive training could equip one to distinguish the cloud of industrial pollution that seems to perpetually hang over Athens from an actual chemical attack.

Moreover, I reminded Springer, in the event of a genuine terrorist attack, putting on a mask and running out of the building seemed an almost certain way to get oneself shot between the eyes, since Greek security forces might quite reasonably assume somebody wearing a mask was more likely to be a terrorist than a journalist.

The Associated Press, which has dozens of staffers in Greece for the Games, has even developed various contingency plans for how to cover the carnage if 20, 30, or even 50 per cent of its complement have been eradicated by an attack.

Athens' own response to potential disruption of the first summer Games to be conducted since the September 11 attacks seems more reasonable. Those entering the Olympic village, the main press centre, or the arenas themselves, must have their hand-luggage and computer bags scanned, and are required to pass through metal detectors — roughly the same procedures in effect at US airports prior to 9/11.

Helicopters perpetually buzz overhead, augmented by a white dirigible equipped with the latest in hi-tech surveillance equipment.

While by no means as obtrusive as the draconian security measures in force at Salt Lake City two years ago, the presence is everywhere. Police, with side-arms, regularly patrol the perimeters of the Olympic venues, including the villages housing the athletes and the media, augmented by ominous-looking soldiers equipped with assault rifles. (A tertiary layer of dark-shirted security men, apparently not armed, sternly walk about, quietly poking through trash bins in their vigilance for anything suspicious.)

The overall effect does inspire a degree of confidence. I have no doubt, for instance, should the terrorists, if there are any, try to lay siege to the chain-length fence behind the terrace of my village apartment, they would be repelled by massive firepower, but one suspects the terrorists, if they exist, would be cleverer than that.

But beyond the security dragnet around the official Olympic complex, one is still left wondering about the *ex officio* venues. A seven-person contingent from the *Boston Globe*, for instance, had been assigned to an Olympic village which ran into construction delays and was not completed in time for the Games.

The entire group was relocated to a ward in the local Maternity Hospital.

"If there are security people there I haven't seen them," a *Globe* scribe told me two days ago, "but each night when we return home we get greeted by a new batch of balloons and teddy bears."
August 12, 2004

Film may rehabilitate legend of Jack Johnson

Ninety-four years ago this week in Colma, California, having more or less exhausted the supply of legitimate heavyweight contenders, world champion Jack Johnson defended his title against middleweight champion Stanley Ketchel.

While it was a lucrative proposition for both, the match loomed as such a mismatch — Johnson outweighed his foe by 25lb — that the combatants reportedly negotiated their own ground rules: Ketchel wouldn't try very hard to win, and Johnson wouldn't embarrass his opponent by knocking him out.

Twelve rounds in, Ketchel abrogated the agreement when he decked Johnson with a right hand. It was an error in judgment for which he would pay dearly.

Johnson got up from the canvas, dusted himself off, and proceeded to hit Ketchel with an uppercut of such ferocity that it not only knocked him cold, but ripped his front teeth from the gums. Ketchel's manager thoughtfully collected his man's front teeth from the ring and had them made into a pair of dice.

John Arthur Johnson was the first black heavyweight champion, at once the most celebrated and most reviled sporting figure of his age. Denied a title opportunity because of his race, he chased his predecessors — first Jim Jeffries, later Marvin Hart and Tommy Burns — around the world in pursuit of a match, with Burns finally succumbing to the lure of a $100,000 purse to fight at Rushcutters Bay in Sydney.

There, in 1908, Johnson administered a sound thrashing for 14 rounds before the authorities intervened to stop the carnage. Johnson was declared the winner.

He later disposed of Jeffries (in an ill-advised comeback attempt that represented the one and only time Jeffries would lose in the ring), and every other white challenger who could be rounded up, simultaneously defying society by thumbing his nose at convention. He drove fast cars, drank and gambled. He married three white women and consorted with several others, and had a proclivity for adopting white prostitutes and inducting them into his private harem.

It was this quirky predilection which ultimately proved his undoing. He was convicted of violating the Mann Act, which made it a federal crime to transport women across state lines "for immoral purposes." Forced to flee the country, Johnson spent seven years in exile, boxing in Spain, France, Mexico — and in Havana, where he would lose his title to Jess Willard.

He eventually surrendered to US authorities in 1920, and spent a year at the federal penitentiary in Leavenworth, Kansas.

He continued to box after his release. Seven of the dozen losses registered on his career record came after the age of 50, including his last bout, a seventh-round knockout in Boston, when he was 60 years of age.

Fifty-eight years after his death, the legend of Jack Johnson is about to enjoy a renaissance. Ken Burns, the acclaimed filmmaker responsible for the classic *Civil War*, *Baseball* and *Jazz* television series, has just completed an epic, four-hour documentary entitled *Unforgivable Blackness: The Rise and Fall of Jack Johnson*, which is scheduled to air on American Public Television next January in conjunction with Martin Luther King Day.

Three months before its public release, *Unforgivable Blackness* has already enjoyed considerable acclaim after screenings at film festivals in Colorado, Toronto and New York.

And earlier this month the US Senate unanimously passed a resolution introduced by Senator John McCain calling for the posthumous pardon of Johnson.

"Now, if we can get their attention, we have to put a little pressure on our friends in the House," McCain told us two weeks ago.

McCain explained that the resolution represents an expression of the "sense of Congress" and not legislation per se. The justice department would then have to submit a formal pardon, which the president would have to sign.

Not to be cynical, we asked McCain, but does *this* president even know who Jack Johnson was?

"I don't know," chuckled the one-time Republican presidential candidate. "But it seems to me the facts are quite compelling."

As it turns out, George W Bush *does* know something about Jack Johnson. The boxer was a native of Galveston, Texas, and Ken Burns discovered that for six years, beginning in 1995, the then-governor of Texas had proclaimed March 31st, the legendary champion's birthday, "Jack Johnson Day" in the state of Texas.

The dossier of evidence supplied by Burns makes a persuasive case that Johnson was ultimately persecuted because he refused to conduct himself as society demanded of a black man. His defiance was one protracted declaration of personal freedom.

Burns has managed to stitch together racially-charged newspaper accounts with rare old fight footage: Johnson's 1910 destruction of Jeffries in Reno, Nevada, after the former champion had been lured out of retirement to assume the White Man's Burden by the likes of novelist Jack London, and his 1912 Las Vegas defence against Fireman Jim Flynn, who is shown repeatedly head-butting Johnson, to no avail.

Burns said he initially became attracted to the Johnson project because he sensed the filmic value in the tale of the boxer's life.

"First of all it's a story of athletic accomplishment," said Burns. "Then there's the question of race. There probably wouldn't be a story of Jack Johnson had he been a white man. And finally there's the matter of sex: as a nation we're preoccupied with a curious combination of puritanical values and prurient interests, and both come into play with Johnson. He was the most intriguing figure of his age — or, perhaps, of any age."

October 21, 2004

Schilling and Bin Laden make their pitches

Each of the six New England States voted for John Kerry on Tuesday night, but it's as if we'd made a pact with Lucifer: let the Boston Red Sox win a World Series and we'll accept as our part of the Faustian bargain four more years of rule by the former president of the Texas Rangers.

Just a week ago the Red Sox ended an 86-year famine when they reversed the "Curse" and won their first World Series since 1918 — the year the team's owner famously peddled Babe Ruth to the New York Yankees for $100,000. Nearly three million New Englanders lined both banks of the Charles River for a waterborne parade on Saturday.

The exhilaration lasted six days. Nobody I know feels like celebrating today.

The Curse of the Bambino might have been exorcised, but the events of Tuesday brought a more sobering reality. It's hard to know who is to blame — Osama Bin Laden or Curt Schilling — but it makes you want to follow the advice of Red Sox first baseman Kevin Millar and buy a big bottle of Jack Daniel's Sour Mash.

Pick up any newspaper this morning and the electoral graphic of the United States might be a 50-year-old, pre-Bangladesh map of the Indian subcontinent. The nation's heartland, which thoroughly embraced George W Bush and, by inference, his adventure in Iraq, is flanked by pockets of sanity on the east and west coasts, along with the Northern Rust Belt.

Not even in the Vietnam era was the country so thoroughly — and so geographically — polarised. In Massachusetts, where I live, Kerry captured 62 per cent of the vote. In New York he commanded 58 per cent of the electorate. The bottom line is: every state in which it is permissible to not only wear cowboy hats and baseball caps with business suits, but to keep them on during dinner, voted for Bush.

Schilling might not have been named the Most Valuable Player of the American League Championship Series or the four-game sweep of the St Louis Cardinals in the World Series which followed, but his courageous performance in both was emblematic of the Boston team's resilience.

Hampered by an ankle injury so severe it will require surgery next week and a three-month rehabilitation process, he submitted to a procedure so radically experimental doctors wouldn't even perform it until they tried it out first on a cadaver.

Using sutures, the surgeons essentially stapled Schilling's tendon to his leg, sent him out to pitch, and then, after he had beaten the Yankees to initiate the team's comeback from a 3-0 deficit in the best-of-seven ALCS, went out and did it all over again for Game Two of the World Series. The blood oozing from the stigmata was clearly visible to the television cameras. It was a dramatic performance that turned his Sox Red for the entire country to see.

His status as an icon thus confirmed, Schilling set about doing what pretty much any other 38-year-old American who earns $14 million a year might do: protecting his pocketbook by hitting the campaign trail as the sporting world's most enthusiastic Bush supporter this side of Don King.

He skipped a scheduled Bush rally in New Hampshire to participate in the Duck-Boat procession down the Charles, but in the days following the World Series Schilling turned up in several battleground states.

Schilling recorded a phone message to New England voters in which he said, in part: *"These past couple of weeks, Red Sox fans trusted me when it was my turn on the mound. Now you can trust me on this: President Bush is the right leader for our country."*

Curt Schilling of the Boston Red Sox pitches against the St. Louis Cardinals during game two of the 2004 World Series at Fenway Park in Boston, Massachusetts.

At a Pennsylvania political rally, Schilling limped out onto the stage and said: "I'm proud to be on a team with a more important mission — the team that's going to get George Bush re-elected. We need to get your friends and neighbours out to vote . . . I know everybody wants to be on a winning team out there, and there's plenty of room on this bandwagon."

And he showed up in Ohio to say "He's (Bush) a leader who is giving our troops everything they need to get the job done, a leader who believes in their mission and honours their service, a leader who has the courage and the character to stay on the offensive against terrorism until the war is won."

Perhaps in an attempt to counterbalance the influence of their star pitcher, the Boston team's ownership and management stumped for Kerry. Red Sox owner John Henry, chairman Tom Werner, and general manager Theo Epstein (30) — the baseball wunderkind who not only engineered the trade which brought Schilling to Boston, but got him to approve the deal by throwing in a $2 million bonus if the Red Sox won a World Series during the life of his contract — appeared at a Democratic rally in New Hampshire.

"It's only been four years," Epstein told the crowd, "but it feels like 86."

Bush carried Ohio, and with it, the nation. It's difficult to gauge Schilling's influence but it's probably safe to say he didn't sway as many voters as did Bin Laden, who released an ill-timed pre-election video in which he specifically attacked Bush, but stopped just short of declaring himself a Red Sox fan.

Many undecided voters may well have reconsidered their posture by concluding that if Bin Laden was against Bush's re-election, they must be for it.

While all of this was going on, the fun-loving Millar revealed on a nationally televised sports programme it had been so cold before Game Six of the play-offs at Yankee Stadium he and team-mates had primed themselves for impending extinction by swilling from a bottle of Jack Daniel's. Having won, they repeated the ritual before the seventh and deciding game, and, having won that one, could hardly go back on the wagon for the World Series.

Millar claimed the tradition continued through the Fall Classic. He said outfielder Trot Nixon had been so impaired he missed a "take" sign from the third-base coach and swung at a 3-0 pitch. (Nixon wasn't so drunk that he didn't hit a two-run double.)

"I'm just glad we won (the World Series) in four games," said Millar, "before those Crown Royal and Jack Daniel's shots started to kill me."

"The (whiskey) story is nice, but it didn't happen," Red Sox centre-field Johnny Damon said on Late Night With David Letterman a few nights later.

Manager Terry Francona, implicated by Millar as a participant in the booze ritual, said: "I talked to Kevin. It's such an embellishment. He's a real idiot."

Right. So what was Curt Schilling's excuse?

November 04, 2004

Putin shows some craft to pocket super ring

This morning's trivia question: which of the following does not own a 2005 Super Bowl ring? (a) Patriots quarterback Tom Brady (b) Patriots owner Robert Kraft (c) Patriots coach Bill Belichick (d) Russian president Vladimir Putin.

If you answered (b), then you must be a faithful reader of *Kommersant* ("the New Russia's first independent newspaper") which first broke the news of the $50,000 misunderstanding at Konstantinovsky Palace last weekend.

Kraft is walking around Wimbledon bare-handed this week. In the lexicon of the National Football League, the ring is the thing. Players don't speak of winning Super Bowls or World Championships, they talk about winning rings. And, since they are extremely valuable, Super Bowl rings have become a currency unto themselves on the memorabilia black market.

Sometimes they are taken at gunpoint. Hookers have been known to slip a client a mickey and walk off with a Super Bowl ring. Eugene (Mercury) Morris left his in a hotel earlier this year and never saw it again. A few rings have been hocked to support drug habits.

And sometimes, apparently, there is a reasonable explanation, such as the one Kraft no doubt offered when his wife Myra noticed the missing ring last Saturday night: "Well, honey, the president of Russia stuffed it in his pocket and walked off with it."

In a private ceremony at his Brookline mansion two weeks ago, the Patriots owner handed out several dozen Super Bowl rings to the members of his team. Although the NFL ponies up $5,000 apiece for the rings, owners frequently augment the cost of more expensive bling, and Kraft must have figured the team's unprecedented feat in winning its third world championship in four years warranted the creation of the gaudiest momento in the history of team sport.

The rings, weighing better than four ounces apiece, were made of 14-carat white gold, and were encrusted with 124 diamonds, including three marquises depicting a trio of Vince Lombardi Trophies. Each included the player's uniform number and name. The reported cost exceeded $20,000 per ring.

With training camp still more than a month away, the ring recipients scattered to the four corners of the earth. In Kraft's case, he preceded his annual Wimbledon visit by joining a delegation of American businessmen on a trade mission to Moscow. The group met the Russian president last Saturday. It should probably be noted here Kraft's previous contribution to East-West diplomacy came three decades ago, when he helped engineer the defection of Martina Navratilova from Czechoslovakia to the United States.

Although Kraft was present in Moscow in his role as CEO of the Kraft Group, whose holdings include extensive investments in the paper and packaging industries, his role as an NFL owner added a certain cachet — at least in the minds of some of his fellow moguls. It was Sanford Weil, the chairman of CitiCorp, who reportedly encouraged

Kraft to show his ring to Putin. Kraft slipped the bauble off his finger so the Russian president could get a closer look, but Putin, aware the TV cameras were rolling, quickly jammed what he perceived as a contraband gift into his jacket pocket and walked out the door.

The caption accompanying a photograph of the exchange in a Moscow newspaper read: *"After the energetic meeting with American entrepreneurs, Vladimir Putin added a highest sport award from the American Football League to his prizes for judo and mountain skis competition."*

It seems plain enough Kraft wasn't trying to bribe a Russian president with a Super Bowl ring.

"It's a Super Bowl ring," Kraft told the former KGB official as he proffered the trophy. "It's a very good ring." The NFL owner stood flabbergasted as the ring disappeared into the Moscow streets. At the risk of creating an international incident, Kraft kept his counsel.

At least that's our understanding of what happened. The interpretation from the Russian side paints a decidedly different picture. *Kommersant's* man on the scene reported Kraft "shyly stuffed something into the hand of Mr Putin. Putin nodded and quickly looked around. But no, he didn't see anybody watching," wrote Andrey Kolesnikov. "Then the curiosity took hold over the president of Russia and he started to look at the present. There was a massive silver ring in his hands. Putin even carefully tried it on, but when he noticed that photo and video cameras were pointing at him, quickly took it off and held it in the fist."

At this point in his analysis, Kolesnikov's imagination appears to have gotten the better of him. "Only sometime after did I realise the true meaning of this event. Of course an American billionaire would not give the Russian president a cheap ring that the winners of the Super Bowl are being rewarded. If he wanted to, Kraft could give Putin such a ring that after putting it on the finger that no personal security service could guarantee security. But the American probably decided the very expensive ring will immediately end up in the State treasury because of existing agreement between the Kremlin and White House. And he thought the only chance to leave a good souvenir for the Russian president is to give him a really kitchy thing."

It's hard to know whether Kraft was more insulted by having his ring appropriated or by having his prized momento described in the Russian press as "a really kitchy thing". It seems plain Kolesnikov shared Putin's belief that the Patriots' owner intended the ring to be a present.

"However, Kraft's manoeuvre didn't turn out as he expected," reported *Kommersant's* man. "Some high-placed source in the Kremlin, on the condition of confidentiality, told me the very next day, the ring was already given not straight to the treasury, but to the Kremlin library."

June 30, 2005

IT CRAWLED INTO MY BAG, HONEST! AND OTHER UNPLAYABLE LIES

Michelle Wie at full tilt: "We don't condone rudeness, but we've got to assume that these people have teenaged children of their own and hence should not have been surprised. Anyone who goes out for a round of golf expecting to pal around with a 17-year-old deserves exactly what he gets."

Amateur shootout shot down by USGA

The Worcester Country Club will stage the 2000 Massachusetts Amateur Golf Championship, and Fordie Pitts Jr had been particularly looking forward to participating this year. Not only would the State Open have been contested on the site of the first Ryder Cup matches, but Pitts would have been playing in the event for the 50th time.

Instead, he will be watching from the sidelines, a disappointed and decidedly bitter spectator. This February, Pitts, along with 14 other golfers, was informed by the United States Golf Association (USGA) that he had been relieved of his amateur status. Barring a last-minute (and extremely unlikely) reversal at an appeal hearing scheduled for Pebble Beach two weeks from tomorrow, Fordie Pitts has, at the age of 69, been declared a professional.

Pitts won his first golf competition — the State Caddie Championship — in 1946. In addition to appearing in 49 Massachusetts Amateurs, he has played in the State Open 30 times, and has also played in the US and British Amateur Championships.

Almost five years ago, at Cohasset Country Club, he scored better than his age when he shot 64 in a US Senior Amateur qualifier. Over the years he had become the most revered Massachusetts amateur since Francis Ouimet.

It probably didn't help much that the event central to the controversy bore his name. Last November 26th, 33 professionals and 99 amateurs gathered at Hyannis Golf Club on Cape Cod — a venue co-owned by Pitts and fellow amateur Joe Keller — to participate in the "Fordie Pitts Shootout".

Each participant paid an entry fee of $125 — $25 of which was earmarked to cover green fees, carts, and refreshments. The remainder was, in Pitts' words, "placed in a cigar box" to be divided up among the winning teams.

"The Fordie Pitts shootout had a cash pool of over $13,000, and the rules clearly do not allow amateurs to play for that kind of money," said Tom Landry, the executive director of the Massachusetts Golf Association (MGA), which handled the initial investigation.

Within a day of the tournament, the MGA was in receipt of an anonymous tip which prompted the investigation. Landry interviewed many of those who had competed in the Hyannis event, and on January 4th, each of the 99 amateurs was sent a letter from the MGA advising them of the organisation's surprisingly lenient decision: to retain his amateur status, each would be asked to sign an admission acknowledging the transgression, and would further be required to forward any cash winnings to the MGA, which would disburse the money to charity through a specially-created fund.

The USGA official who oversaw the investigation explained that the treatment had been "lenient" because the miscreants were all deemed to have been first-time offenders. In any case, 84 of the amateurs signed the letters and returned their winnings by the February 4th deadline. Fordie Pitts did not.

Pitts explained that his initial reluctance to comply with the directive stemmed first from his conviction that he was not in violation of the rules, but also from a desire to protect his fellow participants. ("After all, the thing had my name on it," he pointed out.) Pitts later relented, and in March returned the signed letter, along with a cheque for $600 — a month past the deadline.

The USGA's policy on the subject is spelled out in what would appear to be clear-cut language. In an addendum to the Rules of Golf, the body states: "Organised amateur events open to the general golfing public and designed and promoted to create cash prizes are not approved by the USGA. Golfers participating in such events without irrevocably waiving their right to cash prizes are deemed by the USGA to be playing for prize money."

The language of the R&A rulebook denotes a similar policy, and a golfer in Britain or Ireland would have recognised immediately that participating in such an event would jeopardise his amateur status. Why, then, didn't the Americans?

Part of the problem is that despite its highminded posture, the USGA has traditionally looked the other way on these matters. By allowing "optional" cash pools (which are thus deemed "wagers" and not prize money) and by allowing (though theoretically discouraging) massive calcutta and pari-mutuel wagering, the USGA has allowed the situation to fester.

Were the body to strictly apply its rules, there might not be a dozen *bona fide* amateurs left in the whole country — including the board members charged with administering the rules. Just by way of example: two sons of a former MGA treasurer, Don Page, played in the Fordie Pitts Shootout.

At my own club, the members gather at least four mornings a week, throw $15 or $20 into a kitty, conduct a blind draw for four-man teams, and play better-ball for the pot. According to Mickey Herron, the head professional and director of golf at Hyannis, literally the only difference between what we do at South Shore (and what golfers do at every club in the country) and what took place on the Cape last November comes in the substantial difference in the amount of cash involved.

"Technically, you're playing for prize money, too," said Herron. "The problem is that the rule has been so vaguely interpreted over the years that it's lost its meaning."

Pitts, according to some intimates, felt "bulletproof" in this instance, in part because of his own stature in the golfing community, but mainly because he had modeled his "Shootout" on a similar event Arnold Palmer runs at his Bay Hill course in Florida nearly every day.

Pitts, along with many other top amateurs, has played in the so-called "Arnie Shootout" many times. Since Palmer is effectively the poster boy for the USGA,

Oh happy days: Tiger celebrates sinking the winning putt to claim the 2001, Bay Hill Invitational, following some help from the gallery.

Fordie apparently felt secure in his belief that the governing body would never come after him if it meant it might have to hound down Palmer as well.

Herron added: "Look, I myself had serious reservations about (the Shootout) being a violation, but if it was so obviously wrong, why were so many high-profile amateurs playing in it?

"To me, there are only two explanations," Herron concluded. "One would be that the MGA and USGA people are incredibly stupid. The other would be that they've deliberately kept their heads in the sand."
May 25, 2000

Fans give Woods a comfort blanket

Last Sunday afternoon I was guest host for a radio programme originating from one of those ubiquitous sports bars, this one on Cape Cod. As we waited to go on the air, we were surrounded by a bank of television sets. Several of them were showing various NCAA basketball tournament games from around the country, and one was tuned in to the Bay Hill Invitational golf tournament down in Orlando.

Tiger Woods was still playing the front nine when an errant tee shot scattered the crowd. Tiger's ball was prevented from straying into further trouble when it struck an anonymous spectator and came to rest in the light rough just off the fairway.

I'm not claiming to be clairvoyant here, but I did say, out loud, at the time to one of my colleagues "you know, if we could play with Tiger's galleries we could probably shave eight or 10 strokes a round off our scores."

All right, that's an exaggeration. Attempting to strike a golf ball in front of that many people would make most of us so nervous we'd never get it airborne, but put it this way: if you or I could line every fairway with 10,000 or so strategically-placed, lifesized mannequins we'd find far less trouble off the tee than we do.

The point being that the swarming army of spectators attending Woods's every stroke has grown so large that it has become almost impossible for him to drive a ball into serious trouble without hitting one of his fans first.

As most golfing aficionados are by now aware, Woods made his first successful defence of one of the nine tour titles he won in 2000 at Bay Hill last Sunday, when a spectacular birdie on the final hole gave him a one-shot win over Phil Mickelson.

It may not have been as widely publicised, but Tiger's chances were considerably enhanced when his wild hook off the final tee first struck a spectator named Tony DeKroub and was then picked up by Tony's curious girlfriend, Kathleen Eidsvaag, who dropped it like a hot rock when she discovered that the offending missile was a Nike ball whose logo had been augmented with the word Tiger.

Woods played Bay Hill again on Monday morning in a charity event, before approximately 15,000 fewer eyewitnesses. Had he hit the same tee ball off number 18 that he had a day earlier, it would have at the very least wound up in the trees, and in all probability it would have been out of bounds. He'd have been lucky to make six on the hole.

When a moving golf ball strikes an uninvolved bystander it is, of course, considered a rub of the green. Neither does a penalty obtain when a ball in play is handled by an "outside agency" — such as a dim-witted spectator.

To be sure, these rules apply equally to all competitors, but they remain more likely to help Tiger Woods than any other golfer simply because he usually has a larger crowd of slowmoving targets available than anyone else. This advantage is magnified when he is playing in the final group, as he was last Sunday.

By the time Tiger got to the 18th tee, he had not only his own gallery, but everybody else's, to use as backstops, a fact which was not lost on Woods himself. Even as his drive violently changed course, the expression on Tiger's face remained almost serene — as if he were confident that what did occur inevitably would.

"With that many people over there," he explained afterwards, "it was going to smoke somebody."

Tony DeKroub was unhurt by his inadvertent collision with Tiger's ball, which actually one-hopped off the cart path before it hit him in the neck.

Eidsvaag, for her part, was so mortified by her own thoughtless intervention that she initially denied having picked up the ball at all, but televised footage of the episode shot from an overhead blimp nailed her.

Tracked down by Orlando Sentinel columnist David Whitley and confronted with the incriminating videotape, Eidsvaag eventually confessed. Asked what on earth she could have been thinking when she picked up Tiger's ball, Eidsvaag told Whitley "I don't know. I *wasn't* thinking."

Woods, in any case, was allowed a drop from the spot where Eidsvaag had hastily disposed of the evidence. Then, because his stance was on a paved cart path, he was allowed another, which left him just enough room to nail an amazing 195-yard five-iron to the green, which was followed by an equally impressive 15-foot putt to win the tournament.

The episode was eerily reminiscent of a similar misadventure involving a dead-left Tiger tee shot at last year's PGA Championship in Louisville, which may or may not have been aided by spectator interference.

His Tigership is not, of course, the only golfer who gets help from the crowds. Three years ago, his closest golfing friend Mark O'Meara took advantage of a similarly generous drop (after his "lost" Strata ball materialised in the pocket of a spectator's jacket) to win the British Open at Royal Birkdale.

Even after his good fortune off the tee, Woods still had to make two shots that would have been beyond the mortal limits of most of his peers to win the Bay Hill tournament, and as a crestfallen Mickelson, holding his baby daughter in his arms, watched in amazement, he did just that.

The fact remains: if one of us hits that same shot next week, we're hitting three off the tee.

March 22, 2001

Hitting technology out of bounds

At last month's Masters, the Augusta National chairman Hootie Johnson announced that the club would lengthen some of the par four holes, presumably to keep apace with the frightening increases in distance brought about by modern-day golf equipment.

During the 62nd PGA Seniors Championship at Ridgewood last weekend, Tom Watson's stirring victory over Jim Thorpe overshadowed the fact that one of Watson's playing partners had been booted out of the tournament two days earlier for playing with an illegal driver.

And, two days after Watson wrapped up his first Senior Major title, the United States Supreme Court rendered its verdict on the Casey Martin case, ruling that the disabled professional was entitled to ride a buggy in PGA sanctioned events.

Although Tom Fazio eventually wound up with the commission for the Augusta National redesign, a number of prominent golf architects were privately consulted beforehand. One of them, the outspoken Pete Dye, essentially refused the job, but not before imparting his own advice.

"Gentlemen, let me remind you that you are Augusta National. You make your own rules. You tell people how fast they can drive on Magnolia Lane, you tell them what they can and cannot wear, you don't even have a course rating because you won't let the USGA on your golf course to evaluate it. You don't have to answer to anybody, which puts you in a unique position among high-profile events. You've got a great golf course that's stood the test of time, and all you have to do is rummage around in your pro shop, find the balls they were using 20 years ago, and say 'Gentlemen, this is what you're playing this week.'

"Those balls will cost you two bucks apiece," added Dye as he excused himself from the meeting, "and I just saved you $30 million."

At Augusta in April Jack Nicklaus added his voice to those who believe that the USGA and the R&A, golf's rule makers on either side of the Atlantic, need to curtail aerodynamic properties of today's balls before all of the great courses are overtaken by technology. Thus far, neither group appears to have the stomach for what would be the inevitable next step — a protracted court battle with the folks who make the

Titleist ProV1.

Moreover, the USGA and the R&A dovetailed when it came to outlawing several new drivers, most notably Callaway's ERC-II, which are legal in Europe. After testing over 1,000 drivers, the American body ruled that the club's performance was enhanced by a trampoline, or "spring-like" effect on the ball coming off the club-face. The banning of the ERC-II resulted in one of the uglier contretemps in some years, when elder statesman Arnold Palmer subsequently endorsed the "non-conforming" club and said that he saw nothing wrong with its use by "recreational" golfers.

When a competitor was disqualified for using an illegal driver at Ridgewood last week, it wasn't Palmer, but Jersey's Tommy Horton. Horton was playing the third hole in Friday's second round at Ridgewood when he was approached by PGA rules Official Don Essig, who told him: "I've got some bad news for you. That driver you are using is non-conforming."

"What do you mean?" protested Horton. "It's the 360 TaylorMade."

"No," Essig pointed out. "It's got the 'R' stamped on it, which means it's not the standard 360."

The TaylorMade R360 driver with which Horton played is made in Japan, and is on the United States Golf Association's list of non-conforming clubs. TaylorMade markets a modified version of the 360 in the US which is within the bounds of the rules, but the model preceded by the 'R' is prohibited from use in golf competitions in the United States, Mexico, and other countries under USGA jurisdiction.

Horton said it was all an innocent mistake.

"I simply was interested in the R360 and at one of the tour events in the United Kingdom, the guys at the TaylorMade truck said 'Why don't you try these?'," said Horton. "They gave me a couple to try, and I liked the one I've got now. I had no idea it was non-conforming. Absolutely no idea at all."

Whether he was aware that his driver was in violation of the rules or not, Horton might have gotten away with it had he not drawn a pair of high-profile playing partners for the first two rounds. Being paired with Watson and Lanny Wadkins ensured that his group would spend a lot of time on television, and it was apparently one of the TV announcers who spotted the club.

Initially suspicion had fallen on Watson (a stickler for the rules) as the one who reported Horton, but in a subsequent conversation Watson told me he hadn't even noticed what driver Horton was playing.

Casey Martin's attorneys successfully argued his case on the basis of the Americans with Disabilities Act. Personally, I don't think they even needed it, because history was on their side in the first place. I have in my possession a book with an 1870 painting of General Sir John Low of Clatto, "riding the links at St Andrews on his faithful cream pony."

Five years earlier, it might be noted, Sir John had served as the Captain of the Royal and Ancient Golf Club.

"Other R&A members were never seen on the links without their ponies," relates present-day St Andrews caddiemaster Rick Mackenzie in *A Wee Nip* at the 19th Hole, his seminal history of the caddie's role at the home of golf.

Mackenzie recalls another St Andrews member who "employed two caddies, one to carry the clubs and one to hold the pony while he got off to play his shot, a practice which led to intense arguments between the caddies about who should have the easier job of holding the pony."

May 31, 2001

A birdie Kite should not have bagged

CONCORD, MASSACHUSETTS

I didn't actually *see* Tom Kite's golf ball strike the bird, but then neither did Tom Kite. All Kite knew was that he had struck a seven iron about as well as he could hit it, but all of a sudden the ball came tumbling out of the sky, landed on the bank fronting the 17th green at Nashawtuc Country Club, and rolled into the water.

The golfer and his caddie, Sandy Jones, found it difficult to believe that they'd miscalculated that badly on their club selection, a view that was endorsed by playing partner Bruce Fleisher, who estimated that Kite's tee shot to the par-3 hole was destined to wind up no worse than 12 feet from the pin.

The avian angle had occurred to no one until the party reached the green, when a spectator told Kite his ball had collided with a bird in flight.

"Yeah, right," said Kite, who confessed to thinking "This is a guy who's sat up in the stands drinking Michelob *way* too long."

But by the time he had taken a penalty drop, chipped onto the green, and two-putted for a double-bogey five that effectively ended his pursuit of winner Larry Nelson in Sunday's final round of the Fleet-Boston Seniors' Classic, Kite had heard from half a dozen more spectators who thought they'd seen the same thing.

Tom Kite: bird lovers anxious about the avian obstruction

It was only then that the CNBC television people examined their footage of the episode and confirmed that there had indeed been a midair collision between Kite's Titleist Pro V1 and a bird (subsequently identified as a purple martin) above the pond. In replay, the ball appears to behave like a smart missile, tracking the path of the bird, which then plummets to earth. Once CNBC began to air the replay, the switchboards soon lit up with phone calls from bird-loving viewers concerned about the fate of the bird.

Many of them pointed out that Nashawtuc, located a stone's thrown from Thoreau's Walden Pond, is but a two-minute drive from a Massachusetts Audobon Society shelter. This latter concern would appear to have been misplaced, for by all accounts the martin would appear to have been killed instantaneously.

The episode called to mind a well-chronicled incident earlier this year in which Randy Johnson, the hard-throwing Arizona Diamondbacks pitcher, uncorked a fastball that hit a pigeon halfway to the plate (video footage of that one showed the unfortunate bird literally exploding in a puff of feathers), the principal difference being that Johnson was not penalised for what was deemed outside interference.

Now, had Kite's ball struck, say, a telephone line or an electric wire, he would have been allowed to replay the shot without penalty, but dealing with nature and all her elements is endemic to Kite's sport, and there is no recourse to hitting a bird in flight.

"If a ball in motion is accidentally deflected or stopped by any outside agency, it is a rub of the green and the ball shall be played as it lies," say the Rules of Golf.

It was Kite's misfortune that the ball wound up lost in a hazard. "If it had been Tiger Woods," a friend remarked the next morning, "the ball would have hit the bird and fallen into the hole!"

The skies, which had been threatening all afternoon, had finally opened up just moments before Kite reached the 17th tee. "I've got 154 to carry the water and 162 to the hole. Just a nice, smooth, easy seven iron, and I hit a pretty good shot," he recalled the moment.

"It was starting to rain and the wind was kicking up, and when the ball hit the bank and came back into the water, both Sandy and I saw it fall out of the sky. I'd thought at first it might have caught a gust of wind or something."

The 1997 Ryder Cup captain joined the Senior Tour last year, when a celebrated trio consisting of himself, Tom Watson, and Lanny Wadkins were supposed to breathe new life into the over-50 circuit. Although he won two Senior events in 2000 and is among the statistical leaders in virtually every meaningful category, Kite has yet to win this year.

Like Watson, he has also continued to play the odd event on the regular Tour, particularly when it comes to the majors. Just a week earlier, Kite had fired a blistering 64 in the final round of the US Open at Southern Hills before rushing off to catch a flight for Boston and a two-week stay in Massachusetts that began with last week's FleetBoston event in Concord and continues with the US Senior Open which commences at Salem Country Club this morning.

When Kite signed his scorecard in Tulsa he was in 23rd place. By the time his plane crossed the Mississippi River he was tied for fifth, and the way things were going that day for Mssrs Goosen, Brooks, Cink, et al, it is not unfair to say that had the tournament lasted five more holes Kite might have won it *in absentia*.

Last Sunday he appeared well on his way to duplicating that final round performance. He had begun the day six under par, but gone out in 31 and picked up two more birdies on the back nine to find himself tied for the lead with Nelson with five holes left to play before he made bogey on the par-four 14th.

Even then, Kite reckoned that he was on track for another 64, possibly even 63, until his ball was intercepted by the bird. (The bird, of course, would probably maintain that precisely the opposite had occurred.)

At the conclusion of play, members of the Nashawtuc grounds crew returned to the site and recovered the remains of the offending avian, which had plummeted to earth and landed in the rough left of the pond. It was brought to the clubhouse, where it was identified by amateur ornithologists as a purple martin.

It wasn't Kite's first golf encounter with a bird, but it was certainly his untimeliest.

"You'll hit some birds from time to time," he said. "You know, seagulls out on the West Coast. They're flying all around Pebble Beach, and I've hit a couple of them. But it's unfortunate when you've got a chance to win a golf tournament and stuff like that happens."

Kite termed the incident "a bum break".

"With a little bit better luck, things could have happened," he sighed.

He was right, of course, but in bemoaning his misfortune he overlooked one thing. However unlucky he might have felt his day had been, the bird's luck was even worse.

June 28, 2001

Hinkle plants his place in golf history

TOLEDO, OHIO

When the Lucas County health department dropped in on a Toledo mortuary for a routine unannounced inspection last week, they were startled to discover a pile of eight unburied corpses fermenting in a shack behind the funeral home.

Some of the bodies were in state of such advanced decomposition that they have yet to be identified, but the mystery could be partially resolved this morning, should one of the participants in the US Senior Open down the street at the Inverness Club fail to materialise for his appointed tee-time.

Arnold Palmer was spotted several times around the clubhouse yesterday and has thus been ruled out as one of the mystery decedents.

The lure of $2.6 million in prize money has brought the old-timers flocking to Toledo this week.

Hale Irwin, the leading money winner on the recently-renamed "Champions Tour," won't be in attendance (stretchered off the course after suffering back spasms at the US Open two weeks ago, Irwin withdrew earlier this week), but 156 of the world's best senior golfers (Des Smyth and Christy O'Connor Jnr among them) are playing.

The star of the show, though, figures to be Inverness itself.

The venerable 100-year-old layout has hosted seven Major championships. Byron Nelson spent five years, from 1940-45, as the head professional at Inverness.

Frank Stranahan, America's best amateur golfer between Bobby Jones and Tiger Woods, was an Inverness member. In 1986 I stood beside Inverness' 18th green and watched Bob Tway hole a bunker shot to win the PGA Championship.

(The memory frozen in time from that moment isn't watching the ball disappear into the hole, but the expression on Greg Norman's face when it did.)

Golfing history figures to be frequently evoked this week, and in fact has been from the moment the senior golfers started drifting into town.

Lon Hinkle, for instance, has been interviewed more times this week than he had been in the previous 20 years.

Inverness was initially created by an obscure designer named Bernard Nichols, who laid out a nine-hole course in 1903. Thirteen years later the renowned Donald Ross was engaged to build the present course, and another noted architect, Arthur Hills (a Toledo resident and Inverness member, by the way) re-tooled the course preparatory to the 1993 US Open. But it was Hinkle who was singlehandedly responsible for a make-over undertaken in mid-tournament during playing of the 1979 US Open.

His handiwork, unlike that of, say, Bernard Nichols, remains in evidence to this day.

A journeyman pro who won three tournaments in 1978 and 1979 and hasn't won since, Hinkle hasn't had the greatest luck on the Champions circuit, either, entering just three events this year, and finishing 32nd, 65th, and 72nd. He had to play his way into the Senior Open as a qualifier, but once he did, he brought his bit of history with him.

"I'd finished second in Los Angeles and won the Crosby, so I came here as a real legitimate contender that year," recalled Hinkle, who in the '79 Open found himself paired in the first two rounds with the colourful Juan Antonio (Chi Chi) Rodriguez.

The group had a substantial wait on the tee before driving to the eighth, a par-five which plays to 554 yards. The entire fairway was heavily surrounded by timber, but the pair noticed that there was a single opening in the trees offering a carefully-placed drive a chance to short-cut the hole by playing down the 17th fairway — which was not then and is not now out of bounds.

"We had to wait for the group ahead of us to clear the fairway, so Chi Chi and I were just chatting," recalled Hinkle.

"Chi Chi mentioned the short-cut, and I just kind of looked over and said 'Man, there's a fairway over thataway, but where is the green and how far away is it?'"

Hinkle had the honour. (Had he not, "Chi Chi's Tree" might have entered the golfing lexicon 24 years ago.) He took a one-iron through the gap, leaving him 220 yards to the green. He knocked it on, and two-putted for birdie.

So did Chi Chi.

Word quickly trickled back through the field, and by the end of the day a whole host of golfers had availed themselves of the short-cut, resulting in an emergency convocation of near-apoplectic USGA officials.

In the dead of night, the Inverness grounds crew was ordered to plant a 25-foot blue spruce to discourage the newly-discovered line of play.

"Hinkle's Tree" remains there today.

"By the time I got to the eighth on Friday, I was four-over and fairly disappointed in myself for letting the tournament get away," Hinkle recalled this week. "I looked at the tree as though it had somehow ruined my Open."

What history did not record is that while Hinkle glumly played his way down the eighth fairway like everybody else in the second round, Rodriguez refused to be deterred. Rising to the challenge thrown down by the tournament officials, Chi Chi defiantly teed his ball up on a pencil and hit it over the tree anyway.

"I really enjoyed my days as a contender, and I have some great memories," said Hinkle. "But the defining moment of my career seems to be that tree. I was happy with my career in the late 70s and early 80s, but it's the tree that people associate with my name. I hear about it on a regular basis — but it's not like I did something wrong."

June 26, 2003

Making the most of senior moments

Two summers ago Juan Antonio (Chi-Chi) Rodriguez went 78-74 and out to miss the cut in the Senior US Open at Salem Country Club in Massachusetts, and vowed he'd never play another senior major again.

"I want to play golf and have fun," Chi Chi explained to us from Puerto Rico, where he is living in semi-retirement, a couple of days ago. "I don't want to be embarrassed. This tour was supposed to be about nostalgia. People want to come out and see us play and have a good time, but when you're making double bogeys,

I don't care how old you are, you're not having fun."

And some of the old-timers would be happy to settle for double bogeys. When he came to the final green at Inverness last Friday, in the second round of the Senior US Open there, Arnold Palmer had no chance of making the cut anyway, but his gut-wrenching experience in full few of several thousand spectators ringing the green is instructive.

Palmer's approach shot fell short of the green, landing in a cavernous bunker. He blasted out, but his ball flew the green and came to rest in ankle-deep rough. His next shot was one all too familiar to the weekend duffer: he chunked the ball. It travelled no more than three feet, still in heavy grass, but at least this time he could see it.

From there Arnie chipped on, but his ball went sliding down and off the slick green, travelling nearly back into the bunker from whence he had started his greenside play.

"*Stop!!!*" Palmer shouted at his ball, and, when it did, spectators who had been writhing in their seats at the sight of this public flogging chuckled nervously.

This time Palmer took his putter from the fringe and got the ball to within six feet. When he sank that — and at 73, Arnie doesn't make a lot of six-footers — for a 7, the crowd politely applauded. He smiled, none too convincingly, waved and was back in Pennsylvania by nightfall.

"That's a tough golf course anyway," said Chi Chi Rodriguez, who watched last weekend's action on television. "But besides the length of the course and the rough, those greens were the fastest of any USGA event in history. What's the point of doing that for seniors? We're not supposed to be out there grinding; we're supposed to smell the flowers."

The PGA Senior Tour, now rechristened the Champions Tour, does indeed find itself in an identity crisis. In some respects it is a victim of its early success: its immediate popularity when it was conceived two decades ago sparked a massive growth in purses that annually brought the newly-turned 50s flocking from every caddyshack in every corner of the globe.

By the time the Senior Tour was five years old, for instance, Palmer was no longer competitive. The powers-that-be attempted to remedy this by incorporating a "grand champions" tournament-within-a- tournament for players aged 60 and above, but players Palmer's age are out of their league even there by now.

The television folk, and, one suspects, the USGA, would much preferred to have seen Tom Watson win last week's US Senior, but the living legend fell short of overtaking Bruce Lietzke. Now, Lietzke isn't exactly anonymous — he won 13 tournaments and over $6 million on the PGA Tour — but neither is he the sort of marquee player who is going to carry the standard of the Champions Tour into America's living-rooms.

This is in part a situation of Lietzke's own creation. Twenty years ago, when his children came along, he made a conscious decision to be a stay-at-home father and part-time touring pro. He built his PGA schedule around his family commitments. He coached his son's Little League baseball team, for instance, which meant no summer golf. Lietzke stopped playing the US and British Opens, and as a consequence never earned enough points to qualify for the Ryder Cup, which he last played in 1981.

"Bruce has his priorities the way he wants his priorities," said fellow Kansas Citian Watson. "You can't argue with a man's priorities. Not being able to spend the time we'd like to with our families is a choice most of us out here must make. He chose not to make it."

Watson remains a force on the Champions Tour, but Jack Nicklaus is, at 63, barely more competitive than Palmer. Lee Trevino has followed Rodriguez' lead, and refuses to participate in Senior Majors and, basically, any other event in which he can't use a cart.

At the same time, there are millions to be made. Christy O'Connor Jnr, for instance, took the Senior Tour by storm when he turned 50, and might still be raking in the money but for his unfortunate experience with a Harley-Davidson. Des Smyth finished as medallist in last winter's Champions Tour Q-School, and halfway through the year has already earned over half a million dollars.

The lure of the big money has also brought an influx of previously unsuspected talent. Perhaps the most remarkable example has been Allen Doyle, a career-long amateur who turned professional at 48 in the hope of earning enough money to pay his daughter's college tuition. He made $250,000 in the two years before he turned 50, and has earned over $8 million since.

Doyle said he wouldn't have turned pro at all had the USGA responded positively to his request to play one more Walker Cup, this time as player-captain. When the blue-jackets said no, he turned pro, but not in his wildest dreams could he have imagined what the next half-dozen years would hold.

Allen Doyle: raking in the dough on the Champions tour.

"I'm not a dreamer," Doyle explained last week. "I don't look beyond tomorrow and the next day. The only thing I wanted was, first, to get a chance to get out there and play, and I felt that if I got that I could compete. Remember, in my amateur career I'd played against Tiger Woods and David Duval and Phil Mickelson and Justin Leonard before anybody on the regular tour ever heard of them, and when I was 47 and

48 I was on the tour and played against the guys my age, like Hubert Green and Ben Crenshaw, who were about to turn 50.

"I also had Jay Sigel, who preceded me. Jay probably wouldn't agree, but I kind of felt I was a better player in my 40s than he was, and when he came out he was fourth on the money list," pointed out Doyle.

"I'd seen guys out there who'd come onto the Seniors Tour and done okay, so I had some barometer to judge by. What I tried to key into was just not worrying about all the bullshit, just worry about playing and shooting a score, and at the end of the week if my score totalled up lower than most guys, then I'd done better than most guys," he said with a chuckle. "That's all I tried to do. I didn't imagine I was going to win the money title."

Doyle was a relatively anonymous, 48-year-old PGA Tour rookie when he arrived at the 1996 Greater Milwaukee Open and found a note in his locker asking if he could come by the media room. Though puzzled ("What the hell did they want me in the media room for?"), Doyle dutifully reported to the press tent, where he identified himself.

Next thing he heard was a voice announcing over the loudspeaker "Allen Doyle is now available in the interview room."

"Must have been 50 or 60 guys get up and run in there," recalled Doyle. "I'm wondering 'What did I do? Did I do something wrong?'"

The reason for the unexpected attention became quickly apparent. A 20-year-old Tiger Woods was making his professional debut in the Milwaukee event that week.

"The first guy to ask a question explained it," said Doyle. "He reminded me 'You're the only one in the field who's ever played with the kid'."
July 03, 2003

TPC Boston banks on popular sideshows

NORTON MASSACHUSETTS

Last Sunday afternoon Darren Clarke had a four-shot victory that made him the first man not named Tiger Woods to win the $1 million first prize in the NEC Invitational at Firestone Country Club, Ohio. Informed that this year the winning purse had been increased to $1,050,000, the Ulsterman thereupon declared his intention to spend the extra fifty grand before the night was out.

That evening Clarke must have pushed himself away from his last pint and made his way to the Akron-Canton Airport, where he had a private jet waiting, because he woke up in Rhode Island, which is where he was when we tracked him down on Monday to ask if he intended to play a practice round at TPC Boston, the site of the Deutsche Bank Championship which starts tomorrow.

"Absolutely not," Clarke told us. "I don't know anything about the course, but I'll see it soon enough. Today I'm going to relax and try to get over my hangover."

When Clarke embarked on Sunday's final round, the leaderboard behind him included Brad Faxon, Jim Furyk, Retief Goosen, Jonathan Kaye, Davis Love III, Vijay Singh, Hal Sutton — and Woods. Apparently, for television viewers, only the latter name counted, but it might be added that from that select group, only Kaye was sufficiently obscure to fit among the low-profile winners of this summer's other big events. After two-months' worth of Ben Curtises, Shaun Micheels, and Chad Campbells, viewers were doubtless pleased to see a golfer they'd actually heard of winning a championship.

Darren Clarke: spend it before the night is out.

Deutsche Bank's inaugural American tournament won't get under way until tomorrow (Monday is Labour Day in the US, and ABC wanted a live event to show in the afternoon), but the event is already sold out. Well over 100,000 spectators will visit the new facility in Norton, some 35 miles south of Boston. When Jim O'Mara, general manager of TPC Boston at Norton, is asked how a facility barely a year old landed such a marquee event, he replies: "It doesn't hurt if your club is half-owned by the PGA Tour."

Woods, Clarke, and a handful of other Ryder Cup veterans will be returning to the Boston area for the first time since the events at Brookline in 1999. For the past five years, New England has been bereft of a PGA Tour event. The demise of the annual tournament at Pleasant Valley created a void, both in the hearts of local golf fans and among the movers and shakers of the tour. An old-fashioned operation reminiscent of the tour's early days, Pleasant Valley might have been a relic, but it had been a favourite stop among players.

It might have outgrown its usefulness from a business standpoint, but dropping the tournament had been a move fraught with moral repercussions. Moreover, from a business standpoint, it didn't seem particularly sensible to abandon the nation's sixth-largest television market.

"I think the tour was anxious to get back to the Boston marketplace," said O'Mara, "and everyone was pleased with the course construction and design here. It's a high-quality, championship quality facility with the infrastructure to handle a PGA tournament today.

"There are certain demands when it comes to hosting a PGA event today, and there aren't that many facilities capable of doing it," explained O'Mara last week. "That's basically what happened at Pleasant Valley: there were a lot of great things about Pleasant Valley. The fans loved it. The players liked it there, but the tournament simply outgrew its surroundings."

The PGA Tour had been discussing ways to return to New England for years and ABC was looking for an event to televise over the holiday weekend. As Pleasant Valley had learned, two basic ingredients are required to stage a modern-day PGA event: (1) a well-heeled corporate sponsor, and (2) Tiger Woods — and not necessarily in that order.

IMG, the agency founded by the late Mark McCormack, not only represented Woods but had worked closely over the years with the German bank which had shelled out to get Tiger to commit annually to its event in Europe. Deutsche Bank was looking to enhance its profile in the US and enjoyed a good relationship with Woods.

Then came the master stroke: each PGA tournament is conducted to benefit a charity, usually a locally-based one, but early in the planning stages somebody came up with an ingenious proposal: "What if we made the charitable beneficiary of this one the Tiger Woods Foundation?"

Thus is was when the Deutsche Bank Championship was announced 10 months ago, the tournament was able to reveal Woods's commitment to the event.

The importance of this is illustrated by TV ratings: the drama of Micheel's win in the PGA Championship at Oak Hill two weeks ago might have been great golf, but it was watched by far fewer viewers than would have been glued to their sets had Woods been in contention.

All right, we know how they got Tiger to Boston, but how did they manage to attract Clarke, Furyk, Vijay Singh, Nick Price, Jesper Parvnevik, Greg Norman, and Ben Curtis as well? Jay Monahan, the 33-year-old Deutsche Bank tournament director, offered up a trifecta of the Patriots, Jimmy Buffett, and Fenway Park.

Beginning tomorrow, Gillette Stadium will serve as a car-park for spectators, but a significant segment of the tournament field will be in Foxboro for the Patriots' pre-season finale against the Bears tonight. Musically-inclined golfers will be provided with tickets for Buffett's concert at Norton's Tweeter Centre on Saturday night. Monahan also wangled 36 pairs of tickets for tomorrow night's sold-out Red Sox game against the New York Yankees.

We couldn't resist asking Monahan if any golfers had committed to the tournament *because* they got tickets for the baseball game thrown in?"

"Absolutely," he said, but we suspect Darren Clarke wasn't one of them.
August 28, 2003

Tiger's latest driver woes prove most embarrassing

NORTON MASSACHUSETTS

Tiger Woods may, like the rest of us, be guilty of transgressing some of the original sins, but sloth, indolence, and misogyny are probably not among them, which is why Lisa McGonigle's version of *The Lady and The Tiger* seemed somewhat odoriferous.

Ms McGonigle is a thirtysomething lady from Stoneham, Massachusetts, and earlier in the summer she signed on as a volunteer for the inaugural Deutsche Bank Championship at TPC Boston which concluded this past Monday.

Shortly before the tournament she learned to her delight that the task to which she had been assigned would involve first-hand contact with the 156 players in the field: she had been nominated to drive one of the buggies shuttling golfers from green to tee over the first two rounds.

It is interesting to note here that the PGA Tour, having come down on the wrong side of the Casey Martin issue a few years ago, found itself in the position of *requiring* players to use motorized transportation during a round. Even without 25,000 daily spectators clogging the routes, the layout of the new Arnold Palmer-designed course left some pretty hefty hikes from green to tee, particularly over the first two rounds when competitors were starting on both the first and 10th holes, and it was in the interest of pace-of-play that vehicular transport was deemed expedient.

Ms McGonigle says that Friday's first round passed without incident, but that midway through Saturday afternoon, as Tiger, who had started on the back side, came up the 18th fairway, she was ordered to vacate her spot behind the wheel.

"There are extra carts for Tiger's group because he's Tiger," muttered McGonigle. "[Robert] Allenby (who was playing in Woods's game on Saturday) got in the cart next to mine, and then the gentleman in charge told me the man running Tiger's security had said Tiger didn't want a woman driving his cart. It was "a security issue".

Near tears, McGonigle was heard near the press tent muttering about "that spoiled brat" having ruined her tournament, and the next thing anybody knew the tale had made its way, as a news item, into Sunday's edition of the suburban *MetroWest Daily News*.

By Monday, McGonigle had been reassigned to shuttling disabled spectators back and forth between the handicapped seating areas. Whether this was a normal rotation on the duty roster or reflected official disapprobation remains unlearned, but we do know this much: Lisa was on the phone to both major Boston dailies that morning, and by noon, before Woods had even teed off, an interview describing her tale of woe was playing once an hour on the most powerful radio station in New England.

McGonigle's version of events seemed improbable for several reasons. Even if Woods did, as she claimed, have "a phobia about women drivers," experience has taught us he'd have so thoroughly insulated himself from the episode his fingerprints would have been untraceable.

Unlikely as it seemed, it also occurred to us that it was at least possible that there had been a genuine security issue. Although they're not widely publicised, Tiger still does get the occasional death threat, and while those (so far, anyway) can usually be written off as crank calls, if he *had* gotten one on Saturday, somebody might have deemed it prudent to ensure that whoever drove him from the 18th green to the first tee was licensed to carry a gun.

Efforts to confirm McGonigle's version weren't particularly helpful, principally because both tournament officials and Tiger's official entourage were caught completely off-guard by the charge.

"It's the first I've heard of it," said Deutsche Bank Tournament Director Jay Monahan.

"It's ridiculous," said Mark Steinberg, Tiger's personal agent at IMG.

"There are so many things going on out there and Tiger's so focused that he wouldn't know who was driving a cart anyway. It could be me, it could be you, it could be her. He wouldn't even notice. It's completely laughable."

Monahan and Steinberg did huddle together in the press tent while a WBZ radio producer played a tape of the station's interview with McGonigle, in which she claimed Tiger's refusal to ride with her had been relayed to her by one of Woods's security goons, whom she identified as "Chris".

Except Tiger doesn't *have* a security man named Chris.

Woods didn't learn of McGonigle's charge until he finished his final round, a 67 that put him in a seventh-place tie behind tournament winner Adam Scott. "That never happened," said Tiger, who seemed genuinely stunned.

Of course, even had the accusation been true, Woods, Steinberg, and Monahan could reasonably been expected to deny it, which is why the story continued to have some legs despite an apparent absence of corroboration.

It wasn't until we were on our way out of the course on Monday evening that a more likely explanation emerged. According to a Deutsche Bank publicist, an hour or so before Woods finished his first nine holes on Saturday, McGonigle had a minor mishap in which she grazed a tree on her return trip from the first tee. There was no damage to either cart or driver, but it did occur to those in charge of the player shuttle service that, given the human swarm flocking about Woods's every movement, hitting a tree would be the least of the problems if Lisa strayed from the cart path again.

"Maybe," it was suggested, "we should get somebody else to drive Tiger."

We can't swear this is what happened, but, the supposition is, it's at least possible that one of her fellow volunteers tried to spare McGonigle's feelings by describing it as a "security issue" instead of telling her the truth, which is that they didn't trust her driving the cart through a mob of potential litigants, but in the end it seemed to matter little. As night fell across Massachusetts, her interview blaming Tiger Woods was still playing on the radio.

September 04, 2003

Bamby the gamekeeper sics the dogs on Michelle

In 1925, at the Worcester Country Club, Bobby Jones famously cost himself a chance to win the US Open with a self-imposed penalty when he saw his ball move in the rough after he had addressed it.

The movement was almost imperceptible, and no one else had seen the infraction. Commended for his honesty, Jones replied: "You might as well praise a man for not robbing a bank."

Following a rain delay in Jakarta last March, Colin Montgomerie clearly improved what had been an awkward stance with what was later shown to have been an illegal drop, but escaped prosecution on the grounds that his actions had been blessed by an on-site rules official.

Last Sunday, in Palm Desert, California, young Michelle Wie briefly believed she had finished fourth in her first professional outing, but she was subsequently disqualified from the Samsung World Championship for having taken an illegal drop the previous afternoon.

Beyond the fact that the eyes of the golfing world were riveted on the Hawaiian teenager, the episode became all the more noteworthy because it wasn't a fellow competitor or even a spectator who ratted Wie out to the rules committee. It was a sportswriter.

The journalist's credo holds that one is supposed to report the news, not make it, but then Michael Bamberger isn't your ordinary journalist. In golfing matters he is uniquely qualified, having spent a year as a caddie on the European Tour (primarily on the bag of the eccentric vagabond American pro Peter Teravainen), an experience he would later chronicle in a terrific book, *To the Linksland*.

Bamberger had been assigned to follow Wie throughout last weekend's proceedings at Bighorn, and as a result he was less than six feet away when the offence occurred.

The Panahou High School honour student had turned 16 on the previous Tuesday, and had celebrated her eligibility for a driving licence by renouncing her amateur status, a decision which immediately earned her upwards of $10 million in endorsement deals.

227

She battled with the leaders throughout the tournament, but the episode on the seventh hole in the penultimate round proved her undoing. She hooked her drive into a bush and, after announcing to playing partner Grace Park that she was declaring the ball unplayable, took a penalty drop, albeit one Bamberger reckoned to have been "a full pace" nearer to the hole.

Bamberger said he didn't believe Wie had intentionally cheated.

"I just think she was being hasty," he said, noting that her group was already in danger of being put on the clock for slow play.

At the time Bamberger was still wearing his reporter's hat, so he kept his counsel and waited to approach Wie privately after her round. She expressed confidence that her drop had been within the rules, but the scribe wasn't so sure. During Sunday's play he mentioned the matter to a member of the rules committee, who agreed to review the matter with Wie.

Over the past decade there have been numerous instances of television viewers telephoning in to report rules infractions, and the usual practice is for tournament officials to review the television footage.

LPGA rules official Robert O Smith admitted afterward that had he had to make a decision based on the videotape, the evidence would not have been sufficiently conclusive to make a ruling, but after Wie finished her round and signed her score-card, he invited her and caddie Greg Johnston to accompany him to the scene of the crime. Once they showed him where the ball had initially been and whence she had played her next shot, it became apparent that the drop had been at least "12 to 15 inches" nearer to the hole, and hence illegal.

Had Wie assessed herself an additional two strokes for the infraction before signing her card on Saturday, she'd have cost herself some money, but she wouldn't have been disqualified, but by signing for a score to which she was not entitled, she got the boot for violating Rule 6, making her first professional outing one she is unlikely to forget.

Despite the subsequent outcry, this is hardly the first time a sportswriter has sicced the rules dogs on a player after spotting a violation. (I've done it myself on at least two occasions, with Vijay Singh the perceived culprit both times, but the officials in question proved as accommodating to the player as the folks in Jakarta were to Monty.)

"Adherence to the rules is the underlying value of the game," said Bamberger. "To stand in silence when you see an infraction is an infraction itself."

I'm not sure I'd want to sound that high and mighty, but if he thinks he has spotted a rule being bent, a reporter at the very least has a clear obligation to his readers to find out *why* the player was allowed to get away with it.

Although she was in tears afterward, Wie didn't blame Bamberger for exposing her mistake, and admitted that she should have covered her backside.

"I learned my lesson," she said. "Whether it's three inches or a hundred yards, I'm going to call a rules official every single time."

And when he ran into the scribe in the press tent after his daughter's disqualification, BJ Wie, the player's father, offered his hand and said, simply, "Good job, Michael."

The one person in the Wie party who did fault Bamberger was her caddie. In a week in which her net wealth had increased by $10 million, Wie probably wouldn't miss the $53,126 fourth-place money, but Johnston, out five grand, had to be physically restrained from coming after the reporter.

It was a reaction that Bamby, the former caddie, understood all too well.
October 20, 2005

Wie's way of getting around inane rule

I guess the first thing we all need to remember is that Michelle Wie is 17. We don't let 17-year-olds vote, we don't let them drink, and in some states we don't even let them drive, but we can send them out to play golf with hundreds of thousands of dollars at stake and expect them to behave like adults.

In a more perfect world, Ms Wie would have been back in Hawaii last week, kicking ass in her final week as the captain of her high school golf team and contemplating what she planned to do with the rest of her life after graduation.

But she wasn't. She was in South Carolina, playing in an LPGA event called the Ginn Tribute, and not for the first time she incurred righteous indignation from several competitors because once again she appeared to be flaunting the rules.

We have previously documented Wie's tendency to play fast and loose with the Rules of Golf, and at the Ginn she would seem to have done it again, turning a simple decision over an unplayable lie into a family conference that verged terribly close to violating the proscription on outside advice.

On the par-three fourth at River Towne Country Club, Wie's misdirected tee shot sailed wide to the right of the green and disappeared among some trees. A search party that included Wie, her caddie, David Clark, her parents, and several well-meaning volunteers searched for the ball. When it was found, it was clearly unplayable, leaving Wie to contemplate her options.

When her father, B.J. Wie, suggested going back to the tee, Clark, the caddie, appeared to demur. "That would be three off the tee," he pointed out, but in short order Wie marched back from whence she had come, and hit another tee shot. This one also struck a tree, but at least she could hit it again. She chipped onto the green and took two putts for a triple-bogey six.

Watching in the press tent while this little adventure took place was Wie's agent,

Greg Nared. Although he was not part of the discussion, he overheard someone mention that Wie's big number placed her in some jeopardy of reaching the magic figure of 88.

It seems the LPGA has this bone-headed rule that any non-tour member carding 88 or worse in an official event is automatically excluded from participating in LPGA-sanctioned tournaments for the rest of the year.

Since Wie is not 18, she is not a member, and were she to be barred for the rest of 2007, she would no longer be able to play on sponsors' exemptions — at least on the ladies' tour. (Her status in men's tournaments would not have been affected, but then Wie has never made a cut in a PGA event.)

Nared, in any case, went rushing out to the course, and caught up with Wie as she finished the 16th hole. Next thing anyone knew, Wie had hopped into a golf cart with her agent and was driven back to the clubhouse, where it was announced she had withdrawn because she had "tweaked" her wrist. Up until that moment neither of her playing partners had noticed any sign of this infirmity.

Since Wie was 14 over par at the time and a bogey-bogey finish that would have left her at 88 was not at all inconceivable, the timing of the wrist injury did seem to be more than a happy coincidence.

The severity of the injury did not prevent Wie from showing up for the LPGA Championship, which commences in Maryland today. There, she produced yet another firestorm when at least one of her playing partners in a pro-am event two days ago complained that she had all but ignored the members of her team, each of whom had shelled out $5,000 for the privilege of playing with her.

Tour officials did not penalise Wie over the question of advice, ruling her father had merely offered one of the options available under the rules governing an unplayable lie. The fact remains: her caddie is allowed to transmit advice. Her father is not.

Since there is no way of determining the severity of her injury, there was no inquiry into her seemingly precipitate withdrawal from the Ginn, but some of her fellow competitors appear less than persuaded.

"I don't know the situation, if it's injury or whatever," said Annika Sorenstam two days ago. "I just feel there's a little bit of lack of respect and class just to leave a tournament like that and then come out and practice here."

And while Wie was spoken to about her decorum during Tuesday's pro-am, if any action was taken it was not publicly revealed.

Although they all occurred in the space of five days, the three incidents should be approached separately.

In the first instance, while it's difficult to blame Wie for her father's interference, she should have paid the price and been assessed a two-stroke penalty for accepting outside advice. This isn't the first time B.J. Wie has been guilty of sticking his nose where it doesn't belong, and the LPGA might be well within its rights to ban him from the course.

In the second case, while I don't believe for a second Wie couldn't have completed her round, the regulation she was circumventing is such a stupid and arbitrary rule it's difficult to blame her.

The automatic ban on anyone shooting 88 or higher, for instance, makes no allowance for weather conditions. What if the LPGA pros had to play in conditions like those that visited Muirfield during the third round of the British Open five years ago? On that day, remember, Tiger Woods, Colin Montgomerie, Lee Janzen and David Toms, who caught the worst of the weather, couldn't break 80.

And the last infraction? We don't condone rudeness, but we've got to assume that these people have teenaged children of their own and hence should not have been surprised. Anyone who goes out for a round of golf expecting to pal around with a 17-year-old deserves exactly what he gets.

June 07, 2007

ONE EYED HORSES, NINE-TOED WRESTLERS, AND OTHER BOOBS

The Best There Ever Was: Michael Jordan, number 23 of the Chicago Bulls.

Jordan writes the perfect scenario

Under ordinary circumstances, a team winning its third consecutive National Basketball Association championship would be a cause for widespread celebration, but in Chicago (and indeed, throughout the nation) the joy has been muted in the five days since Michael Jordan's Bulls accomplished that feat.

Rather, the refrain has been a gloomy *Gotterdammerung*. The Chicago team's fans find themselves lamenting with some trepidation the departure of the Phil Jackson, the coach who assembled and presided over this dynasty, the possible retirement of Jordan, and the almost-certain break-up of a team which has won six titles in the past eight years.

For the NBA the outlook is even more foreboding. Although the league has stuffed its coffers with marketing money during the Jordan era, its contract with its players expires on July 1st, and a fiscally-inspired lockout looms. This prospect has already imperiled the World Championships scheduled for Greece later this summer, and could lead to NBA players being banned from the 2000 Olympics in Sydney. But it pales in comparison to the image problem the NBA could face were it to abruptly find itself bereft of its standard-bearer.

For the better part of 10 years, Michael Jordan's has been the public face of the NBA. Beyond his undeniable greatness with a basketball in his hands, Jordan is a handsome, articulate, and witty fellow whose appeal transcends generational and racial lines.

Jordan has also been the star whose brightness has eclipsed many of the league's more unseemly moments. Earlier this season, for instance, the Golden State Warriors' Latrell Sprewell attempted to strangle his coach, P J Carlesimo. He was booted off the team and his contract was terminated, but his appeal resulted in a court reducing his suspension to one year and re-instituting his contract, beginning next season.

A *Sports Illustrated* expose two months ago revealed that NBA players, whose racial make-up is predominantly black and whose average salary is well over $1 million a year, also average approximately one illegitimate child apiece. (While some players have none, apparently some have as many as six or seven by as many different women.) Despite their almost obscene wealth, claimed the magazine, many players have been reluctant to acknowledge or support their out-of-wedlock children.

Add to this that not a month goes by without a sex or drugs scandal involving an NBA player, and the horrifying prospect of what NBA commissioner David Stern might confront in a post-Jordan era becomes clearer. Suffice to say, the league will do everything in its power to persuade its marquee player to remain on board.

Jordan earns over $40 million a year, and only a miniscule part of that comes from his Bulls salary. He also has enjoyed lucrative deals with Nike, with cereal companies, fast-food chains, and, of course, his film appearances. (Who could forget *Roger Rabbit*?) After the one-man show he put on in the Bulls' finale, Jordan's future is tied to a more complex puzzle.

Michael Jordan was a great player before Phil Jackson came along, but, by way of illustration, one can vividly recall a play-off game between the Bulls and the Celtics a dozen years ago when Jordan (this was so long ago that he even had hair) scored 63 points in the old Boston Garden. His team, however, lost the game — and lost the series to the Celtics, 3-0.

It was Jackson who convinced Jordan that by sublimating his individual gifts he could become the catalyst for a winning team, and, indeed, that is precisely what happened.

In the process he also became such a larger-than-life public figure that he lost any sense of privacy, a circumstance which after a dozen years drove him from the game. I recall with no great sense of pride that during a period of less than two years around this time I found myself on four different occasions in the midst of a media pack nipping at Jordan's heels. I was not particularly comfortable about any of them.

First there was the "gambling scandal". On a night between play-off games in New York, Jordan had hired a limousine to drive a small party, including himself and his father, to Atlantic City, where they had played blackjack until the wee hours. When the Bulls lost the following evening, the excursion was blamed in some quarters.

The following October, I was in Chicago for the American League baseball play-offs when Jordan stole the limelight by abruptly announcing his retirement from basketball, and I was in Florida the next spring to record the beginnings of Michael's ultimately unsuccessful attempt to carve out a second career as a major league baseball player.

And, just a few months later, I was slogging through the swamplands of the Lumbee Indian territory bordering North and South Carolina after the bizarre murder of Michael Jordan's father. Two teenagers (one an Indian, the other black) were eventually apprehended and convicted of the slaying, but not before speculation had blamed everything from the Ku Klux Klan to his son's gambling debts.

All of which begins to explain Jordan's relatively uneasy relationship with the members of my profession, and why, whether he decides to retire or return, we will probably be among the last to know.

Jackson, the Zen-quoting intellectual coach, has already cleaned out his office. If he doesn't wind up meditating on his Montana ranch, he will be coaching another team. Scottie Pippen, who has played Keith Richards to Jordan's Mick Jagger, who has been underpaid for many years and is, in his own mind at least, under-appreciated, allowed his contract to expire and is probably headed elsewhere.

Dennis Rodman, the eccentric and heavily tattooed defensive and rebounding specialist (and sometime transvestite), is definitely gone as well.

Two weeks ago one would have made it even money that Jordan's competitive instincts would have brought him back in spite of it all, but that was before he wrote such a perfect exit scenario for himself.

In the sixth and deciding game, with Pippen all but immobilised with a back ailment, Jordan took over the game single-handedly. His 45 points, over half his team's total, included the game-winning shot in the 87-86 victory, and, for the sixth time since 1991, Michael Jordan was named the Most Valuable Player of the NBA Finals.

"He's a guy that always comes through in the clutch," said Jackson. "He's a winner and he's proven it so many times over and again. How many times does he have to show us that he's a real-life hero?"
June 19, 1998

Farewell to the best there ever was

The other shoe dropped yesterday. Exactly one week after a settlement ended the National Basketball Association's six-month labour dispute, the game's most visible player, and arguably its best ever, officially announced his retirement.

Michael Jordan's decision was not entirely unexpected. Since the moment he sunk the winning basket to defeat the Utah Jazz in last June's NBA Finals, it had been widely speculated that he would ride off into the sunset on the strength of that dramatic moment.

Jordan, loyal to his union brethren, had turned up at just enough union meetings to keep management guessing, and delayed formalising his retirement until after the lockout so as not to undermine the players' negotiating position.

It was a selfless gesture, albeit one that didn't cost him much, and one that should not have surprised those who recalled Jordan's stance in the 1994-95 baseball strike, one which coincided with his first retirement from the Chicago Bulls.

In October of 1993, only 30 years old and seemingly in his prime, Jordan stunned the basketball world by announcing that he would not be returning to the Bulls, who had won their third consecutive NBA title the previous summer. While he cited the media's obsession with his large gambling losses and the recent murder of his father, James, among his reasons for walking away, mainly, he said, he wanted to spend more time with his family.

Just four months later, Jordan became the most-watched spring-training phenomena in baseball history when he worked out at the Florida facility of the Chicago White Sox, with whom he had signed in his search for a new challenge.

Playing baseball at the major league level is the aspiration of every American boy, even Michael Jordan, although he had not played the sport since high school.

Having been among the media throng charged with chronicling Jordan's exploits that spring, I can attest that, while he did not display major league abilities then, had he been a callow 18-year-old rookie instead of a 30-year-old one, not a man alive could have safely bet against his eventually reaching that plateau.

He spent the 1994 season attempting to learn to hit the curve ball for the White Sox minor league affiliate in Birmingham, batting a meagre .202 and striking out an average of once every four at-bats.

Any other thirty-something player would have been given his outright release after a year like that, but management had other plans for Jordan: he could have gone straight to the major leagues the following spring in return for being the owners' poster boy in a running labour dispute.

The major league Players' Association had gone on strike in August of 1994, killing off that year's World Series, and the rancour had lasted throughout the winter. The baseball owners prepared to open the season using rosters of "replacement" players, and there was no shortage of aspiring baseballers willing to sacrifice their principles for one taste of playing at the major league level.

Jordan might not have given the scab players credibility, but he would have ensured packed houses wherever the ersatz White Sox played. Having been assured of a chance to fulfil his dream by playing in the big leagues, he instead walked away again, refusing to betray the major leaguer players — who had not, it should be noted, exactly welcomed him with open arms when he arrived in Sarasota the previous spring.

Say what you will about him, Michael Jordan is and was a stand-up guy. He proved it then and he demonstrated it again with the exercise which concluded yesterday.

Jordan rejoined the Bulls that March, but his basketball was a bit rusty and Chicago were eliminated in the 1995 Eastern semi-finals. They have won every year since. In fact, beginning with the 1990-91 season, Chicago have won six of the last eight NBA titles. The only two they *didn't* win in this decade were between 1993 and 1995 — the two years Jordan didn't play a full season. He also won a national collegiate title at North Carolina and two Olympic gold medals — in 1982 as an amateur, and as a member of the 1992 "Dream Team" in Barcelona when professionals were allowed to compete for the first time.

His career scoring average of 31.5 points per game is the highest in NBA history. Jordan is a 12-time All-Star, 10-time scoring champion and five-time Most Valuable Player. He was the 1985 Rookie of the Year, even though he had yet to mould himself into a great complete player. I can recall watching him — and this was so long ago that he had hair — score 63 points against the Boston Celtics in a 1986 play-off game, one which the Bulls lost, for not entirely unrelated reasons. Just two years later, Jordan was voted the NBA's Defensive Player of the Year.

A statue of Jordan, erected outside Chicago's United Center during his 1994-95 baseball hiatus, bears the inscription:

The Best There Ever Was, The Best There Ever Will Be

Jordan also changed America's perception of black athletes as commercial spokesmen. He flogged everything: breakfast cereal, long-distance service, hamburgers, soft drinks, hot dogs, batteries, underwear, and, especially, athletic footwear. He also starred in a movie, *Space Jam*, with Bugs Bunny, Daffy Duck and Bob Hoskins.

He was criticised for his excessive losses at blackjack tables in casinos around the country, although God knows he could afford it — Jordan's worth is estimated at $500 million — and was hardly a likely target for gamblers looking to squeeze a player. In 1997 alone, he earned $78 million — $30 million in basketball salary and $48 million in endorsements. Assuredly, he had his blind spots, and most of them occurred in the proximity of a golf course, where Jordan found himself among that all-too-familiar strain of inveterate golfer — the eight-handicapper who, for reasons having more to do with vanity than ability, insists on playing to a three. It is a bit of self-delusion that has cost him many thousands of dollars over the years.

Once, during a practice session preceding a 1993 play-off game at Madison Square Garden, we were in the process of negotiating a *mano-a-mano* match as we watched his team-mates on the floor.

"What's your handicap?" asked Jordan. That ever-bemused smile on his face, his eyes swung around to meet mine without his ever moving his head.

Without missing a beat I replied: "I only have one eye."

The next day the *Post* ran an expose chronicling an all-night gambling junket he and his father had made to Atlantic City the night before a play-off game. Michael was abruptly at war with the press again, and we never did play our match.
January 14, 1999

Cinema based on a corrupt premise

Among the sheaf of letters I collected from my office mailbox the other day, one in particular caught my attention. It was addressed to "George (The Racist) Kimball."

The writer, who did not sign his name, objected to the inclusion of O J Simpson (in the Number One spot) on a "Football Hall of Shame" I had been asked to compile for another of those turn-of-the-century lists.

"Why doesn't anyone want to consider that the gigallo (*sic*) was the primary

Rubin (Hurricane) Carter: Dylan doesn't sing 'that' song anymore.

target and that Nickole (sic) just happened to be in the wrong place," wonders the unsigned note. The note also included the writer's conclusion, to wit: ". . . that you're a racist bastard."

As I had taken pains to point out in the text to which the anonymous letter-writer objected, O J actually came away with a split decision in two trials resulting from the 1994 double homicide. He was acquitted in a murder trial characterised by police bungling and an indifferent prosecution, but found responsible for taking two lives in a subsequent wrongful death suit brought in civil court.

Although a small lunatic fringe insists on clinging to the notion that Simpson was a wrongfully-accused victim of society, it is difficult to imagine that, say, 30 years from now a Hollywood director will re-open the case by making a film predicated on the bald-faced assertion that O J was *innocent*.

Yet a similarly unlikely scenario will begin playing itself out in theatres across the country tomorrow, when Norman Jewison's widely-acclaimed *The Hurricane* opens for nationwide release.

The film, purportedly based on the life and times of one-time middleweight contender Rubin (Hurricane) Carter, actually opened at selected theatres on December 29th, in order to make it eligible for the 1999 Academy Awards.

In 1966, Hurricane Carter, a good-but-not-great middleweight who had already spent more than half of his life behind bars, was accused along with an accomplice, John Artis, of an after-hours triple-murder in a saloon in Paterson, New Jersey. The pair were tried and found guilty. Despite having his cause embraced by the liberal establishment, Carter would spend the next two decades in prison. He never fought again.

The Hurricane, alas, is very good theatre but very bad history, as one might have anticipated from a movie which notes in its credits "based on the novels *(sic) Lazarus and the Hurricane* by Sam Chaiton and Terry Swinton, *The 16th Round* by Rubin "Hurricane" Carter, and the 1970s ballad by Bob Dylan entitled *The Hurricane*."

Almost a quarter-century later, I can recall my own reaction after a disk-jockey friend played me an advance copy of Dylan's 1976 protest ballad. Two phrases in particular stuck in my craw. First, Dylan's bland assertion that Carter had been imprisoned "for something that he never done." And second, the song's repeated refrain that Carter *"could have been the champion of the world."*

There is no doubt that both the police and the prosecutors cut many corners in their zeal to convict Carter and Artis, but the contention that it was an outright frame-up rests on shaky ground indeed.

However, far from being deprived of a title shot, Carter got his in 1964. This fight, conveniently ignored by Dylan, is depicted in the film. In Jewison's version The Hurricane beats Joey Giardello to a bloody pulp, but the champion, despite literally never laying a glove on Carter, is awarded the decision on the scorecards of all three judges, who must, the viewer is left to believe, have been motivated by the same bitter racism of the New Jersey police.

Here's the problem I have with this attempt at revisionist history: I don't know for a fact whether Rubin Carter pulled the trigger in the Lafayette Grill, but neither does Bob Dylan or Norman Jewison.

Although Carter is shown being convicted haphazardly by an all-white jury, in fact there were two separate trials, and he was found guilty both times — the second by a racially-mixed jury. Although his arrest is depicted as a case of mistaken identity, the film fails to note that a shotgun and a bullet were recovered from the car in which Carter and Artis were driving shortly after the murder.

More egregiously still, the film invents a malevolent, police detective named "Della Pesca" who devotes his entire life to hounding Carter into prison at every turn, from the age of 11 onward. Della Pesca never existed.

Put it this way: every time Carter was tried on the merits of the murder case, he was found guilty. When the conviction was finally thrown out in 1985 by a federal judge (grimly portrayed by Rod Steiger in the film), it was because the prosecution had "fatally infected the trial" by basely appealing to racism as a motive and by withholding evidence. In other words, not even the judge who sprung them claimed that Carter and Artis were innocent, but rather that their trial had been indisputably unfair.

Left unrecorded are the facts that, once freed, Carter was shortly arrested and charged with assaulting Lisa Peters, the female member of the arcane Canadian commune which had worked for his release, or that Bob Dylan became so embarrassed once Carter's true character emerged that he has refused to perform *The Hurricane* for the past 20 years.

As the credits roll at the film's conclusion, Jewison, in his haste to bring viewers up to date, informs the audience that "the real killers have never been caught."

Ironically, the film's denouement is a grainy clip of a 1994 ceremony in which the real Rubin Carter is shown being presented with a "championship belt" by the real Jose Sulaiman, the president-for-life of the World Boxing Council. The film claims that this was the first time someone who had not won his title in the ring had been thus honoured. (Which is not true; Sulaiman dispenses WBC belts the way some men hand out business cards.)

That Sulaiman is widely regarded as a petty despot who exemplifies all that is wrong with the corrupt world of boxing never seems to have occurred to the director. That he interprets Sulaiman's approval as a triumph of vindication for Rubin Carter illustrates how little of the real world of boxing he understands. Or of the real world, period, for that matter.

January 06, 2000

Storm in a D-cup

For the past couple of weeks they have been the subject of a debate and controversy that has dominated America's sports pages. The baseball season may be headed into its stretch run, the National Football League opened play last weekend, and the Sydney Games are almost upon us, but all anybody seems to want to talk about is Jenny Thompson's tits.

I should point out right now that I haven't actually seen them.

Neither have any of *Sports Illustrated's* readers, although legions of them appear to have become exercised about the matter. As far as I can determine, the only ones who have seen Jenny's boobs are Heinz Kluetmeier, the veteran photographer who took the picture in question, and Jenny Thompson's boyfriend, who was there when Kluetmeier shot it.

Three weeks ago, just before the US Olympic swimming trials, Thompson surprised everyone by appearing in her bathing suit, sans top, in a colour photograph in the pages of America's premier sports magazine. The photograph depicts her confidently smiling at the camera.

Her breasts are modestly covered by her clenched fists, and if anything, the pose suggests pugnacious challenge, as *Sports Illustrated* columnist Rick Reilly noted a few weeks later, something along the lines of *"Want to wrestle? I'll win."*

The publication of Thompson's topless photograph resulted, predictably, in the usual scores of subscription cancellations, and both Thompson and the magazine have been under attack since from a bizarre coalition of the Christian right and the neo-feminists, the former describing the shot as "soft-core pornography" and the latter categorising it as "exploitative" of women.

It should be noted here that Jenny Thompson hardly qualifies as a bimbo. She is 27, a Stanford graduate from Massachusetts and owns five Olympic Gold Medals. (All of them in swimming relay events; she will be looking to add to her collection this month in Australia.) She has already been accepted to Columbia University's medical school, and plans to be doctor once her competitive career has ended.

Ironically, in the photograph in question, Thompson is wearing patriotic-looking red, white, and blue swimsuit bottoms and a pair of bright red boots. In other words, her outfit virtually duplicates what the roly-poly sideshow heavyweight Eric (Butterbean) Esch wears into the ring every time he fights.

You want to talk obscene? I'll flat-out guarantee you this much: Butterbean's boobs are a *lot* bigger than Jenny's.

Moreover, as *Washington Post* columnist Sally Jenkins pointed out in a courageous defence of Thompson, even though it appeared in a magazine which publishes an annual nipple-fest with each February's laughably-entitled Swimsuit Issue, "the photograph is utterly harmless — there is not a single, actual, verifi-

Jenny Thompson: not the photograph that caused the fuss.

able nipple in sight.

"The self-appointed moralists and feminist guardians completely miss the point, and misread the photograph," said Jenkins. "The picture isn't offensive. It may even be an important image for this reason: Thompson isn't showing off her breasts. She is showing off her muscles. It's a crucial distinction."

In fact — and again, since we can't see them, this would be purely conjecture — Thompson's boobs would appear to be among her least-developed features. That each of them can be concealed by a small fist suggests that she is probably not a *Playboy* centerfold candidate.

Since the publication of the photograph, some of the nation's top sports columnists have been ready to rip one another's throats out. Jenkins and Reilly vigorously defended Thompson's pose. Linda Robertson of the *Miami Herald* not only wants to send Thompson to her room, but wants to send Jenkins and Reilly with her. George Vecsey of the *New York Times* also addressed the subject last Sunday, but couldn't seem to make up his own mind about where he stood.

"I read every word of the excellent article, liked Thompson a lot, and enjoyed the photo of her confidence, her muscles, her posture, her athleticism," wrote Vecsey. "Anybody who says her pose was not partly about sex is being hypocritical, but then again, so am I, because I looked more than once before I asked 'Gee, I wonder if she should be doing this'?"

"Wow," wrote Reilly. "Jenny Thompson has a nice pair, doesn't she? Massive. Firm. Perfectly shaped. "Her thighs, I mean."

"Too bad she took the top off and put the boots on," complained Robertson in the *Miami Herald*, "because the muscles are secondary to the covered breasts. The strategically placed hands and the incongruous footwear distract from the magnificent muscles. Sadly, Thompson's confident smile barely gets noticed."

"Thompson," opined Robertson, "looks as silly and as exploited as the Miss America contestants who parade around in swimsuits and high heels with fake smiles."

Donna LoPiano, the president of the Women's Sports Foundation, complained in a letter Jenkins forwarded to me that "Sports Illustrated seldom covers women for their athletic exploits and frequently portrays women as sex objects rather than athletes," coverage LoPiano deemed "objectionable and demeaning to female athletes."

Interestingly, both Robertson and LoPiano (Jenkins collectively describes them as the "Old Girl Network," while Reilly calls them "grumpy women" who "have their girdles in a wad") pointedly suggest that the *Sports Illustrated* pose depicts the partially-clad swimmer's "genitalia" — even though 14 years ago another group of feminists, this one seeking the right to bathe topless at a local beach, went to court and won a hard-fought battle when an Appeals Court judge ruled that breasts do *not* constitute genitalia.

And again, what's the big deal? You can't see them anyway. "It's not a sexual picture at all," Kluetmeier, the photographer, told Sally Jenkins. "It was not about taking her clothes off. She's the perfect Olympian, and the Greeks and the Romans would have fought to sculpt her. People who interpret it any other way have an agenda."

Thompson herself seems surprised by the furor all of this has generated.

"I wasn't naked," she recalled before departing for Australia this week. "I was fully covered, and I don't see anything wrong with what I did.

"It was an expression and a celebration of strength and the beauty of muscles. It was more about, 'look at how strong my body is,' and not 'look at me, I'm a sex symbol or sex object'," Thompson said. "I wasn't giving a seductive look in the pose. It was more 'Here I am, this is me, and I'm going to the Olympics'."

Fittingly, the last word on the subject should go to the subject's Mom. The response of Jenny Thompson's mother Margrid to the controversy?

"I think everyone should lighten up."
September 07, 2000

April Fools hit by sucker punch

Seventeen years ago this week, readers of *Sports Illustrated* were treated to the astonishing story of Sidd Finch, an English-born, French horn-playing mystic who, having being schooled in a Tibetan monastery, turned up at the New York Mets' Florida training camp that spring, asking for a try-out as a pitcher.

Finch's fastball was clocked at a world-record 168 m.p.h, but less than a week after his arrival, Sidd (short for Siddartha) had disappeared, having given up the sport because he was unable to accept baseball concepts which contravened his Tantric principles — among other things, he found offensive the concept of "stealing" a base.

That Finch's saga was recorded by the incorrigible humorist George Plimpton, coupled with the fact it appeared in an issue dated April 1st, should have been a dead giveaway, but the magazine received over 2,000 Sidd Finch letters the week after the story was published. For months afterward the switchboards of both *Sports Illustrated* and the Mets were kept busy fielding phone calls from irate fans demanding the team track down Sidd Finch and sign him at any cost.

Over the years the Sidd Finch story assumed almost legendary proportions as the grandaddy of all April Fool's Day sporting hoaxes. Surely someone must have wondered in the meantime what might have happened had it taken place in the so-called "information age," and over the past few days we finally got a chance to find out. On Monday morning Charles Jay, whose *TotalAction Fight Page* serves as a clearinghouse linking worldwide boxing reports of the day, published an "exclusive" revealing, barely a week after it had been announced, that the June 8th Lennox Lewis-Mike Tyson fight in Memphis was off.

Tyson, revealed Jay, had pulled out of the bout after learning that once his debts had been paid from his promised $17.5 million purse he would be fighting Lewis virtually for free.

Now, in terms of plausibility, Tyson baulking at the fight under these conditions was no more preposterous than, say, the morning's other big news, which was that the Queen Mother had passed away at 101, and my first reaction was to scour the wires to see how other newspapers might have been playing the story.

A more careful reader of Jay's account would probably have noticed the first letter of each paragraph combined to spell out A-P-R-I-L F-O-O-L, and there were other clues. In "confirming" the dissolution of the fight, for instance, it quoted a spokeswoman at the Pyramid in Memphis called "Rosie Ruiz," Rosie Ruiz having been the name of the notorious fraud who cheated her way to the gold medal in the 1980 Boston Marathon after completing most of the route via subway.

Another cited source was an alleged press aide to Memphis Mayor Willie Herenton named "Irving Clifford" (Clifford Irving was the author of a biography of Howard Hughes which later proved to be a hoax), while another was "Alan Smithee," that being the recognized *nom de plume* employed when a Hollywood director or screenwriter deems a product so unsatisfactory he refuses to have his name associated with it.

If those clues weren't sufficient, Jay quoted former University of Memphis basketball coach Larry Finch ("who, along with his brother Sidney and three other former Memphis players are investors in the group" backing Lewis-Tyson) as saying: "You can't believe everything you hear, everything you read. We just didn't pay close enough attention. It's like they write things in code. Things have been moving at 168 m.p.h., but does anybody even know what day it is?" And 168 m.p.h., remember, was the velocity of Sidd Finch's fastball.

To their credit, most American newspapers held off on breaking the "story," though at least one was taken in. Spotting the item on Jay's website, *Las Vegas Review-Journal* columnist Joe Hawk telephoned his office asking them to clear space on the front page of the sports section for a story of major importance. Hawk's breathless revelation that Lewis-Tyson was off made it into 1,300 newspapers before Jay explained the hoax to *Review-Journal* boxing writer Kevin Iole.

Lewis' trainer Emanuel Steward, in Las Vegas for the US Amateur Boxing Championships, apparently read Hawk's story and was immediately on the phone to the heavyweight champion, demanding to know why he hadn't been informed the fight had been cancelled. (A baffled Lewis replied he didn't know any more about it than Steward did.)

If most US newspapers exercised more restraint than the *Review-Journal*, Total Action's immediate competitors on the Internet appear to have been more gullible. Fightnews.com, did its best to discredit Jay's "exclusive" while clearly never recognising it as a hoax. Fightnews editor Scott "Flattop" Pope quoted an anonymous source within the Tyson camp, refuting Iron Mike's alleged abdication from the big fight, while proudly trumpeting the news that in response to Pope's query, Pyramid representatives had denied even having a spokeswoman named Rosie Ruiz.

In Tuesday's editions, the Las Vegas newspaper felt constrained to publish a box containing an apologetic retraction: "A story appearing on page 1C in a small number of Monday's editions of the *Review-Journal* was an April Fools' Day hoax and incorrect. The Lennox Lewis-Mike Tyson world heavyweight championship fight, scheduled June 8th in Memphis, Tenn., has not been postponed or cancelled."

Jay also received an irate letter from Joe Hawk, complaining that his "irresponsible shenanigans" had led to the NCAA basketball tournament, the opening of Major League baseball's season, and hometowner Andre Agassi's winning his "700th career tournament" (sic) being knocked off the front page of the *Review-Journal*.

Perhaps because he had played it so close to the line with his prank, Jay was briefly concerned when he received an e-mail from Pat English, the lawyer for Main Events, the lead promoter of the Lewis-Tyson fight, accusing him of stooping to a new low in journalism and threatening legal action over lost ticket sales. It was only when Jay carefully re-read the missive from English that he realised the first letter of each paragraph also spelled out A-P-R-I-L F-O-O-L-S.

April 04, 2002

University resorts to naming and shaming

Ten years ago, just before Super Bowl XXVI in Minneapolis, I was summoned to a press briefing by the Native American activist Clyde Bellecourt. Mr Bellecourt was the founder of the American Indian Movement (AIM), whose headquarters is in the Minnesota city which was staging the 1992 NFL championship game between the Buffalo Bills and the Washington Redskins.

It should hardly come as a shock that progressive-minded Native Americans find the latter nickname offensive.

"How would people in Washington like it," Bellecourt asked me that day, "if they named a team 'the Washington Niggers'?"

Most people ignored the AIM's informational pickets at that Super Bowl, but Bellecourt's point was well taken.

Although the ownerships of the Redskins and the Kansas City Chiefs, the Atlanta Braves and the Cleveland Indians, to name a few, resolutely insist the sobriquets are respectful and not derogatory, Indians can probably be forgiven if they don't quite see it that way.

Though the team ownership would have people believe the nickname was intended as a tribute, the evolutionary process went like this: when a Boston team joined the NFL back in the 1930s, it shared both its stadium and its nickname with baseball's Boston Braves.

When the football team relocated to Fenway Park — home to the Red Sox — some years later, it became expeditious to lose the Braves handle, but not the logo, so they readily converted to Redskins. Eventually the Redskins moved to Washington and the Braves first to Milwaukee, then to Atlanta.

In their present incarnation, the Braves regularly annoy the Native American population.

At any given Atlanta home game, half the people in the stands are in possession of $5 foam-rubber tomahawks purchased from the concession stands, which they brandish in unison several times a game as the stadium rocks with a Hollywoodesque version of a tribal war chant.

The Notre Dame mascot — sans pipe.

The Braves are owned by the sportsman-*cum*-media tycoon Ted Turner, who was married for some time to the actress and prominent political activist Jane Fonda. After Ms Fonda was caught on camera several years ago performing this ritual along with the other Braves fans, she was taken to task by Bellecourt and his followers, who eventually extracted the promise that Jane would never again perform the Tomahawk Chop.

The Cleveland baseball team's mascot, "Chief Nok-a-Homa," is a grotesque caricature of a happily stupid (or, possibly, stupidly happy) Native American.

This is a point to which Irish, or at least Irish-American, people should be particularly sensitive.

Possibly the best-known mascot in America is the University of Notre Dame's leprechaun. Intended to depict the school's nickname "The Fighting Irish," the Notre Dame mascot is a pugnacious, green-clad, pipe-smoking little pipsqueak apparently spoiling for a fight with anyone who crosses his path.

Several years ago I chanced to interview the Notre Dame leprechaun, who turned out to be a student of Polish extraction. And this past football season, Notre Dame, in defiance of all logic, had an African-American leprechaun.

And while it might be the most prominent, Notre Dame's isn't even the most offensive leprechaun mascot in the land, as a visit to the Fleet Center for any Boston Celtics home game would quickly attest.

Mike Barnicle, the former Boston Globe columnist, once described "Lucky," the Celtics' mascot, as "nothing more than a cheap shot at Irish-Americans.

"The Celtic mascot looks like someone you might see hanging around the bus station begging for nips," wrote Barnicle. "They might as well have the little jerk throwing up on his shoes or falling down Broadway during the annual St Patrick's parade."

Anyway, back to the noble savages. Professional sports franchises have far too much money tied up in team-logoed merchandise to even consider bowing to the objections of Native Americans on this point, but over the past few decades a few of the more progressive colleges have been struck by pangs of conscience. The University of Massachusetts, who were the Redmen when my father played football there 60 years ago, are now the Minutemen. Dartmouth and Stanford, both once called the Indians, have been transformed, respectively, into the Green Wave and The Cardinals.

At high school level, a few states have even enacted legislation to banish the racial stereotypes. In North Carolina, for instance, Indian mascots are supposed to be eliminated from public schools by the end of next year, but that proactive measure represents the exception rather than the rule.

Enter "The Fightin' Whities". For some months the Native American community at the University of Northern Colorado in Greeley had vainly protested the fact that Eaton High School in that town calls its sports teams the "Fightin' Reds".

Rebuffed in their efforts to bring about peaceable change, the Indians went on the warpath and retorted in kind.

Last week an intramural basketball team at the university unveiled its new nickname and mascot. Although all of the Northern Colorado players in question are Native Americans, they have decided to call themselves the Fightin' Whites. Their mascot — presumably available on non-game days for saloon openings, Bar Mitvahs, and St Patrick's Day parades — is a rotund, pasty-faced, middle-aged Caucasian spouting the team motto, *"Everythang's gonna be all right!"*

"The point is, how does it feel to be made fun of? Let's do something that will let people see the other side of what it's like to be a mascot," explained Solomon Little Owl, the university's director of Native American services who came up with the Fightin' Whities idea.

"I am really offended by this mascot issue, and I hope the people that support the Eaton mascot will be offended by this."

March 14, 2002

When accidents add insult to injury

A bit over a week ago, with appropriate fanfare, *Penthouse* magazine published what were purportedly topless photographs of the Russian tennis player and international ice hockey groupie Anna Kournikova.

Kournikova protested that the photos in question were not of her, a stipulation to which virtually anyone owning a computer would have immediately attested. One of the most widely-circulated photos on the internet was taken of Anna at Wimbledon a few years ago, when, about to receive serve, she leaned so far forward that she fairly spilled out of her tennis dress at the moment the photographer snapped the picture.

And as any teenage boy in America could have told you, if those were Anna's breasts, then the ones in *Penthouse* plainly were not.

A few days after the issue had hit the stands, *Penthouse* was forced to issue an apology. The magazine now faces two lawsuits, one from Kournikova and the other from the clothing heiress to whom the bosoms represented as those of the tennis player actually belonged.

Should Kournikova prevail in court, she will collect considerably more money than she's been earning on the tennis circuit of late, although events in Rome earlier this week indicate that her career may at last be on the upswing.

We don't know if you were paying attention or not, but Kournikova registered her biggest win in years this past Tuesday when Venus Williams defaulted her second-round match in the Italian Open.

Venus, it turned out, had injured her right wrist . . . while picking up her racquet bag.

The injury indisposing Williams will doubtless take its place alongside, say, that of Wade Boggs, the Boston Red Sox third baseman who once wound up on the Disabled List after injuring his back attempting to pull off his cowboy boots in his hotel room.

Come to think of it, I recall a colleague mentioning that the most surprising aspect of that particular injury was that Boggs (later the defendant in a celebrated palimony case) didn't have a companion on hand to remove his boots *for* him.

Roger Craig, the old Brooklyn Dodgers and New York Mets pitcher who later became a successful major league manager, once cut his hand on a bra strap. (And it wasn't even Anna Kournikova's.)

Last fall place-kicker Bill Gramatica knocked himself out of the play-offs when he leaped to celebrate a successful field goal and strained a groin muscle, putting himself in the company of Atlanta Braves catcher Terry Harper, who once separated a shoulder high-fiving a team-mate.

The Braves, in fact, deserve their own subsection in the Stupid Sports Injuries

Hall of Fame.

Pitcher Tom Glavine once broke a rib while vomiting airline food on a team charter flight. Another pitcher, John Smoltz, suffered severe burns when he tried to iron a shirt he was wearing at the time.

I was in the New York Mets' clubhouse the night outfielder Vince Coleman unpacked a new set of irons he had just had delivered. Demonstrating his golf swing, Coleman whacked Doc Gooden, that night's pitcher, in the back, knocking him out of the start.

I was also at Busch Stadium in St Louis the night Coleman was doing pre-game stretching exercises in the infield and didn't notice the approach of the automatic tarpaulin-roller. The dastardly machine rolled right over his leg, putting Coleman, who had stolen 110 bases that year, out of the 1985 National League Championship Series.

Denver Broncos quarterback Brian Griese suffered a concussion last year when he tripped in team-mate Terrell Davis' driveway and knocked himself out. (Cold sober, they claim.) Florida Marlins' second baseman Bret Barberie once missed a game because he accidentally rubbed chili juice into his eyes.

Early in his Seattle Mariners career, Ken Griffey Jr was forced to sit after a game when he put his protective cup on wrong and incurred a pinched testicle.

Glenallen Hill, then an outfielder with the Toronto Blue Jays, wound up on the Disabled List from cuts incurred when he smashed a glass table in his sleep. Hill turned out to have been a closet arachnophobiac: he subsequently explained that he had woken from a dream in which he was being attacked by spiders.

The Baltimore Orioles' Mark Smith injured a hand by sticking it in an air conditioner to see why it wasn't working.

Rickey Henderson, the well-travelled future Hall of Famer now with the Red Sox, missed a game as a member of the Toronto Blue Jays when he contracted frostbite . . . in August.

Irving Fryar, then with the New England Patriots, was injured at half-time of a game in which he wasn't even playing. Inactive for the game, he decided to drive home at half-time, and when he came to a fork in the road decided to go neither left nor right but straight, running into a tree and knocking himself out.

Fryar was also injured during the 1984 NFL play-offs when he cut his hand in a "kitchen accident," which, while true, turned out to only have been part of the story. It subsequently developed that Fryar was indeed in the kitchen when he tried to take a knife away from his wife, who was trying to use it on him.

Which doesn't mean kitchen accidents can't be self-inflicted. At a "Texas Welcome Home" luncheon celebrating the onset of a new season, Rangers outfielder Oddibe McDowell sliced his hand open attempting to butter a dinner roll.

While with the Houston Astros, Nolan Ryan once missed a game when he was

Anna Kournikova : all body parts displayed in *this* photograph *are* authentic.

bitten on his pitching hand by a coyote.

Milwaukee Brewers pitcher Steve Sparks dislocated a shoulder trying to tear a phone book in half, and the Rangers' knuckleball reliever Charlie Hough once broke a finger while shaking hands.

Two years ago Florida pitcher Ricky Bones was placed on the disabled list after he hurt himself changing channels on the television set in the Marlins' clubhouse.

All of which places Venus Williams in good company. Not to make light of her injury, but just imagine what might have happened if, instead of her racquet bag, Venus had tried to lift, say, her wallet.

May 16, 2002

President of baseball Hall of Fame talking Bull

❝ The oddest thing about it," Ron Shelton was saying the other day, "is that baseball, of all sports, has such a strong tradition of dissent. Think about it: In what other game do the fans and players sit back and watch while someone stops to have an argument with the umpire? They go cheek-to-jowl, they each speak their pieces, and eventually the game resumes. I don't know of any other sport that allows that. If you do it in basketball or soccer, you're thrown out of the game," said the Hollywood director. "In hockey, they just start a fight, but in baseball, dissent is a ritualised part of the game."

In a voice-over toward the end of Shelton's 1988 film *Bull Durham*, the actress Susan Sarandon, who plays a cerebral Baseball Annie, quotes the poet Walt Whitman: *"I see great things in baseball. It's our game. The American game. It will repair our losses and be a blessing to us."*

Widely considered the best baseball movie ever made, *Bull Durham* was scheduled to be officially recognised as such this weekend. Months ago the Baseball Hall of Fame had arranged a *Bull Durham* weekend, which was to include a special screening, along with personal appearances by Shelton and actors Kevin Costner, Tim Robbins and Sarandon, and Robert Wuhl.

The Hall of Fame's president, Dale Petroskey, was a deputy press secretary in the administration of Ronald Reagan, and served in similar capacities for a succession of Republican politicians. Sarandon and Robbins have been vocal in their opposition to the administration's foreign policies, and specifically to the war against Iraq.

In short order, the *Bull Durham* weekend was off. By fiat, Petroskey cancelled the event, publicly disinviting the couple in a letter he released to the media before he even bothered sending it to them.

In his letter Petroskey wrote: "The president of the United States, as this nation's democratically elected leader, is constitutionally bound to make decisions he believes are in the best interests of the American people," and "The National Baseball Hall of Fame — and many players and executives in Baseball's family — has honoured the United States and those who defend our freedoms." He went on to lecture Robbins on his "obligation to act and speak responsibly," and voiced his fear that "your very public criticism . . . ultimately could put our troops in even more danger".

Plainly, under the guise of removing politics from the issue, Petroskey was making a heavy-handed political statement of his own. (*"Move over, Hootie,"* said Shelton.)

I should probably point out in addition to directing Robbins, Sarandon, and Costner in *Bull Durham*, Shelton directed me in *Play it to the Bone*. In any case, Ron is a former minor league player, and *Bull Durham* was his rollicking but touching portrayal of life in the bush leagues.

"I was appalled, but not shocked," Shelton told me this week after Petroskey ran *Bull Durham* out of Cooperstown . "But then, I'm appalled at a lot that's going on in this country right now."

"The arrangements for this have been under way for nearly a year," said Shelton. "We were looking at it as a weekend that was going to be without politics, just a celebration of a little movie we made 15 years ago."

So how did Petroskey justify his act of prior restraint? "What we were trying to do was take politics out of this," he claimed. "We didn't want people to espouse their views in a very public place, one way or another. The Hall isn't the place for that."

Oh, Bull.

Even that sentiment would be more credible had Petroskey not leaned on his Republican connections just last year to invite George W Bush's press secretary, Ari Fleischer, to the Hall of Fame to provide his views on "the current political scene," which, of course, included the "War on Terrorism."

Robbins, in any case, responded to the cancellation by firing back a letter of his own.

"I had been unaware that baseball was a Republican sport," noted the actor. "I reject your suggestion that one must be silent in times of war. To suggest my criticism of the president puts the troops in danger is absurd. If people had listened to that twisted logic we'd still be in Vietnam."

Robbins went on to inform the Hall of Fame president: "Your subservience to your friends in the administration is embarrassing to baseball. You belong with the cowards and ideologues in a hall of infamy and shame."

The cancellation, while applauded in conservative circles, provoked outrage. Petroskey was bombarded by over 25,000 letters and e-mails. Roger Kahn, the distinguished baseball author who was to speak at the Hall of Fame later this summer, cancelled his own appearance in protest.

Even Costner, who hadn't finalised his plans to appear at the weekend, was critical of Petroskey's decision, even though he is a dyed-in-the-wool Republican who introduced Bush at the 2000 Republican National Convention.

"I've never talked to him about it," said Shelton, "but I imagine Kevin supports the war. He's basically pretty conservative."

Even Major League Baseball, in a statement, moved to distance itself from Petroskey's act of censorship.

The Hall of Fame president subsequently admitted he botched his handling of the affair, but made no move to correct his error. "With the advantage of hindsight, it is clear I should have handled the matter differently," he wrote on the Hall of Fame website.

"Nobody was going to talk about the war," insisted Shelton, who, though he has been quieter about it, is no more enthusiastic about the Iraq war than Sarandon and Robbins. "I work very hard at not being a celebrity, so I might express myself differently than Tim and Susan. But I share their view — which is, incidentally, the view of most of the rest of the world," he pointed out.

"Still, one's point of view isn't supposed to matter as much as the ability to express it."
April 24, 2003

Useless stud made his exit as an entree

The heart-warming tale of an under-sized, bargain-basement priced colt which captured the fancy of the nation during the times of the Great Depression has apparently struck a chord. Americans, many of whom have never been near a race track, have spent the past summer reading Laura Hillenbrand's best-selling *Seabiscuit: An American Legend*, and since its release earlier this month they've been queuing up at theatres to watch *Seabiscuit*, a feel-good film chronicling the same subject.

In the midst of all this evocative nostalgia we might spare the time to shed a tear for Ferdinand. So far as we know, there are no plans afoot to make a movie about the 1986 Kentucky Derby winner's life and unfortunate end, and if they did make one they'd probably have to clean it up for family audiences.

Since the unseemly events concluded sometime last year, this mystery may never be completely unravelled, but the question today is, apparently, Who Ate Ferdinand?

The unsettling development came to light a few days ago when *The Blood-Horse*, a glossy high-end publication devoted to the thoroughbred industry, published the results of an investigation by reporter Barbara Bayer, who had unsuccessfully tried to track down Ferdinand in Japan, where he had supposedly been standing at stud.

Bayer, it turns out, was about a year too late. Ferdinand had evidently run out of ammunition, rendering him somewhat less than studly, and his decidedly unsentimental Japanese owners opted to cut their losses by having him, uh, recycled. Now the only question seems to be whether he wound up as dog food or, since horse-sashimi is considered a delicacy in The Land of the Rising Sun, as the entrée on some unsuspecting diner's dinner plate.

Now, you might suppose Ferdinand would have been entitled to expire with dignity, but while we sentimental creatures think of euthanasia, the Japanese are usually more pragmatic about these matters. No-longer-useful horses there are routinely put to death by being clubbed in the head, or (presumably if they're not headed for somebody's dinner table) injected with disinfectant.

We'd always had a warm spot in our heart for Ferdinand, who had won just two of nine career starts when he arrived at Churchill Downs that May. Thanks to a tip from trainer Charlie Whittingham, we'd been all over the 17 to 1 winner in the 1986 Run for the Roses, when he was steered home by Bill Shoemaker, and departed Louisville that spring with pockets brimming with cash. It was the fourth and last Derby win for Shoe, who would be paralysed in an automobile crash a few years later.

Since Shoemaker's win on Ferdinand came just weeks after 46 year-old Jack Nicklaus had won his last Masters, there were a lot of "vintage wine" stories written that spring, but Ferdinand himself did not survive to enjoy his own dotage.

Ferdinand was the son of English Triple-Crown winner Nijinsky II, and, a year after his Derby upset, was voted horse of the year when he defeated Alysheba in the Breeders Cup Classic.

As a sire, he was by all accounts no Nijinksy. Retired to stud at his birthplace, Claiborne Farms in Kentucky, he performed without great distinction and was eventually purchased by Japanese interests five years later.

At the time Japanese breeders were aggressive in their pursuit of American and European bloodstock. Bayer learned in her investigation that Ferdinand spent six breeding seasons at Arrow Stud on the island of Hokkaido. He was bred to 77 mares in his first year in Japan, but that number fell to just 10 in 2000. At that point he was sold to a Japanese horse dealer named Yoshikazu Watanabe, but covered just six mares in 2001 and two more in 2002 before his involuntary demise.

For reasons which are probably understandable, Watanabe was not particularly forthcoming in revealing the details of Ferdinand's fate. He first told Bayer that the horse had been "given to a friend," a story later amended to claim that the 19-year-old champion had been gelded and donated to a riding club. Finally, Watanabe 'fessed up to the truth.

"Actually, he isn't around any more," he told the *Blood-Horse* reporter. "He was disposed of late last year."

"In Japan, the term 'disposed of' is used to mean slaughtered," wrote Bayer. "No one can say for sure when and where Ferdinand met his end, but it would seem clear that he met it in a slaughterhouse."

Among those encountered by Bayer in Japan was a Japanese groom named Toshiharu Kaibazawa, who had attended Ferdinand during his years at Arrow Stud.

Kaibazawa described the late Ferdinand as "the gentlest horse you could imagine. He'd come over when I called to him in the pasture. And anyone could have led him with just a halter on him. He'd come over to me and press his head up against me. He was so sweet.

"I want to get angry about what happened to him," Kaibazawa told the *Blood-Horse*. "It's just heartless, too heartless."

By the way, not only was Shoemaker 54 years of age when he won the Kentucky Derby on Ferdinand, Whittingham, the Hall of Fame trainer, was 73 years of age.

Ferdinand was 19 at the time he was killed, because, explained Watanabe, "he was getting old".

July 31, 2003

Eyeballing victory on the road to Kentucky

LOUISVILLE

The presence of two one-eyed horses (and one one-eyed owner) in Saturday's Kentucky Derby has proved irresistible to the turf writers who have flocked to Churchill Downs' backstretch this week. You'd think it had never happened before, but it has.

In 1982 owner Tom Gentry ran a one-eyed horse named Cassaleria in the Derby. I was introduced to Gentry by my fellow Kentucky Colonel Billy Reed, who assumed, correctly, that the maverick owner of a one-eyed horse would find a kindred spirit in a maverick, one-eyed sportswriter.

Gentry spent the days before the Derby commuting between his farm in Lexington and Louisville by helicopter, and each trip brought a new shipment of goodies, including Cassaleria t-shirts and large, blue-on-yellow buttons with the slogan *"Thine Eye Has Seen The Glory,"* which he would toss to the milling crowds. The locals grew to so anticipate these deliveries that by late in the week when Gentry's 'copter swooped down it looked like the last days of Saigon in the Churchill Downs parking lot.

On the eve of the Kentucky Derby, Gentry invited me to a Cassaleria party in the owners' car-park. He had hired for the occasion what had to be the largest Winnebago in captivity, well-stocked with catered *hors d'ouvres* and with a bar at each end. When I arrived shortly after the running of Friday's Kentucky Oaks, it had everything but fellow guests.

An elegant looking black woman, whom I took to be the caterer, stood admiring the food, while on a leather seat near the bar lounged a 30-ish black man dressed in tuxedo trousers and a white shirt. Assuming he was the bartender, I ordered a drink, and when he didn't move fast enough for my liking, repeated the request.

He eyed my strangely, but eventually uncoiled himself from his comfortable position, and handed me a beer.

Only when Gentry showed up and I was introduced did I come to realise that I was actually the third guest to have arrived. The first had been Marilyn McCoo and her husband, Billy Davis Jr, or two-fifths of the Fifth Dimension. It was Davis who had fetched my beer.

Cassaleria, alas, did not fare well the following afternoon, and finished 13th, a furlong or two behind winner Gato Del Sol.

Essentially forgotten for 22 years, Cassaleria name has been invoked a lot this week. Pollard's Vision, a three-year-old, who lost an eye to a mysterious equine malady called "Mare Reproductive Loss Syndrome," which swept Kentucky blood-stock farms a few years ago, has a chance to win Saturday's Run for the Roses, as does Imperialism, trained by 21-year-old Kristin Mulhall. (Were Imperialism to wind up in the Winner's Circle, Mulhall would not only be the first woman but the youngest trainer ever to saddle a Derby winner.) Imperialism's defect is congenital: he was born with his right eye sunken in its socket, likely the result of one of his hooves being pressed against it in the womb. He can't see a horse coming from behind on that side until it draws even with him.

That Pollard's Vision was visually challenged had become apparent by last July's Keeneland Yearling Sale at which he was purchased, for $70,000, by David Moore, a one-eyed retired banker, and was named, by Moore's daughter Charlotte, for Red Pollard, the one-eyed jockey who rode the legendary Seabiscuit.

According to two-eyed trainer Todd Pelcher, in the absence of the defect the colt might have brought as much as $400,000.

Pollard's Vision made his debut last summer at Belmont Park, finished 22 and a half lengths off the pace, and promptly tossed his rider, John Velasquez, as he crossed the finish line. He bounced back, though, beating the field with a 12 and-a-half-length victory at Saratoga in August, and more recently won the Illinois Derby.

When Kristin Mulhall purchased Imperialism for owner Steve Taub three months ago, the Kentucky Derby was the last thing on her mind.

Mulhall says she wasn't aware of Imperialism's handicap until he stumbled off the plane in California, where she keeps her stable. The young trainer (who exercises her own horses) attempted to ride him that day, but the horse spooked and nearly tossed her over the rail. She immediately fitted him with a hood fitted with a blinker on his right side.

Once she got the colt on the track, Imperialism surprised everyone. He won his first two races for Mulhall at Santa Anita — the Grade II San Vicente Stakes, followed by the San Rafael Stakes. He then finished third in the Santa Anita Derby, but was moved up to second after a foul claim (against Rock Hard Ten) was allowed.

Although they are just the second and third one-eyed horses to make it to the starting gate in Louisville on the first Saturday in May, Pollard's Vision and Imperialism aren't unique to the Sport of Kings. Horseplayers still recall an animal named One-Eyed King, a successful stakes horse in the 1950s, and a gelding named One-Eyed Tom nearly got to Churchill Downs a decade before Cassaleria did. (One-Eyed Tom failed a starter's test when he broke out of the gate and ran in the opposite direction, and was not allowed to run in the 1972 Derby.)

Old-time railbirds also rattle off the names of Mystic Eye, Funny Fellow, and Real Connection, all of whom raced with success despite having one eye.

If being blind in one eye doesn't seem to be a terrible impediment (to sports-writers or to thoroughbreds), though, consider the case of a horse named Burk's Charge. *Lexington Herald-Leader* turf writer Maryjean Wall recalled this week that after Burk's Charge crashed into the inside rail at Pimlico back in 1995, he was discovered to have been blind in *both* eyes, a particularly curious development since the mishap occurred in the ninth race of his career.
April 29, 2004

Hero Rulon could yet dip a toe in pro circuit

ATHENS

Like Brazilian soccer players, some athletes are destined to be known forever by their Christian names, and Rulon the Wrestler is one of them. Most Americans wouldn't know a Greco-Roman match from a rugby scrum, but they all know Rulon Gardner.

No disrespect to that Zeus fellow who won the original Greco (the "Roman" part was an expansion franchise that came along later) gold medal, but putting a full-nelson on that Kronos fellow at Olympia was probably a piece of cake compared to tossing around Alexander Karelin, the previously undefeated Russian legend Rulon had to beat to win gold in the 130kg category in Australia four years ago.

That shocking victory in a sport in which Americans do not traditionally excel turned an affable, roly-poly Mormon from Wyoming into an instant celebrity, with late-night network chat-shows all wrestling over Rulon.

Over the intervening four years, Rulon has nearly frozen to death after being stranded overnight in a Rocky Mountain snowstorm, had a toe amputated, gotten divorced, wrecked a motorcycle, and, more recently, dislocated his right wrist playing in a celebrity charity basketball game. He was a long shot to *get* to Athens, much less defend his championship.

When the half-dozen Americans who would represent the United States in Greco-Roman wrestling arrived at Eleftherios Venizelos International Airport three weeks ago, the first sight they encountered was an Olympic billboard displaying the message, in English, "Welcome home." Rulon let out a whoop of joy.

"My sport is one of the two original Olympic sports," Rulon explained at the time. "Winning an Olympic gold medal was a dream come true, but to do it here, in the birthplace of the Olympics, would be even greater. I can't tell you how much it would mean to me."

If Rulon had been an overwhelming underdog against Karelin in Sydney, he was an underdog in Athens last week for entirely different reasons.

Two winters ago an ill-advised snowmobiling adventure got him lost overnight in six feet of snow in the Wyoming wilderness.

Despite two dunks in an icy river and 12 hours up to his armpits in snow, he survived, but the experience nearly cost him both legs. In the end doctors were able to save his feet, apart from the middle toe on his right foot, which had to be amputated.

As a result of this mishap, Rulon retains an unusual souvenir in his refrigerator back home. He keeps the pickled toe in a jar of formaldehyde. It won't stay there forever; Rulon's long-range plan is to bury the digit in the grave of his dog Bo, who died a few years ago.

"That way part of me will always be with him," the wrestler explained.

Last year in Colorado he crashed his motorcycle on the way to a training session. Rulon came away with bumps, bruises, and the odd scratch, but the bike was totalled. A few months after that he was playing in the celebrity hoops game when he went diving into the bleachers in pursuit of a loose ball and dislocated his wrist. Greco-Roman wrestlers can make do with nine toes, but two functioning wrists are fairly essential.

"My wrist ended up on top of my forearm," recalled Rulon. "I had to pop it back in myself. Later, the doctors had to put three pins on the top of my hand."

Somehow, Rulon fought his way through these sundry maladies to win this year's US trials, which is how he came to spend his 33rd birthday last week attempting to do something not even Zeus had been able to pull off.

And while Rulon did win his second Olympic medal in Athens, this time it wasn't the gold. A 4-1 overtime loss to Georgi Tsurtsumia of Kazakhstan in their semi-final match had left him wrestling for third place last Tuesday night.
September 02, 2004

Larry Wiseman plays his bugle at sunset in front of the more than 53,000 names of U.S. casualities carved

TO
ABSENT
FRIENDS

A great talent sorely missed

By the time he got around to making that pilgrimage to Ireland he'd always talked about, he already knew he was a dying man. Michael James McAlary was 41 when he died of cancer on Christmas Day. He was eulogised as the New York Daily News' Pulitzer Prize-winning columnist, but those of us who knew him best remember him for what he really was: a reformed sportswriter.

He was the grandson of a Belfast man who emigrated in the 1920s to live the life of an illegal immigrant in Brooklyn. When the grandfather's wife died and a subsequent fire consumed the family home, life became unbearable for him. He ran off and disappeared, never to be heard from again.

Six children, including Mike's father John McAlary, were left to be scattered in foster homes. There were eventually 30 grandchildren, none of them having so much as a photograph of the family patriarch. It was later learned that he had died working as a hired hand on a Maryland farm.

"The old man died an illegal immigrant," McAlary wrote of the shared tragedy,

Mike McAlary: Pulititzer prize-winner — living his dream.

"never knowing what he'd missed — or how he had been missed."

When I met Mike McAlary 25 years ago, he was a teenage prodigy, covering the Volvo tennis tournament in New Hampshire as a stringer for the *Manchester Union-Leader*. He was a hotshot kid, already a terrific writer but eager to learn, and the tournament, an idyllic little affair held annually up in the White Mountains, gave him his first showcase and his first exposure to big-time journalism. By day he would chronicle the exploits of Jimmy Connors and Ivan Lendl, and by night he would accompany Mike Lupica, Bud Collins, and myself on our tours of the North Conway pubs, sipping a coke in a corner booth while he absorbed it all.

He went on to become sports editor of his college newspaper at Syracuse University, and by the time I arrived at the old *Boston Herald American* in 1980, Mike was already there, serving his apprenticeship on the sports desk.

He was, in truth, badly misused, little more than a glorified copy boy on a newspaper whose predicted death was almost a daily occurrence. The word was out that if it didn't find a buyer within a year, the Hearst Corporation was going to euthanise the paper, and morale was low. Worse, Mike, when he wasn't transcribing horse racing reports, was given the most trivial sort of writing assignments.

For a young fellow who had covered Jimmy Connors when he was 16, it was a bit of a comedown to be writing stories about high school games that might, if he was lucky, be read by the subjects and their mothers, and it began to show in Mike's work. His increasingly careless stories did not go unnoticed by the newspaper's powers-that-be. One day the editor, Don Forst, summoned me his office and asked me to have a word with McAlary, so a few nights later in the Eliot Lounge, we had our little chat.

"'Look,' I told him, 'you may think you have no future on a paper that has no future, and you may be right about that. But you do have a future in this business, and when all those silly stories are printed, they have your name on them. What you have right now is an opportunity to write your own resume'."

A decade later Mike thanked me for what he termed "the best advice I ever got."

Within a year, he was off to the Big Apple. New York was in the throes of an escalating newspaper war. Rupert Murdoch's afternoon *Post* had decided to take on the tabloid *Daily News'* stranglehold on the subway crowd by publishing a morning edition of its own, and the *News* retaliated by creating an afternoon paper. It was this latter for which Mike was hired to work.

The next year the News folded its p.m. edition, and Mike went straight to the Big Leagues. He was hired to cover the Yankees for the *Post*.

"God, it was breathtaking to be in your twenties and covering New York baseball!" he would later recall.

He and George Steinbrenner, the blustery mogul who owned the baseball team, were soon on a first-name basis. Steinbrenner called Mike "Malarkey," and Mike referred to The Boss as "the anonymous owner of the New York Yankees."

The world of sports would not satisfy his ambition for long. He needed an even bigger stage, and when he was hired by *Newsday* as a city-side columnist a few years later, he got it. New York newspapers were soon fighting over him. At increasingly obscene salaries, he went from there back to the *Post* and, eventually, back to the *News*. When that happened, Murdoch even filed a lawsuit in an attempt to keep him.

The gritty panorama of the New York streets provided him with the fodder for three books. The first of these, *Buddy Boys*, chronicled the exploits of two corrupt New York cops.

Five years ago he suffered a near-fatal automobile accident. Only the air-bag saved his life, but he was in a coma for five days and received the last rites twice. His family was warned that brain damage was a real possibility.

He survived that experience, only to learn he had cancer.

McAlary was in the midst of a chemotherapy session when he got a call about a horrifying episode of police brutality in a Brooklyn precinct house. Mike tore out of his hospital to another in Coney Island to interview a Haitian security guard named Abner Louima, who had while in custody been sodomised by several white cops using the wooden handle of a toilet plunger. It was an incident so cruel and reprehensible that it had even disgusted fellow cops, some of whom were responsible for tipping off McAlary.

His coverage of those events won him last year's Pulitzer Prize. He accepted America's highest journalism award grimly aware of his own fate.

"It was," he said, "kind of like hitting a home run in my last at-bat."

He made periodic forays back to his roots in the world of sports. The latest came this autumn, when he wrote insightfully about Darryl Strawberry, the Yankees's outfielder who, on the eve of the World Series, was stricken with the same form of cancer McAlary had.

The year before last he also visited Ireland, with his tour guide and friend John Timony, then the Deputy Police Commissioner of New York and now Philadelphia's Top Cop.

Mike and Alice had four children, the oldest 13. He had caught the worst break imaginable, but he refused to lament his fate.

"If you question why the bad things happen you have to question why the good things happen, too," he pointed out, "and I've been luckier than most. I got a chance to live my dream."

December 31, 1998

A life of promise ends with a gunshot

LAS VEGAS

I last saw Mitch Halpern eight days before he died, moments after he had disqualified Rosendo Alvarez in his WBA light-flyweight championship fight against Beibis Mendoza. It had not been — and I'm sure Halpern would have admitted as much — one of his better nights in the ring.

As a rule, the best referees are the ones you don't notice much, but on this particular evening Mitch repeatedly insinuated himself into the action. Although both contestants seemed eager to mix it up on the inside, Halpern had repeatedly stepped in to warn Alvarez for what he perceived to be low blows, even though none of them seemed to bother Mendoza much. Finally, after twice ordering a point deducted from the Nicaraguan's scorecard, Halpern halted the action midway through the sixth round and awarded the fight — and the title — to Mendoza.

The disqualification had seemed dubious, if not unwarranted, and Halpern seemed, well, agitated as he defended it.

"We have rules and regulations here in Nevada," he said. "How many times am I supposed to warn him?"

That was on August 12th. Last Sunday evening, in his home in Las Vegas, Mitch

Halpern took a gun and put a bullet through his brain. His friends and colleagues have been trying to make sense of it ever since. Halpern was 33 and widely regarded as one of the more promising referees around. He had already surpassed Richard Steele, his mentor, and appeared to have been designated the heir to the retired Mills Lane as Nevada's top referee.

Steele recalled that the young Halpern had approached him one night as he stepped out of the ring and informed him that he, too, would like to become a boxing referee.

"I told him to meet me at the gym the next Monday," recalled Steele after the death of the man he described as his "son".

"I've had plenty of guys say the same thing, and most of them never show up," said Steele. "Mitch was there on Monday. He worked harder at it than anyone I've ever known. He wanted to be the best, and he was. He took everything I knew and added his own natural ability."

Halpern had worked 87 world title fights, including the first Evander Holyfield-Mike Tyson fight, the second Lennox Lewis-Holyfield bout, and last year's Felix Trinidad-Oscar De La Hoya welterweight unification fight. But he was perhaps better known for one at which he did not officiate.

He had been named to work the 1997 Holyfield-Tyson rematch at the MGM Grand. At a rules meeting two nights before the fight, Tyson's camp — the boxer did not attend, but his hangers-on were present *en masse* — vehemently protested, claiming that Halpern's failure to control Holyfield's roughhouse tactics in the earlier meeting was indicative of a bias toward their man. They even claimed that if Halpern weren't replaced, Tyson might not show up.

The Nevada Commissioners remained adamant, and were prepared to call Team Tyson's bluff, but Halpern, in an effort to defuse the controversy, asked to have his name withdrawn from nomination 24 hours before the fight. The commission seemed relieved, and the bout went on with the veteran Lane, a tough, no-nonsense, law-'n'-order ex-Marine and former prosecutor, in charge.

That turned out to be the night Tyson tried to devour Holyfield's ears. I have often wondered — and I can't be alone in my curiosity — whether, under the circumstances, the younger referee would have had the stones to disqualify Tyson that night as quickly as did Lane. (And even Lane, it might be noted, didn't disqualify Tyson immediately after he bit Holyfield for the second time. He only did it after the round — when he looked up and saw the televised replay of the incident.)

In any case, Lane retired, both from the ring and from the bench, to life as a television judge after that fight, and, more or less by acclamation, Halpern inherited his role as Nevada's top referee.

The Mendoza-Alvarez fight which proved to be Halpern's last was hardly a plum assignment. It was for a vacant title recently lifted from Thailand's Pitchnoi Siriwat, and was originally slated to take place the evening before, on the undercard of the Tim Austin-Arthur Johnson bantamweight title bout at the Paris. It was moved to promoter Don King's Holyfield-John Ruiz card only when WBA welterweight champion James Page failed to show up for his scheduled defence against Andrew (Six Heads) Lewis, and Showtime needed a co-feature to fill that evening's telecast.

Everyone is entitled to an off-night, but in retrospect, Halpern's performance that evening was so uncharacteristically bad that, well before the disqualification, I turned to my friend Mike Katz at ringside and said, "It looks like Mitch is so pissed off that he didn't get the heavyweight fight that he's determined to put his stamp on this one".

Katz pointed out, correctly, that this hypothesis would be more persuasive had the Holyfield-Ruiz assignment gone to anyone but Steele, Halpern's guru.

Eight nights later Halpern killed himself.

"It was an obvious suicide," Metro Las Vegas homicide lieutenant Wayne Peterson said. "He died of an obvious, self-inflicted gunshot wound."

Nearly two decades ago, another prominent Las Vegas referee, Richard Greene, committed suicide under similar circumstances.

Greene had been the third man in the ring for the Ray Mancini-Duk Koo Kim lightweight title fight, in which Kim had absorbed such a beating that he was carried from the ring unconscious and died some days later. Speculation had it that Greene was distraught over his perceived shortcomings in failing to stop the bout earlier, and felt that he might have saved the Korean if he had.

Halpern's work in Mendoza-Alvarez was bad, but it wasn't *that* bad.

He had a chance, said Steele, "to be the best referee of all time."

Who knows what demons lurk in the minds of men? Halpern was divorced, but had a four-year-old daughter and a fiancee. He had a promising future.

But don't they all?

August 24, 2000

Tycoon with a heart of gold

My last encounter with Ely Callaway came last April, a chance meeting beneath the oak tree behind the clubhouse at Augusta National. Our conversation lasted but a few minutes. At the time neither of us had any reason to suspect we'd never see each other again.

Two weeks later, during surgery to remove his gall bladder, it was discovered that the grand old man was suffering from inoperable pancreatic cancer. Although no public announcement was made, word spread like wildfire throughout the golfing community, and when he "resigned" as president and CEO of Callaway Golf on May

15th, it was assumed, probably correctly, that the move was made to ameliorate the panic his inevitable end might otherwise have triggered with respect to the company's publicly-traded stock.

A warm and generous man, he died at 82 a week ago this morning. Although I didn't know him well — our personal relationship, in fact, covered just the last five years of his life — I considered him a friend, but then, so did virtually everyone who ever met him.

When a few of us were looking to play golf the day before Super Bowl XXXI in San Diego, my friend Dave Anderson, the *New York Times* sports columnist, rang up his former colleague Larry Dorman, who had resigned his position as the *Times'* golf correspondent to become a vice president of Callaway Golf.

Arrangements were duly made for us to play a club called The Farms in Rancho Santa Fe, but Dorman advised that we would be required to play with a member. When we arrived at the course we learned that the member assigned to our fourball was Ely Callaway himself, and by the time first-tee negotiations had concluded, it had been determined that Mr C would be my partner and cart-mate.

He spoke in the courtly accent of his native Georgia and was a distant cousin of Bobby Jones, but Ely Reeves Callaway had come to golf fairly late in life — far too late to develop much of a game of his own.

He had brought along that day two dozen balls imprinted with the Callaway logo. He explained that while Callaway Golf had engaged 200 people for the previous two years doing 'R&D' (research and development) on a proposed Callaway ball, the results had yet to meet with the company's standards and "we haven't made a single golf ball."

The balls we were playing that day had been made by another manufacturer and stamped with the Callaway name. He kept the first dozen for his own use, and presented me with the other box, but before the round was complete, he was borrowing the gift balls back from me.

"Now," he said with a laugh after the latest errant missile had disappeared into the jungle, "you can see why I'm going into the golf ball business."

During the course of the round he suggested that I try out his driver, the then-evolutionary Biggest Big Bertha. I did, was pleased with the results, and at the end of the day he handed it over as a present. A few days later, on a tour of his plant, he ordered that another be specially-made for me.

On Monday, the day after the football game, at Mr C's invitation, we inspected the Callaway plant in Carlsbad and when, during the course of the tour I was measured for specifications, which revealed that I should be using a driver with two degrees more loft, Ely ordered that one be made for me on the spot.

When, less than an hour later, the still-warm weapon, shrouded in bubble-wrap, was presented, I momentarily wrestled with piggish sportswriter thoughts of being

Ely Callaway: a Georgian by birth, a North Carolinian by upbringing, and a business tycoon by trade.

the only guy on the block to own two Biggest Big Berthas, but in the end reminded Callaway that I already had one — his own — in the boot of my rental car, and offered to return that one.

"All right," he said with a smile. "You can just throw it in the back seat of my car, the blue BMW out there."

During World War II, Callaway, owing to his experience in the clothing business, served as an officer in the Quartermaster Corps of the United States Army, overseeing the purchase of materials and the manufacture of uniforms,and emerged from the conflict a 25-year-old Major.

For the next quarter century he worked at Burlington Industries, one of the most prominent clothing manufacturers in the United States, eventually becoming the company's president. He left Burlington in 1973 following a dispute over control, walking away with a generous settlement.

With that money as a stake He purchased a small California vineyard, and built it into another hugely successful operation, selling it for $14 million eight years later. He then purchased, for $400,000, Hickory Stick, another small boutique company, which produced replica antique putters. He changed its name to Callaway Golf, and by 1988 was doing $5 million worth of business annually.

Ten years later Callaway's annual sales had increased to $800 million per year. The company he leaves as his legacy is now the largest clubmaker in the world.

Callaway Golf might have created the most popular driver on the planet and, eventually, a premium golf ball, but ironically (considering that his initial foray into the business had come as a manufacturer of putters) the company was never able to produce a decent putter. Ely Callaway was shrewd enough to recognise this short-coming, and corrected it by acquiring the Odyssey line of putters.

The Midas touch he displayed with his business acumen did not extend to his love life. During our round in San Diego I had mentioned that at Scotland's Skibo Castle the previous summer I had met and played behind his wife. Callaway's reply was a noncommittal grunt, indicating that he was not particularly interested in pursuing the topic.

When we were invited over to his house for drinks after that day's golf the reason became apparent. Apart from the fact that it had been meticulously tidied up by a maid, there was no sign of a female presence in the home, and it was clear that the latest companion had run off to join her predecessors in the ever-swelling legion of former Mrs Callaways.

He was a Georgian by birth, a North Carolinian by upbringing, and a business tycoon by trade. The politics of such men are usually predictable, but once again Ely Callaway ran against the grain. The visit to his home revealed no photos of himself with Nixon, no personal letters from Ronald Reagan and George Bush. Instead the memorabilia in his study made it apparent that his political heroes and friends had been John F Kennedy, Jimmy Carter and Bill Clinton.

While cynics might have rated his highly public attempt to rehabilitate John Daly as a misbegotten publicity stunt, for Callaway it was a gesture from the heart. Daly, the 1991 PGA and 1995 British Open champion, had lost his sponsorship deal with Wilson and had been suspended from the Tour (in the wake of bizarre episodes on the golf course, busted-up hotel rooms, and threatened past and current wives regularly dialing up 911) when Callaway rode to the rescue.

Callaway paid off Daly 's huge gambling debts, said to total be in the millions, restructured his finances to put him on a living allowance while seeing to the distribution of his alimony and child-support payments, and paid him handsomely — all on the provision that the golfer refrain from gambling and drinking.

When Daly resumed both vices last year, Callaway made good on his own promise and dropped him like a hot rock, but he made no attempt to recover the money he had paid out on Daly 's behalf. Mr C would not, in fact, have even rated the doomed episode a mistake at all, any more than he would have conceded that he was dead wrong on the ERC issue.

After rigorous testing, the United States Golf Association dovetailed with the R&A and banned the new driver (on the grounds that the springboard clubface provided extra distance by creating an excessive "trampoline-like" effect), Callaway elected to keep making and marketing the club, in the United States anyway, hoping no doubt to reach a settlement like Ping did with their Ping Eye2 irons, which they stopped making after a court case with the USGA.

The USGA took no position on the club's legality, and while no money changed hands, the remaining stock of Ping Eye2s was instantly transformed into collector 's items.

It is unfortunate that it a similar deal wasn't achieved in Ely Callaway's lifetime. He might have relished being described as a golfing "maverick," but "outlaw" was a term he found it difficult to abide.

July 12, 2001

Slammin' Sammy one in a zillion

It was partly out of self-interest that I decided to walk Augusta National's par-three course with Sam Snead on the eve of the 1993 Masters tournament. Since Sam would be teeing off in the first group, he'd also be the first to finish, giving me a nice tidy column and a head-start into the evening's festivities.

But there was also ample historical justification for following Snead that day. Back in 1960 he had won the inaugural par-three contest, thereby initiating a traditional jinx: then, and in 42 successive events, no man has ever won the Wednesday

Slammin' S... more gin than tonic.

par-three contest and then gone on to win a green jacket over the weekend.

Sam was in rare form that afternoon. In between his clowning on the tee, jawing with his playing partners, and bantering with the galleries, he made four birdies on his way around the course. His final score of 23 was respectable enough, particularly for an 80-year-old man, but he knew somebody would do better.

With that we repaired to the clubhouse bar, where for the next several hours Sam entertained a transient audience while doing his best to drink Augusta National out of gin, or tonic, or both.

Late that afternoon a green-jacketed club emissary approached and tugged at Snead's sleeve. The four-under had been equalled, but not bettered.

Slammin' Sammy was in a four-way tie for first place, and his presence was requested on the tee.

Since I'd been with him all day, I was probably the only one, with the possible exception of Snead himself, who knew exactly *how* much alcohol he'd consumed, but after sending his caddie to get his clubs, Snead dutifully made his way back to the tee of the first play-off hole.

It was a downwind, downhill shot, and Sam overclubbed. He hit an eight iron which bounced once on the fringe to the left of the green and bounded into the water behind.

He waited until his three colleagues, all of them less than half his age, had teed off, then shook each of their hands.

"Good luck, fellas," he said. "See you back at the bar."

He was back at the clubhouse before the ice had even melted in the drink he'd left there.

There were reports later that he'd been involved in a smash-up driving out of the club. I wasn't surprised.

Snead, who died last week, four days short of his 90th birthday, won a record 81 official PGA Tour events. In the modern era that would have made him a zillionaire, but he never won more than $50,000 in a single year.

Of course, he handsomely supplemented his income by hustling all comers, and over most of his lifetime he was the object of a bidding war between his two "home" courses, the Greenbriar in White Sulphur Springs, West Virginia, and the Homestead across the mountain pass in Virginia. He shuttled back and forth between the two so frequently that either could claim him as a native son even when he happened to be in the employ of the other.

As part of the Millennium Open two years ago, the R&A brought a host of past champions back to St Andrews, and put them on display in a four-hole exhibition match on the eve of the tournament. Before he teed off that Wednesday afternoon, Sam was recalling his first visit to the Auld Grey Toon back in 1946.

In those days the railroad line still ran right into St Andrews, and the one bearing

Sammy pulled in alongside the left-hand side of the Old Course. Snead, who wasn't even aware that he'd arrived at his destination, pointed out the window at the links and observed to a startled seatmate *that looks like it used to be a golf course.*

That week he went out and won the British Open, but then refused all entreaties to defend his championship the next year. He explained that it was too far to travel, and that besides, he couldn't afford it. First-prize money back then was pittance, and, said Snead, "it cost me more than that to get there".

Once Snead engaged in a heated debate with Ted Williams, the Boston Red Sox outfielder widely considered the greatest student of hitting, if not the greatest hitter, in baseball history.

"In golf you're trying to hit a stationary target," Williams noted. "Putting wood to a baseball travelling a hundred miles an hour is the most difficult thing to do in any sport."

Snead acknowledged Williams' initial argument.

"But," he pointed out, "we have to *play* our foul balls."

A portent that the end might be near occurred early last month, when Snead joined Byron Nelson on the first tee at Augusta to strike his ceremonial first shot. He might have lost a bit of distance over the years, but for as long as anyone could remember he still drove it straight down the middle. But this time he hit a screecher which caught a spectator full in the face, breaking the man's glasses.

I thought back to one of the last conversations I'd had with Snead, which occurred a couple of years ago at a chance meeting in a rental-car courtesy-van at the Las Vegas airport.

We were each surprised to see the other. Sam told me he was in town for an appearance at a golf show over at the Convention Center. I'd been invited to play that afternoon in a media event publicizing the LPGA Championship.

"Where are you playing?" Snead asked.

"The Desert Inn," I told him.

"Where's that?" he asked.

When I told him and began to describe the course, one of Las Vegas' oldest, and he said "Hmm. I may have played there," I had to laugh.

"Sam," I told him. "You won a *tournament* on that course. Your picture is on a plaque in the clubhouse."

Boy, I thought to myself, getting old sure is a bitch.

It was only later that afternoon that the fuller implication of that encounter occurred to me. If Snead was on that bus, he was obviously going the same place I was, meaning that a few minutes after our conversation he had climbed behind the wheel of a car and driven it out of the parking lot.

Now, there was a frightening thought.

May 30, 2002

Clearly, greatness is not hereditary

From what I've tasted of desire
I hold with those who favour fire.
But if it had to perish twice,
I think I know enough of hate
To say that for destruction ice
Is also great
And would suffice.
                    — Robert Frost

He voiced his life's ambition in simple terms any of us could understand: *"When I walk down the street, I want people to stop and say 'There goes Ted Williams, the greatest hitter who ever lived'."*

His plans for an afterlife were, unfortunately, somewhat more vague.

Not yet dead a week, the Splendid Splinter has become the object of a nasty little war among his offspring. While his daughters (along with most of his baseball friends) maintain that Williams expressed a desire to have his remains cremated, no sooner had the great man expired than his son, John Henry Williams, had his father's body flown to Arizona, where it was drained of blood, filled with a special freezing solution, and left to float inside a pod filled with liquid nitrogen.

By submitting Williams to this scientifically dubious process, his son apparently hopes to make the baseball immortal *truly* immortal. Or perhaps, as his sisters suspect, he is attempting to keep his options open while he figures out a way to squeeze a few dollars more out of his meal ticket.

An outfielder who played 19 seasons, all for the Boston Red Sox, Williams was the last man to bat .400, a feat rarely performed before he did it in 1941 and never accomplished since.

He carried an even .400 average into the final day of the season that year, in which the Sox were scheduled to play a meaningless double-header against the Philadelphia Athletics. Manager Joe Cronin offered to let him sit the day out to protect the statistical milestone. Ted insisted on playing, went 6-for-8 over the two games, and finished with a .406 mark for the year.

His lifetime statistics place him among baseball's elite, but his numbers might have been even more stratospheric had he not lost five years from what should have been the prime of his career to wartime service. He spent three years flying combat missions in the Second World War, and was called up for two more during the Korean conflict. As a Marine Corps fighter pilot he was John Glenn's wingman, and, with one wheel down, once crash-landed a burning plane on the deck of a carrier and walked away unscathed.

As it was, he hit 521 home runs. Give him back those five years, and another he

Ted Williams: the greatest hitter
who ever lived.

lost when he broke his elbow running into an outfield wall during the All-Star game, and we're probably talking Babe Ruth numbers.

He was unquestionably blessed with extraordinary physical gifts. He is said to have had the quickest wrists of any man to play the game, and his eyesight was the stuff of legend: to settle a bet among his wartime buddies, he was able to read, word-for-word, the label of a record spinning at 78 rpm — and the label was in Spanish.

He endured a love-hate relationship with the Boston fans, whose adulation he spurned, and, for most of his career, one of mutual animosity with the sportswriting fraternity. On the occasion of his 500th home run, he paused after crossing the plate and spat in the direction of the press box.

Following his retirement as a player, he had an unhappy, four-year fling at the helm of the Washington Senators/Texas Rangers, and proved only that he could not only hit .400, but manage .400 as well. He embarked on a second career as a sport fisherman, and was every bit as adept with a fly rod as he had been with a baseball bat in his hands, or at the controls of a warplane.

His domestic life was, by contrast, an abysmal failure. He was by all accounts, including his own, a bad husband to his three wives, and not a particularly good father to any of his three children. His efforts to atone for this oversight later in life led to the undignified mess in which his affairs lie today.

For the last decade his youngest offspring had increasingly taken control of his father's life, overseeing a market for memorabilia that turned a man who was once reluctant to sign a single autograph into a regular fixture at baseball card shows all over the country. Williams was only too happy to share his doddering years with the fawning son.

Several years ago, an FBI sting resulted in the arrest of three unscrupulous memorabilia dealers who were attempting to flog Ted Williams' 1946 World Series ring on the Internet. The culprits' defence was that they were acting with the connivance of John Henry Williams, who had supplied the ring. He denied it and claimed that the ring had been "stolen," but the three men were acquitted, suggesting that the jury valued the word of the career criminals over that of Williams' son.

The Greatest Hitter Who Ever Lived died at 83 last Friday in a Florida hospital. John Henry whisked the body off to the Alcor Life Extension Institute in Arizona to be cryogenically frozen. Barbara Joyce Williams Ferrell, John Henry's sister and Ted's oldest daughter, said she recognised the scheme for what it was as soon as her brother proposed it.

"I knew right away what it was," she said. "He's just trying to make money off Daddy. He said the way they're going with medical science and DNA, we could freeze dad's body, or we can freeze his head," she said. "He said 'We could sell the DNA'."

There are only two conceivable motives for having resorted to this cryogenic process. One is the far-fetched proposition that John Henry actually expects to bring his father back to life. The other is that he hopes to flog the great man's genes on the Internet.

Baseball memorabilia collectors would probably pay handsomely for a splinter of the Splinter, but that Williams' DNA will bequeath baseball greatness is genetically dubious. At this point, in fact, the only conclusive example of what Ted Williams' DNA will produce is John Henry Williams himself. You wouldn't want another one of those running around the house.

July 11, 2002

NFL negligent for not recognising true American hero

Thirty-eight years later it remains the highlight of any Olympic film: when he took the baton from Dick Stebbins for the anchor leg in the 4x100 metres relay final, the US sat in fifth place. Bob Hayes, who had already won the 100 metres gold medal in Tokyo, proceeded to run down the anchormen of Jamaica, Russia, Poland, and France over that final straight to win.

Hayes was clocked at 8.6 seconds for his 100 metres split, which was later described, accurately, as "the most astonishing sprint of all time". (Okay, he had the benefit of a running start, but consider when Tim Montgomery broke the world record for the distance in Paris last week, his time was 9.78 seconds.) The 39.06 time for the US team in that relay shattered the world record by half a second.

Watching in the stands in Tokyo that day was Jesse Owens, the 1936 American Olympic hero, who was seated with Hayes' mother.

"Jesse told me 'you go out there and run, and we'll take care of your Mom'," Hayes reminisced in his hometown newspaper two months ago. "When (Emperor) Hirohito put that medal around my neck, all I could think about was here's this kid from the ghetto, from the 'hood, standing with the highest level of a foreign government. Then I looked up at the stands and saw my Mom with tears in her eyes. It's my best Olympic memory."

And the Olympics may not even have been the highlight of Hayes's athletic career. I was there at Tulane Stadium eight years later when Hayes helped the Dallas Cowboys defeat the Miami Dolphins in Super Bowl VI.

When they buried Bob Hayes in Jacksonville, Florida, yesterday, he went to his grave the only man to have won both Olympic gold medals and a Super Bowl ring.

"A lot of track guys give football a shot, but Bob is the only one who really did anything with it," Hayes's old Dallas team-mate Calvin Hill recalled to a Jacksonville newspaper last week. "My old track coach at Yale wasn't given to hyperbole, but he said what he saw in that final leg of the '64 Olympic relay, you may never see again."

Hayes already held world records in the 100 and 220-yard dashes, as well as in the indoor 70, when he prepared for his senior football season at Florida A&M. At the behest of the US Olympic Committee, President Lyndon B Johnson contacted Jake Gaithers, the coach at the predominantly black university, requesting he hold Hayes out of gridiron competition lest he be injured.

"Mr President, let me tell you something," Gaithers later recalled. "I carried this boy for four years, and I know. I guarantee he won't get hurt."

"How can you 'guarantee' this?" asked Johnson.

"Because Bob Hayes is a *football player*," replied Gaithers. "He just happens to also be the world's fastest human."

The Cowboys had drafted him before the Olympics, and his lightning speed forced a revolution in defensive concepts. More than any other man, Hayes was responsible for the development of modern-day zone coverages, simply because no defensive back alive could handle him.

In an 11-year NFL career he caught 71 touchdown passes (more than seven of the 15 wide receivers currently immortalised in the Pro Football Hall of Fame), and averaged 20 yards per catch. (Only one Hall of Famer, Miami's Paul Warfield, averaged more.) He was installed in the National Track and Field Hall of Fame in 1976, but when his name came up for eligibility for election to the Pro Football Hall of Fame in 1981, Hayes didn't get a sniff. Over the five-year window in which his name was on the ballot he never even made the 15-man short-list.

Voters will cite various reasons for this omission — Hayes went to only three Pro Bowls in 11 years, he had only one 100-yard receiving day in his 15 post-season appearances, and scored just one playoff touchdown — but it says here the actual reason he was shunned was that in 1979 he served 10 months in a federal penitentiary after pleading guilty to delivering narcotics to an undercover police officer.

Hayes fought his battles with drugs and alcohol, and made four trips to rehab clinics before defeating his demons. Why his personal life should disqualify him from membership in an organisation that continues to honour OJ Simpson is mystifying.

Acknowledging his drug and prison experiences "destroyed my life," Hayes went to his grave tormented by his exclusion from this final honour.

"There's a lot of pain in my heart because what I accomplished was second to none," he said in a 1999 interview in which he described himself as "an outcast".

For many years Hayes was even ostracised by the Cowboys' organisation. It was only a year ago Dallas owner Jerry Jones, aware that Hayes (who had battled prostate cancer, liver and kidney problems, and undergone triple-bypass heart surgery) didn't have long to live, made him the 11th member of the Cowboys' Ring of Fame.

"I'm thrilled, I'm grateful, I'm blessed," Hayes told the crowd at his induction at

Texas Stadium last September. "I played for the world's greatest professional sports team in history. Once a Dallas Cowboy, always a Dallas Cowboy."
September 26, 2002

Plimpton had no problem having fun

"There are people who would perhaps call me a dilettante, because it looks as though I'm having too much fun. I have never been convinced there's anything inherently wrong in having fun."
— George Plimpton, 1927-2003

When I began covering sports in Boston in the early 1970s, a popular trivia question had obtained some currency: "Who is the only man to play for the Red Sox, Celtics, and Bruins?"

The answer to the trick question was John Kiley, the Fenway Park organist who also pulled keyboard duty at the old Boston Garden, but those who guessed "George Plimpton" wouldn't have been far wrong.

George Ames Plimpton, who died a week ago today, trained with the Boston

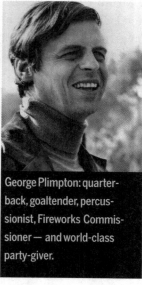

George Plimpton: quarterback, goaltender, percussionist, Fireworks Commissioner — and world-class party-giver.

Celtics and played for several minutes of an exhibition game with what was then the foremost basketball dynasty in the world. He also took a shift as an ice-hockey goaltender for the NHL Boston Bruins, and while he never did play with the Boston Red Sox, he did once pitch to Willie Mays at Yankee Stadium. ("I retired him on a pop fly," Plimpton recalled.)

More famously, Plimpton played quarterback for the Detroit Lions, an experience which he chronicled in *Paper Lion*. He somehow turned four downs (in which his team lost an aggregate 32 yards) into a self-deprecating best-seller which was subsequently made into a film. He also had flings with boxing (he had his nose bloodied by the light-heavyweight champion Archie Moore), the PGA tour (*The Bogey Man*), the circus (in a trapeze act), and spent a month as a percussionist with the New York Philharmonic.

Having inadvertently founded a school of literature which came to be known as "participatory journalism," Plimpton became trapped by his own schtick. (Publishers flogged his biography of Truman Capote, for instance, with the tag-line "By the author of *Paper Lion*.") But George Plimpton would have been an important figure in the world of arts and letters had he never ventured near the arena of fun and games.

In 1953 he co-founded the *Paris Review*, arguably the most influential literary journal of the latter half of the 20th century, and was at least nominally its editor for the next 50 years. In that capacity he interviewed Ernest Hemingway for the magazine's "Writers at Work" series, and was instrumental showcasing writers who would later confirm his judgment: Plimpton was among the first to publish Philip Roth and VS Naipaul, and, his friendship with Capote notwithstanding, gave early exposure to the works of Jack Kerouac.

Plimpton was not, as has been widely reported in the days since his death, the first to publish Kerouac. The *Paris Review* was founded three years after Kerouac's first novel, *The Town and The City*, was issued by Harcourt Brace Jovanovich in 1950, but a 1953 issue of the *Paris Review* did feature *"The Mexican Girl"* which was excerpted from *On The Road*, three years before that novel was published.

George was also a world-class party-giver. In 1973 he celebrated the 20th anniversary of the *Paris Review* with a party which took place on a chartered boat which circled Manhattan. The guests (I was included, since I had been published in the *Paris Review* 10 years earlier) were serenaded by a jazz quartet fronted by the drummer Elvin Jones, and the *piece de resistance* came when the vessel stopped near a barge anchored in the East River for a spectacular fireworks show. (Plimpton had managed to have himself appointed to the previously non-existent position of "Fireworks Commissioner" for New York.)

Although I'd been at a few of Plimpton's New York hooleys, I hadn't known him well, but a few months after the cruise I ran into him in the Boston Celtics locker-room following a game. I was struck by the warmth with which his former "teammates" embraced the Harvard-educated man of letters, whose upper-crust accent and manners would have suggested aloofness. That evening several of them accompanied Plimpton and myself on a pub crawl.

He comfortably moved in circles of society and power (he was a classmate of Robert Kennedy at Harvard, and was not only with Kennedy in Los Angeles the night he was shot, but helped the former NFL lineman Roosevelt Grier subdue the assassin. ("I had my hands around his neck," he recalled of his encounter with Sirhan Sirhan.) He also had bit parts in numerous films, and once wryly noted he had appeared in more movies than he had written books. Noting that his cameo appearances included *Lawrence of Arabia*, *Reds*, *When We Were Kings*, and *Good Will Hunting*, all of which won Academy Awards, he joked, "It would seem to me that a film director should require my presence if he sees an Oscar in the future."

One afternoon nearly three decades ago Plimpton came to Boston on a book tour promoting *Mad Ducks and Bears*. He was fretting with some remorse because he had just learned that a seemingly inconsequential passage about a lad named Puffer who played on a boy's team coached by the former lineman Alex Karras had resulted in unforeseen consequences. Schoolmates had taken to taunting young Puffer, who had developed bed-wetting habits and was now in therapy. Puffer's parents were threatening to sue Plimpton, who did not seem disturbed by that prospect, but was filled with self-recrimination over any humiliation he might have unwittingly inflicted on the boy.

For all his exploits on the playing fields, Plimpton had an unexpected response when he was asked which sport had been the most daunting: none of them. Rather, it was his stint with the New York Philharmonic, which was at the time coached by Leonard Bernstein.

"All sports are predicated on error, but in music, you cannot make a mistake," Plimpton recalled in a 1999 America Online interview.

"The fear of doing this, particularly since I can't read music, was frightening, to put it mildly. Evening after an evening of pure terror in London, Ontario, playing an instrument called the bells. I destroyed Gustav Mahler's Fourth Symphony by mis-hitting an instrument called the sleigh bells. I dream about that from time to time, and wake up covered with sweat. It's a funny answer, but I think it's true." October 02, 2003

Dr Gonzo finally exacts his fatal price

When Arthur Bremer shot George Wallace at a presidential campaign rally in Maryland in the spring of 1972, the widespread assumption was that it portended some wider, deep-rooted conspiracy, and we all sprang into action. By nightfall I was at Hunter S. Thompson's house in Washington, where he had recently been dispatched as National Affairs editor for *Rolling Stone*.

Four of us were working the story for two different countercultural publications, and decided that our initial legwork could be accomplished most efficiently by a shared delegation of responsibility.

Francie Barnard, another *Boston Phoenix* reporter, and I spent the next day re-tracing the steps of the would-be assassin and the segregationist Alabama governor through the Washington suburbs. Hunter and his *Rolling Stone* cohort Tim Crouse would, in the meantime, work the story from their end by interviewing campaign and federal sources.

When Francie and I returned that evening laden with notes and taped interviews with the Maryland constabulary, we discovered Thompson and Crouse in the back garden, both half-stoned and sipping cocktails. They'd never left the house.

I was reminded of that evening a few years later with George Plimpton's account of the 1974 Muhammad Ali-George Foreman fight in Zaire. Thompson and another cohort, Bill Cardoso, had travelled to Africa to chronicle the event, and then spent a month wandering about The Dark Continent after Foreman's training-camp cut forced a month's postponement. By the time the fight took place, Thompson had contracted malaria and decided to skip the trip to the stadium. When Plimpton and Norman Mailer arrived back at their hotel the morning after The Rumble in the Jungle, they discovered Hunter floating naked in the swimming pool.

"Who won?" he asked.

By then, of course, Hunter's legend had been firmly established. Having invented a public persona, he was then forced to endure three decades of trying to justify it. Thirty years of trying to be Hunter Thompson would have constituted an impossible task for any human, and in the end it consumed him.

I'd first met Hunter in 1968 when he walked into the offices of the Scott Meredith Literary Agency around the publication date of *The Hells Angels,* but even then his legend had preceded him. I was at the time subletting an apartment from the poet and translator Paul Blackburn, who'd just received a Guggenheim grant to go off to Spain. Paul's wife, Sara, was an editor at Random House who had midwifed the sale of Hunter's book, so I had advance warning that this wild man who'd just walked in off the New York streets with a cowboy hat perched on his head might be a kindred spirit.

After *The Hells Angels* became a surprise best-seller, Hunter began to have second thoughts about the contract he'd signed with Random House, which essentially gave the publisher an option on his next book on the same terms — including the same paltry advance — as the first.

When the publisher stood firm, Hunter countered by submitting a manuscript of *The Rum Diary*, a terrible first novel which had been collecting rejection slips for a decade. The issue degenerated into lawsuits and countersuits, and Scott Meredith, though nominally the author's agent, covertly sided with the publisher, having erroneously concluded that he'd have to deal with Random House a lot longer than he'd have to deal with Hunter Thompson. Meredith had for years been indulging Mailer's eccentricities, and figured Thompson couldn't be any worse. He figured wrong.

With the issue pending in the courts, Scott Meredith began to withhold money due Hunter for ancillary rights, including foreign sales, from the Hell's Angels book. Although I was a very junior editor at the agency, I was able to function as Thompson's mole, staying after hours to furtively photocopy documentation of the foreign-rights sales and passing the information to Hunter and his lawyers. Meredith never did figure how Thompson was securing his background intelligence.

That episode ended badly. The Blackburns preceded their European trip with a visit to an arts institute in Aspen, where one evening Paul caught Sara *in flagrante* with Hunter, precipitating a divorce. Paul went off to Spain by himself, so I got the apartment for an extra year, Random House didn't get its second book and Hunter never did recover all his *Hell's Angels* money.

Hunter S. Thompson: left the Niemans, among others, agog.

A year or two later we were both writing for the short-lived *Scanlan's Monthly*. A blown *Playboy* assignment covering the Kentucky Derby in the company of British artist Ralph Steadman wound up in the pages of Scanlan's, giving birth to what Cardoso would christen "gonzo" journalism.

If the tour de force was considered an act of genius, Hunter's own recollection was probably more accurate.

"I'd blown my mind, couldn't work," he once told an interviewer. "So finally I just started jerking pages out of my notebook and numbering them and sending them to the printer. I was sure it was the last article I was ever going to do for anybody."

Even while relentlessly developing the persona, he struggled to maintain a sensible demarcation with his private life. In 1969, I drove to Aspen with my brother and another friend. When I phoned Hunter, he instructed me to drop my companions in town and to visit alone. I spent several pleasant hours enjoying the quiet hospitality of Hunter, his then-wife Sandy, and his young son, Juan, after which we rejoined the others at the Hotel Jerome bar, where, as if on cue, he transformed himself and spent the rest of the evening dutifully performing his Dr Gonzo act. We stayed up all night, and greeted the dawn sitting on his back porch in Woody Creek plinking — if you can call blasting away with a .44 Magnum "plinking" — at an elaborate configuration of gongs he had set up on the fence abutting his property.

By 1970, we were each involved in a countercultural run for the sheriff's office: I was on the ballot in Douglas County, Kansas, Thompson ran in Pitkin County, Colorado. We had arrived at our decisions independently, but, once nominated in our respective jurisdictions, we did hold a summit meeting of sorts that summer.

"George Kimball just left after a vicious three-day strategy session," Hunter reported in a letter to Realist editor Paul Krassner that August. *"He's running for sheriff of Lawrence, Kansas, but with no hope of winning. This is a strange phenomena . . . with no prior collusion. Very odd."*

By 1971, Hunter had assumed his post at *Rolling Stone*. Having relocated to Massachusetts, I occasionally covered music for the same publication. That spring I got a letter from Hunter (re-published in *Fear and Loathing in America*) which began: *"George, I've just been talking to Jann Wenner about you, suggesting that he get you into writing some articles in addition to that record-review gig. My motives were mixed, of course. Aside from your undeniable mastery of the medium, I want Wenner to have the experience of dealing with somebody more demonstrably crazy than I am — so that he'll understand that I am, in context, a very responsible person."*

Being described as more nuts than Hunter S Thompson, even by Hunter S Thompson himself, was a pretty frightening thought.

At *Rolling Stone*, Hunter wore two hats: his own, and that of "Raoul Duke, Sports Editor." In this latter connection we covered two Super Bowls together. For the first, the 1973 game between the Dolphins and the Redskins, we stayed for a week with Cardoso and his wife at their Hollywood house, thereby presaging the break-up of yet another marriage.

A year later we covered Super Bowl VIII in Houston. There took place the Battle of the Blue Fox, in which, to Thompson's delight, we watched a pair of undercover cops subdue an entire pool-cue and broken-bottle-wielding motorcycle gang when a brawl broke out in a Texas strip joint.

Another night that week, Thompson sat in a Houston saloon and produced a sheet of paper from one pocket and a Swiss army knife from the other, depositing the resultant bits of confetti into his drink. When Leigh Montville, then of the *Boston Globe,* asked me what he was doing, I replied, correctly, "blotter acid." Montville groaned. Hunter was supposed to be our designated driver that night.

We managed to make it safely back to the hotel before the chemicals kicked in, but later that night, grabbing a religious tract which had been slipped under his door, Thompson delivered a thundering homily, roaring out Biblical passages from the 14th floor of the atrium at the Houston Hyatt Regency.

One night in the early 1970s, someone with an odd sense of humour invited Hunter and me, along with the venerable *Boston Globe* columnist George Frazier, to address a gathering of the Nieman Fellows over dinner at a Back Bay gentlemen's club. Attuned to Thompson's tastes, the Harvard undergraduate charged with shepherding us through the procedure had thoughtfully provided a quart of Wild Turkey, which was long gone even before the cocktail hour commenced, with predictably disastrous results.

The next morning Hunter and I excused our comportment by reflecting that we had, after all, behaved pretty much the way the Niemans had expected us to behave, but poor Frazier was so traumatised by the evening that for the remaining few years of his life he winced in mortification whenever it was mentioned.

Another botched assignment — this time to cover a convention of police chiefs in Sin City for Rolling Stone — turned, quite by accident, into a masterpiece. When *Fear and Loathing in Las Vegas* appeared in 1973, no one had read anything quite like it, and, alas, they never would again. It was by far the best thing Thompson wrote, and he spent the rest of his days in a vain attempt to re-achieve that promise while simultaneously attempting to fulfil the expectations of the doting cult of worshippers he had unwittingly spawned.

There had been only sporadic contact in recent years, but when my daughter moved to Colorado last month I did give her Hunter's number and e-mailed him that he might expect a phone call.

Last Sunday Hunter killed himself with a bullet through the head. Juan found the body when he stopped by the house the next morning. There will be those who will now try to claim that Hunter, who always lived for today without a thought for tomorrow, left this earth on those very terms.

My daughter phoned from Denver when she heard the news.

"I never did get to meet him," she said. "I'm sorry now that I didn't at least call."

"It wouldn't have made much difference," I told her. "I guess he just wanted to prove how crazy he really was."
February 24, 2005

Memories of an old heroic friend

Over a year has passed since the last time I got together with Emery Hicks. I was covering an NFL play-off game in Kansas City, and we'd arranged to meet afterwards. His reliability was legendary, so I was surprised he wasn't waiting when I returned to my hotel.

After I got to my room he phoned from downstairs. Hicks explained the sight of a large, crippled black man lounging around the lobby had seemed to put so many people ill at ease he'd grown uncomfortable himself, and decided to wait outside.

We headed off for a bistro named Frondizi's, which might have been created with Hicks's epicurean tastes in mind. The restaurant had a four-page menu accompanied by a 50-page wine list. We spent three hours catching up, by the conclusion of which Emery was in no shape for the 35-mile drive back to Lawrence.

This presented yet another problem. The room I'd checked into had a single bed and I told him, "Hicks, I love you like a brother, but I'm not sleeping in that bed with you!"

The hotel manager agreed to move me to a room with two beds. As tired as we both were, we lay there in the darkness talking about the old days and the future, about wives, children, and grandchildren. It was barely dawn when Hicks shook me and explained he was leaving.

"I just remembered I have a chemo treatment in Lawrence this morning. I've got to go."

I'd known he had been suffering from non-Hodgkins lymphoma but had been assured it was in remission and everything was under control. This was my first inkling it might not be. We spoke on the phone several times after that, but that was the last time I saw him alive.

Although he never played a down in a regulation NFL game, Hicks' prowess on the field remains the stuff of legend at the University of Kansas. In a poll undertaken a few years ago he was named the starting linebacker on the college's all-time team, alongside Football Hall-of-Famers Gale Sayers and John Riggins and NFL stars John Hadl, John Zook, Dana Stubblefield and Gilbert Brown.

The most accomplished running back in the state of Oklahoma as a schoolboy, he had been switched to defence at KU, and become the most fearsome linebacker in the old Big Eight Conference. In the 1969 Orange Bowl, a game which 36 years later still represents the crowning moment of Kansas football, he made three straight stops to prevent a touchdown after Penn State had reached the two-yard line. (The Jayhawks lost 15-14). He was drafted by the Oakland Raiders, but the knee injuries which would follow him all his life had begun to take their toll, and he was cut just before the 1970 season. He made it back to Lawrence in time to serve as the best man at my wedding that fall.

The ceremony was one of those free-form outdoor, countercultural affairs. The refreshments included two varieties of punch, one of them undiluted and the other liberally spiked with psychedelic substances. The highlight of the day came when someone — Hicks swore it wasn't him, but I always had my doubts — served my new mother-in-law from the latter.

He never got another NFL shot, but he did spend five years playing for the Hamilton Tiger-Cats in Canada before his knees gave out. One year when the Ti-Cats reached the championship game I travelled to Canada for the Grey Cup, but Hicks was hurt and didn't play. A few years after that he came up to Boston to visit me, but eventually he returned to Oklahoma and spent two decades working the oil fields before moving back to Kansas.

He was born on August 10th, 1947, but when he got to college a mix-up in the records had listed his birthday as May 1st. Since the latter gave him a draft lottery number of 327, he decided not to correct the oversight until years later.

"It might have saved my life," he pointed out.

The late 1960s were turbulent times, and Lawrence had been a particular hotbed of unrest. A sometimes uneasy alliance existed between leftist white countercul- turalists — ie, hippies — and the radical black movement, while varsity athletes tended to be more conservatively aligned and kept their distance from both groups. Hicks may have been the only man I knew who moved easily through all three camps, although the closest he ever came to radicalising the football team came when he helped lead a strike prior to the 1969 season that succeeded in appointing a black cheerleader and allowing the players to grow longer hair.

He had come from an impoverished background in Oklahoma, and the full scholarship to Kansas didn't provide much cash. Then, as now, players received an allotment of tickets for home games, which they were expected to discreetly sell at inflated prices to alumni and boosters. Hicks, as far as I know, never sold his tickets: he either gave them to his friends or traded them for pot. The result was he had to earn his pocket money hustling pool.

In the end it wasn't the lymphoma that killed him, but rather an infection his ravaged immune system was powerless to repel. The memorial service in Lawrence was delayed until last Friday, because many of his old team-mates would be in town for the annual alumni game at Memorial Stadium that weekend.

By the time I last saw him the knee had given out, and it had been fused by surgery. He couldn't bend it at all, and had to climb backwards when he went up or down stairs.

I found myself thinking about that night a lot after he died. Here was a man whose life had been defined by his athletic prowess, and now he could barely walk. He was in the grip of a life-threatening disease, but in the time we spent together that night in Kansas City there hadn't been a moment of self-pity.

That we could all live — and die — like that.

April 21, 2005

Ringside observer with soul of a poet

When China entered the Korean Conflict in the fall of 1950, the Red Army came pouring across the 38th Parallel and quickly overwhelmed remnants of the United States Marine Corps at Chosin.

The massive counter-attack had been directed toward the South Korean army, which had promptly fled en masse, leaving its American allies to be slaughtered or taken prisoner. When Pat Putnam reflected on that experience late one night at the old Flame bar in Las Vegas, he described it as having been reduced to "two million Chinese and one little Irishman".

Already wounded, Putnam, along with several hundred of his comrades, was captured and shipped off to a POW camp in Manchuria, where he spent the next 17 months surviving on a diet of maggots and rice. When he was released, at the conclusion of the hostilities, he weighed 85lb.

For the rest of his life he refused to darken the door of a Chinese restaurant, but he harboured even more ill-will toward the Koreans, who had abandoned him to his fate, than to his captors themselves.

Thirty-five years later, Pat was covering a boxing match at Caesars Palace when the promoter, Bob Arum, introduced him to a visiting dignitary from the South Korean Boxing Federation — "Lieutenant General Kim of the Army of the Republic of Korea".

"Turn around," Cpl Putnam ordered the general, "so I can see if I recognise you."

Patrick Francis Anthony Nolan Putnam, who died on Sunday at 75, was a hard-drinking, hard-living scribe with the soul of a poet. The dean of American boxing writers, he established himself at the Miami Herald in the early 1960s, an era which coincided with the arrival in that city of a promising heavyweight named Cassius Clay.

A daily habitué of the old Fifth Street Gym in Miami Beach, Putnam covered Muhammad Ali's career from its inception and was the first to break the story of Clay's impending conversion to Islam. He should also — the truth can now be told — have been credited as the co-author of some of the young pugilist's more imaginative verse.

For a quarter-century he reigned as *Sports Illustrated's* boxing writer extraordinaire. He authored more than 50 cover stories for the world's pre-eminent sports magazine, and in 1982 he was the recipient of the Nat Fleischer Award for Distinguished Boxing Journalism.

The 1987 "Fight of the Century" between Marvelous Marvin Hagler and Ray Charles Leonard was shrouded in some controversy. Sugar Ray was returning to the ring after an absence of three years, and the medical community was divided over the question of whether, having undergone surgery for a detached retina, he should be fighting at all.

When the boxers appeared at a press conference on the eve of the fight, Arum preceded the question-and-answer session with a decree ruling out any questions about Leonard's eye. From far in the back of the room, Putnam raised his hand and was duly called upon.

"Hey, Ray," he asked. "How many fingers am I holding up?"

The week of a big fight Putnam would hold court from his barstool — at the Galleria Bar at Caesars by day, at the Flame by night — and trainers, promoters and fellow scribes would flock to him there. After the fight he would have arranged to meet the winner, and sometimes the loser, in his hotel suite. The result would invariably be the finest and most insightful prose written about the event, and those of us committed to one-hour deadlines and quickie quotes could only read with envy.

Boxers trusted Putnam, sometimes because they erroneously assumed him to have been one of their own, but his pug's nose hadn't been acquired in the ring, or even in one of his celebrated saloon scraps. In the late 1960s he had broken nearly every bone in his body in a Long Island automobile accident and underwent a facial reconstruction. The result was the best the doctors could do with what passed for a nose.

Months after he had recovered, Putnam received a bill from the authorities demanding payment for a utility pole he had destroyed in the head-on collision. Pat reluctantly agreed to pay the money, but only on the condition that he get possession of the pole.

"That's a pretty expensive souvenir," the man at the county clerk's office told him.

"I don't want it for a souvenir," replied Putnam. "I just want to practice driving around it."

At a party the night before the 1976 Sugar Bowl in New Orleans, Pat and I came upon a lively crap game under way in the hallway of a French Quarter hotel. We watched for long enough to realise that the game was crooked, and had even figured out exactly how the proprietors had rigged the proceedings. I left to get us a couple of drinks, and, when I returned, there was Pat on his knees.

Determined to beat the grifters at their own game, he was rolling the dice on the carpet.

On another occasion, Pat, Michael Katz, Angelo Dundee and I had flown from Baltimore to Miami for the 1982 Aaron Pryor-Alexis Arguello fight, extinguishing the plane's supply of Bloody Marys en route. By the time we arrived at our destination I was unsure that I could operate my rental car.

"No problem," said Pat. "I'll drive."

He did get us safely to our hotel. Only later did I realise that he'd gone the wrong way out of the Hertz lot, driven across a set of steel spikes, and punctured all four tires on the rental car. They were belted radials, so I drove with them that way for the rest of the weekend.

When his longtime friend and colleague, Bob Waters, passed away some years ago, we took a train out to the Island for the funeral. When he spotted the great man's body in repose beneath a bed of roses, Putnam vouchsafed: "Holy shit! Bob won the Kentucky Derby."

In recent years we'd communicated mostly by telephone and e-mail. Pat had been in poor health and had given up travelling to big fights since his retirement from Sports Illustrated, but he'd kept his hand in as a frequent contributor to the boxing website Thesweetscience.com. The final instalment of his four-part series on another "Fight of the Century" — the 1910 Jack Johnson-Jim Jeffries fight in Reno — appeared the day after he died.

Pat will be buried today following a funeral Mass at St John the Evangelist Church in Schenectady, New York. I'm anxious to learn whether his family will respect his final wish, which was that his tombstone read, simply, *"Keep Off The Grass"*.

December 01, 2005

The true tale of the original contender

Not long after his premature retirement from the ring half a century ago, Roger Donoghue served as Marlon Brando's boxing instructor for *On The Waterfront*, in which Brando would portray a washed-up pug called Terry Malloy.

On the set one day, the screenwriter, Budd Schulberg, asked Roger if he could have been a champion had he pursued his pro career. "Well," Donoghue replied after giving the matter some thought. "I could have been a contender."

Incorporated into Schulberg's Academy Award-winning script, "I could have been a contender" not only became the most memorable line of the film, but arguably the most famous of Brando's career.

In the late 1960s, at the old Lion's Head in Greenwich Village, the patrons used to look forward to Donoghue's visits with much the same sense of anticipation as the denizens of Harry Hope's saloon awaited the arrival of Hickey in *The Iceman Cometh*. Roger had by then become a beer salesman, and when he dropped in a couple of times a month to monitor the supply of Rheingold and McSorley's Ale, he could be counted upon to buy a round for the house.

These visits would often last an hour or more, and while his audience often included prominent novelists, folk-singers, actors and newspapermen, Roger would be the centre of attention, regaling the clientele with tales from the worlds of theatre and boxing, often punctuated by animated shadow-boxing.

Although he had been a successful welterweight in his day, he rarely spoke of his career. I eventually learned why.

The son of an Irish immigrant cab driver in Yonkers, Donoghue had turned pro at 18, and by 1951 had won 25 of his first 27 fights when he was matched against Georgie Flores in a featured bout on the Kid Gavilan-Billy Graham card at Madison Square Garden.

Donoghue scored an eighth-round knockout in his Garden debut, but Flores was taken to hospital on a stretcher and died without regaining consciousness.

Roger donated his entire $1,500 purse from the bout to Flores' family, and while he boxed a few more times, his heart was no longer in it. He lost two of his last three fights and retired at the age of 21.

Although he rarely spoke of it, he was haunted by the episode for the rest of his life. In a 1979 New York Times interview, he related the tale of being approached by a youngster who said, "You killed a man. I'm going to tell everybody."

"You don't have to tell everybody," Roger replied softly. "They already know."

After *On The Waterfront*, Donoghue served for some time as Brando's minder, but he was less successful at keeping "Buddy" — as he would invariably refer to the actor — out of trouble than he had been in turning him into a credible middleweight.

Years later, when Brando was filming the original *Godfather*, Roger would cash in an old marker, scoring a plug for his company: in the memorable scene in which James Caan, as Sonny Corleone, beats the piss out of his brother-in-law Carlo, a Rheingold beer truck is prominently parked in the camera shot.

He also taught James Dean to box. Dean was going to play Roger in a film based on Donoghue's life, but the project died with Dean in that 1955 car crash.

A ringside fixture at New York fights, Donoghue became a *bon vivant* who moved easily between the worlds of pugilism, the arts and New York saloon society. He rarely missed a Broadway opening, seemed to know every actor in town and wrote a musical himself. Schulberg was a lifelong friend, and it was Norman Mailer who introduced him to his wife, the painter Fay Moore.

I hadn't seen Roger since the Lion's Head went out of business a decade ago, but last year his name came up in a conversation with the boxing editor and broadcaster Steve Farhood.

Steve had set aside one evening a month to visit a home for senior citizens on the Lower East Side, where he would show old fight films for the residents.

To his surprise, Farhood related, he had learned that one of the residents was a former professional welterweight named Roger Donoghue. I filled him in on what I knew of Donoghue's story, asked that I be remembered, and promised to drop by for a visit sometime.

"He may or may not remember you at all," warned Farhood. "He has Alzheimer's Disease. Sometimes he doesn't remember much."

The next time I ran into Farhood, I asked if he had mentioned me to Roger.

"He's not there any more," he replied. "He was deteriorating so rapidly that he had to be moved to an assisted-living facility in Brooklyn."

It was there that Roger died, at 75, last week. Somewhat infuriatingly, the obituary in his hometown Westchester newspaper began with the words *"Roger Donoghue, the former boxer from Yonkers who killed a man in the ring in 1951 . . ."*
August 31, 2006

Noting the passing of a man for all seasons

I had just turned 30 when I got a fan letter from David Halberstam. It was a short note, telling me how much he enjoyed the sports columns I was then writing for the *Boston Phoenix.*

I was flattered, though probably not as deeply as I should have been. A decade earlier Halberstam had won a Pulitzer Prize for his reporting from Vietnam for the *New York Times,* but he had only a year or two earlier published *The Best and the Brightest*, the book that would catapult him to prominence.

That note was my first inkling Halberstam was interested in sports. He even mentioned he'd suggested to his publisher they contact me about doing a book. If that happened, somebody at Random House must have dropped the ball.

Over the ensuing three decades Halberstam would go on to write 20 more books, and at least half a dozen of them revolved around the world of sport: beginning with *The Breaks of the Game,* (of which Bob Ryan, the dean of American basketball writers, said "there has never been anything better written about the NBA, before or since"), he authored books on rowing (*The Amateurs*), baseball (*The Summer of '49, October 1964,* and *The Teammates*), Michael Jordan and the NBA (*Playing for Keeps*), and football (*The Education of a Coach*), a touching portrayal of the Patriots' Bill Belichick and his father, Steve.

And when he was killed in a California car crash on Monday, Halberstam was on his way to visit Y.A. Tittle, the old New York Giants' quarterback, for a book he was writing about the 1958 NFL Championship game.

Between his Vietnam reportage for the *Times* and *The Best and the Brightest*, if Halberstam had never written about anything else his position in the pantheon of great journalists would be secure. And if he'd never published anything but his sports books, that body of work would still rank him among the best to ever write about that world.

Although *The Best and the Brightest* is a scathing chronicle of how the US stumbled into its Vietnam disaster, when Halberstam was first dispatched to Southeast Asia by the *Times* he was still in his 20s and still a true believer. His subsequent cynicism stemmed from first-hand experience, but it wasn't long in developing.

As early as 1963 John F Kennedy demanded Halberstam be replaced at the Saigon bureau. (The *Times* not only refused, but cancelled a scheduled Halberstam vacation, lest anyone in Washington misinterpret his absence.) Kennedy's successor Lyndon Johnson described Halberstam as a "traitor to his country," and as White House files were unearthed in the wake of Watergate, it unsurprisingly came to light Halberstam's name occupied a prominent place in Richard Nixon's infamous "Enemies List."

"I'm jealous," then-*Boston Globe* columnist Marty Nolan told Halberstam. "But you were also on JFK's Enemies List. That one was a lot shorter."

Although he had introduced himself in that long-ago letter, nearly two decades would elapse before I met Halberstam, and since we were both in the presence of royalty that day in the press room at Fenway Park we barely had the opportunity to exchange pleasantries. Ted Williams was also there that afternoon, and was the centre of attention. Some years later David would write *The Teammates*, a touching account of the friendship between Williams and his fellow 1940s-era Red Sox players, Johnny Pesky and Bobby Doerr, and the dynamics of that relationship half a century later.

An esteemed financial writer once told me "You think I understand all this stuff? I make *them* explain it to *me*." That was the gift Halberstam brought to his forays into the world of sport. By assuming a posture of near-total naiveté, he would elicit patient explanations from his subjects in a manner that not only illuminated the topic at hand, but forced the principals to examine themselves in ways that might never have consciously occurred to them.

His widow, Jean Sandness, this week described Halberstam's sports books as "his entertainments — his way to take a break," but in an interview a few years ago David refused to draw distinctions between "the supposedly serious books and the supposedly not-so-serious books." He was a man for all seasons, and they were all serious to him. His obituaries described him as a "journalist, historian, and biographer," and not as a sportswriter, although he was that, too. A Renaissance man, Halberstam not only moved easily between those disparate worlds, but delighted in orchestrating mix-and-match occasions that brought them into juxtaposition.

The Teammates, for instance, was dedicated to "my teammate, Neil Sheehan," his Vietnam-era colleague who authored *A Bright and Shining Lie*. "He loved pulling people together," said Belichick. "He knew everything and everybody, but not in a know-it-all way."

After back-to-back sports books, Halberstam had just completed *The Coldest Winter*, a book about the Korean War. The night before he was killed he had delivered a lecture on "Turning Journalism Into History" at the University of California, and was en route to his interview with Tittle when the car in which he was riding was broadsided by another vehicle. He had just turned 73 a few weeks earlier.

David Halberstam: a man for all seasons.

Far be it from me to suggest another man's epitaph, but a couple of possibilities spring to mind. In Vietnam, he revealed in a "letter" to his then two-year-old daughter published 25 years ago, "I kept on my desk a small quote from Albert Camus which he had written during France's war in Algeria: *'I should like to be able to love my country and love justice'*."

Another nomination might come from a recent interview at a New York TV station, in which Halberstam answered a question about his indefatigable work habits by quoting the basketball player Julius Erving: *"Being a professional is doing the things you love to do, on the days you don't feel like doing them."*
April 26, 2007

RED ROCK PRESS FIRST FOR SPORT
redrockpress@eircom.net

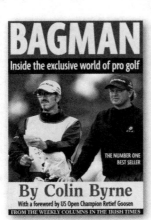

Number 1 best-seller detailing the peripatetic life of Irish caddie Colin Byrne and the world of professional golf.

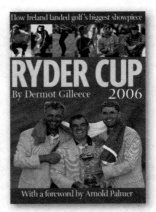

Stunningly illustrated book on how Ireland captured golf's biggest showpiece by Ireland's leading golf writer, Dermot Gilleece.

Winner

William Hill Sports Book of the Year Award.

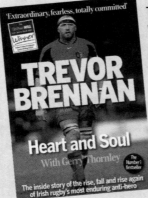

Trevor Brennan's award winning book, and his inspirational story as told to Gerry Thornley, caught the imagination of the Irish sporting public, becoming the biggest selling book over Christmas 2008 and the most talked about sports book of the year.

Winner

Irish Book of the Year Awards, Energise Sport, best sports book.

A remarkable, inspiring and beautifully crafted account of Grania Willis's determination to scale Mount Everest.

Catherina McKiernan's life story from humble rural background to internationally acclaimed runner as told to Ian O'Riordan